W9-ABN-271

TECHNICAL COLLEGE OF THE LOWCOUNTRY
LEARNING RESOURCES CENTER
POST OFFICE BOX 1288
BEAUFORT, SOUTH CAROLINA 29901-1288

Bloom's Modern Critical Views

Bloom's Modern Critical Views

GEORGE ORWELL
Updated Edition

Edited and with an introduction by
Harold Bloom
Sterling Professor of the Humanities
Yale University

CHELSEA HOUSE
P U B L I S H E R S
An imprint of Infobase Publishing

TECHNICAL COLLEGE OF THE LOWCOUNTRY
LEARNING RESOURCES CENTER
POST OFFICE BOX 1288
BEAUFORT, SOUTH CAROLINA 29901-1288

Bloom's Modern Critical Views: George Orwell—Updated Edition

Copyright © 2007 Infobase Publishing

Introduction © 2007 by Harold Bloom

All rights reserved. No part of this publication may be reproduced or utilized in any form or by any means, electronic or mechanical, including photocopying, recording, or by any information storage or retrieval systems, without permission in writing from the publisher. For more information contact:

Chelsea House
An imprint of Infobase Publishing
132 West 31st Street
New York NY 10001

ISBN-10: 0-7910-9428-6
ISBN-13: 978-0-7910-9248-0

Library of Congress Cataloging-in-Publication Data
George Orwell / Harold Bloom, editor. -- Updated ed.
    p. cm. -- (Bloom's modern critical views)
  Includes bibliographical references and index.
  ISBN 0-7910-9428-6 (hardcover)
  1. Orwell, George, 1903-1950--Criticism and interpretation. I. Bloom, Harold. II. Title.
II. Series.

  PR6029.R8Z638 2007
  828'.91209--dc22   2006031145

Chelsea House books are available at special discounts when purchased in bulk quantities for businesses, associations, institutions, or sales promotions. Please call our Special Sales Department in New York at (212) 967-8800 or (800) 322-8755.

You can find Chelsea House on the World Wide Web at http://www.chelseahouse.com

Contributing Editor: Pamela Loos
Cover designed by Takeshi Takahashi
Cover photo © The Granger Collection, New York

Printed in the United States of America

Bang EJB 10 9 8 7 6 5 4 3 2 1

This book is printed on acid-free paper.

All links and web addresses were checked and verified to be correct at the time of publication. Because of the dynamic nature of the web, some addresses and links may have changed since publication and may no longer be valid.

Contents

Editor's Note

My Introduction, written in 1986, seems to me altogether accurate twenty years later. Orwell was more a fabulist than a writer of novels, and essentially always was a pamphleteer, who aspired to join an English tradition that includes Defoe, Swift, Edmund Burke, Carlyle and Ruskin, among many others.

As a prophet, Orwell achieved his apotheosis in 2004, when the United States endorsed Karl Rove's version of *1984*: Dubya as Big Brother, War as Peace, and mountains of Doublethink and Doublespeak in our Empire of Oceania. I write in 2006, when our current fusion of plutocracy and theocracy intensifies weekly.

Unfortunately, Orwell wrote Period Pieces, whose shelf life momentarily may be prolonged, but doubtless will rub down and away as the Age of Karl Rove wanes. In praise of Orwell, he was at heart a Catalan Anarchist, personally heroic, and a moral essayist of authentic honesty and integrity.

The actual essays in this volume present something close to Orwell's full range. Though there are useful critiques of *1984* and of *Animal Farm* here, the reader is advised to seek out the Chelsea House volumes that concentrate upon each of those political fables.

Adriaan M. de Lange analyzes the essay of "Shooting an Elephant," and finds in it Orwell's characteristic rejection of imperialism, while Roger Fowler surveys three versions of Orwellian "realism": descriptive, naturalistic, surrealistic.

Dostoevsky's Underground Man is seen as the ancestor of Orwell's Big Brother by Adrian Wanner, after which Patricia Rae explores Orwell's *The Road to Wigan Pier* as a kind of progressive anthropology.

Antony Shuttleworth, questing for the "real" Orwell in *Homage to Catalonia* and the novel *Coming Up for Air*, finds unintended limitations in the writer's truth-telling.

In an overview of the *Collected Essays*, William E. Cain makes the surprising observation that Orwell's freshness results from his stylistic "perversity," or writing against his own grain (as it were).

1984 is seen by James M. Decker as purely a warning and not an ideological statement, while Paul Kirschner judges *Animal Farm* to be both a literary parody and a social admonition.

In this volume's final essay, Annette Federico praises the novel *Coming Up for Air* as a vision of cheerful, ordinary human decency.

HAROLD BLOOM

Introduction

There is an equivocal irony to reading, and writing about, George Orwell in 1986. I have just reread *1984*, *Animal Farm*, and many of the essays for the first time in some years, and I find myself lost in an interplay of many contending reactions, moral and aesthetic. Orwell, aesthetically considered, is a far better essayist than a novelist. Lionel Trilling, reviewing *1984* in 1949, praised the book, with a singular moral authority:

> The whole effort of the culture of the last hundred years has been directed toward teaching us to understand the economic motive as the irrational road to death, and to seek salvation in the rational and the planned. Orwell marks a turn in thought; he asks us to consider whether the triumph of certain forces of the mind, in their naked pride and excess, may not produce a state of things far worse than any we have ever known. He is not the first to raise the question, but he is the first to raise it on truly liberal or radical grounds, with no intention of abating the demand for a just society, and with an overwhelming intensity and passion. This priority makes his book a momentous one.

The book remains momentous; perhaps it always will be so. But there is nothing intrinsic to the book that will determine its future importance.

1

Its very genre will be established by political, social, and economic events. Is it satire or science fiction or dystopia or countermanifesto? Last week I read newspaper accounts of two recent speeches, perorations delivered by President Reagan and by Norman Podhoretz, each favorably citing Orwell. The President, awarding medals to Senator Barry Goldwater and Helen Hayes, among others, saw them as exemplars of Orwell's belief in freedom and individual dignity, while the sage Podhoretz allowed himself to observe that Orwell would have become a neoconservative had he but survived until this moment. Perhaps irony, however equivocal, is inadequate to represent so curious a posthumous fate as has come to the author of *Homage to Catalonia*, a man who went to Barcelona to fight for the Party of Marxist Unity and the Anarcho-Syndicalists.

V. S. Pritchett and others were correct in describing Orwell as the best of modern pamphleteers. A pamphlet certainly can achieve aesthetic eminence; "tracts and pamphlets" is a major genre, particularly in Great Britain, where its masters include Milton, Defoe, Swift, Dr. Johnson, Burke, Blake, Shelley, Carlyle, Ruskin, and Newman. Despite his celebrated mastery of the plain style, it is rather uncertain that Orwell has joined himself to that company. I suspect that he is closer to the category that he once described as "good bad books," giving Harriet Beecher Stowe's *Uncle Tom's Cabin* as a supreme instance. Aesthetically considered, *1984* is very much the *Uncle Tom's Cabin* of our time, with poor Winston Smith as Uncle Tom, the unhappy Julia as little Eva, and the more-than-sadistic O'Brien as Simon Legree. I do not find O'Brien to be as memorable as Simon Legree, but then that is part of Orwell's point. We have moved into a world in which our torturers also have suffered a significant loss of personality.

II

Orwell's success as a prophet is necessarily a mixed one, since his relative crudity as a creator of character obliges us to read *1984* rather literally. What works best in the novel is its contextualization of all the phrases it has bequeathed to our contemporary language, though whether to *the* language is not yet certain. Newspeak and doublethink, "War Is Peace," "Freedom Is Slavery," "Ignorance Is Strength," "Big Brother Is Watching You," the Thought Police, the Two Minutes Hate, the Ministry of Truth, and all the other Orwellian inventions that are now wearisome clichés, are restored to some force, though little freshness, when we encounter them where they first arose.

Unfortunately, in itself that does not suffice. Even a prophetic pamphlet requires eloquence if we are to return to it and find ourselves affected at least as much as we were before. *1984* can hurt you a single time, and most likely when you are young. After that, defensive laughter becomes the aesthetic problem. Rereading *1984* can be too much like watching a really persuasive horror movie; humor acquires the validity of health. Contemporary reviewers, even Trilling, were too overwhelmed by the book's relevance to apprehend its plain badness as narrative or Orwell's total inability to represent even a curtailed human personality or moral character. Mark Schorer's response in the *New York Times Book Review* may have seemed appropriate on June 12, 1949, but its hyperboles now provoke polite puzzlement:

> No real reader can neglect this experience with impunity. He will be moved by Smith's wistful attempts to remember a different kind of life from his. He will make a whole new discovery of the beauty of love between man and woman, and of the strange beauty of landscape in a totally mechanized world. He will be asked to read through pages of sustained physical and psychological pain that have seldom been equaled and never in such quiet, sober prose. And he will return to his own life from Smith's escape into living death with a resolution to resist power wherever it means to deny him his individuality, and to resist for himself the poisonous lures of power.

Would it make a difference now if Orwell had given his book the title "1994"? Our edge of foreboding has vanished when we contemplate the book, if indeed we ought to regard it as a failed apocalypse. Yet all apocalypses, in the literary sense, are failed apocalypses, so that if they fade, the phenomenon of literary survival or demise clearly takes precedence over whatever status social prophecy affords. The limits of Orwell's achievement are clarified if we juxtapose it directly to the authentic American apocalypses of our time: Faulkner's *As I Lay Dying*, Nathanael West's *Miss Lonelyhearts*, Thomas Pynchon's *Gravity's Rainbow*. Why do they go on wounding us, reading after reading, while *1984* threatens to become a period piece, however nightmarish? It would be absurdly unfair to look at *1984* side by side with Kafka and Beckett; Orwell was in no way an aspirant after the sublime, however demonic or diminished. But he was a satirist, and in *1984* a kind of phantasmagoric realist. If his O'Brien is not of the stature of the unamiable Simon Legree, he is altogether nonexistent as a Satanic rhetorician if we attempt to bring him into the company of West's Shrike.

Can a novel survive praise that endlessly centers upon its author's humane disposition, his indubitable idealism, his personal honesty, his political courage, his moral nature? Orwell may well have been the exemplary and representative Socialist intellectual of our time (though Raymond Williams, the crucial Marxist literary critic in Great Britain, definitely does not think so). But very bad men and women have written superb novels, and great moralists have written unreadable ones. *1984* is neither superb nor unreadable. If it resembles the work of a precursor figure, that figure is surely H. G. Wells, as Wyndham Lewis shrewdly realized. Wells surpasses Orwell in storytelling vigor, in pungency of characterization, and in imaginative invention, yet Wells now seems remote and Orwell remains very close. We are driven back to what makes *1984* a good bad book: relevance. The book substitutes for a real and universal fear: that in the political and economic area, the dreadful is still about to happen. Yet the book again lacks a defense against its own blunderings into the ridiculous. As social prophecy, it is closer to Sinclair Lewis's now forgotten *It Can't Happen Here* than to Nathanael West's still hilarious *A Cool Million*, where Big Brother, under the name of Shagpoke Whipple, speaks uncannily in the accents shared by Calvin Coolidge and Ronald Reagan. Why could not Orwell have rescued his book by some last touch of irony or by a valid invocation of the satiric Muse?

III

What Max Horkheimer and T. W. Adorno grimly called the Culture Industry has absorbed Orwell, and his *1984* in particular. Is this because Orwell retains such sentimentalities or soft idealisms as the poignance of true love? After all, Winston and Julia are terrorized out of love by brute pain and unendurable fear; no one could regard them as having been culpable in their forced abandonment of one another. This is akin to Orwell's fantastic and wholly unconvincing hope that the proles might yet offer salvation, a hope presumably founded upon the odd notion that Oceania lets eighty-five percent of its population go back to nature in the slums of London and other cities. Love and the working class are therefore pretty much undamaged in Orwell's vision. Contrast Pynchon's imaginative "paranoia" in *Gravity's Rainbow*, where all of us, of whatever social class, live in the Zone which is dominated by the truly paranoid System, and where authentic love can be represented only as sado-masochism. There is a Counterforce in *Gravity's Rainbow* that fights the System, but it is ineffectual, farcical, and can be animated only by the peculiar ideology that Pynchon calls sado-anarchism, an ideology that the Culture Industry cannot absorb, and that I suspect Adorno gladly would have embraced.

I don't intend this introduction as a drubbing or trashing of Orwell and *1984*, and *Gravity's Rainbow*, being an encyclopedic prose epic, is hardly a fair agonist against which *1984* should be matched. But the aesthetic badness of

1984 is palpable enough, and I am a good enough disciple of the divine Oscar Wilde to wonder if an aesthetic inadequacy really can be a moral splendor? Simon Legree beats poor old Uncle Tom to death, and O'Brien pretty well wrecks Winston Smith's body and then reduces him to supposed ruin by threatening him with some particularly nasty and hungry rats. Is *Uncle Tom's Cabin* actually a moral achievement, even if Harriet Beecher Stowe hastened both the Civil War and the Emancipation Proclamation? Is *1984* a moral triumph, even if it hastens a multiplication of neoconservatives?

The defense of a literary period piece cannot differ much from a defense of period pieces in clothes, household objects, popular music, movies, and the lower reaches of the visual arts. A period piece that is a political and social polemic, like *Uncle Tom's Cabin* and *1984*, acquires a curious charm of its own. What partly saves *1984* from Orwell's overliteralness and failures in irony is the strange archaism of its psychology and rhetoric:

> He paused for a few moments, as though to allow what he had been saying to sink in.
>
> "Do you remember," he went on, "writing in your diary, 'Freedom is the freedom to say that two plus two make four'?"
>
> "Yes," said Winston.
>
> O'Brien held up his left hand, its back toward Winston, with the thumb hidden and the four fingers extended.
>
> "How many fingers am I holding up, Winston?"
>
> "Four."
>
> "And if the Party says that it is not four but five—then how many?"
>
> "Four."
>
> The word ended in a gasp of pain. The needle of the dial had shot up to fifty-five. The sweat had sprung out all over Winston's body. The air tore into his lungs and issued again in deep groans which even by clenching his teeth he could not stop. O'Brien watched him, the four fingers still extended. He drew back the lever. This time the pain was only slightly eased.
>
> "How many fingers, Winston?"
>
> "Four."
>
> The needle went up to sixty.
>
> "How many fingers, Winston?"
>
> "Four! Four! What else can I say? Four!"
>
> The needle must have risen again, but he did not look at it. The heavy, stern face and the four fingers filled his vision. The

fingers stood up before his eyes like pillars, enormous, blurry, and seeming to vibrate, but unmistakably four.

"How many fingers, Winston?"

"Four! Stop it, stop it! How can you go on? Four! Four!"

"How many fingers, Winston?"

"Five! Five! Five!"

"No, Winston, that is no use. You are lying. You still think there are four. How many fingers, please?"

"Four! Five! Four! Anything you like. Only stop it, stop the pain!"

Abruptly he was sitting up with O'Brien's arm round his shoulders. He had perhaps lost consciousness for a few seconds. The bonds that had held his body down were loosened. He felt very cold, he was shaking uncontrollably. His teeth were chattering, the tears were rolling down his cheeks. For a moment he clung to O'Brien like a baby, curiously comforted by the heavy arm round his shoulders. He had the feeling that O'Brien was his protector, that the pain was something that came from outside, from some other source, and that it was O'Brien who would save him from it.

"You are a slow learner, Winston," said O'Brien gently.

"How can I help it?" he blubbered. "How can I help seeing what is in front of my eyes? Two and two are four."

"Sometimes. Winston. Sometimes they are five. Sometimes they are three. Sometimes they are all of them at once. You must try harder. It is not easy to become sane."

He laid Winston down on the bed. The grip on his limbs tightened again, but the pain had ebbed away and the trembling had stopped, leaving him merely weak and cold. O'Brien motioned with his head to the man in the white coat, who had stood immobile throughout the proceedings. The man in the white coat bent down and looked closely into Winston's eyes, felt his pulse, laid an ear against his chest, tapped here and there; then he nodded to O'Brien.

"Again," said O'Brien.

The pain flowed into Winston's body. The needle must be at seventy, seventy-five. He had shut his eyes this time. He knew that the fingers were still there, and still four. All that mattered was somehow to stay alive until the spasm was over. He had ceased to notice whether he was crying out or not. The pain lessened again. He opened his eyes. O'Brien had drawn back the lever.

"How many fingers, Winston?"

"Four. I suppose there are four. I would see five if I could. I am trying to see five."

"Which do you wish: to persuade me that you see five, or really to see them?"

"Really to see them."

"Again," said O'Brien.

If we took this with high seriousness, then its offense against any persuasive mode of representation would make us uneasy. But it *is* a grand period piece, parodying not only Stalin's famous trials, but many theologically inspired ordeals before the advent of the belated Christian heresy that Russian Marxism actually constitutes. Orwell was a passionate moralist, and an accomplished essayist. The age drove him to the composition of political romance, though he lacked nearly all of the gifts necessary for the writer of narrative fiction. *1984* is an honorable aesthetic failure, and perhaps time will render its crudities into so many odd period graces, remnants of a vanished era. Yet the imagination, as Wallace Stevens once wrote, is always at the end of an era. Lionel Trilling thought that O'Brien's torture of Winston Smith was "a hideous parody on psychotherapy and the Platonic dialogues." Thirty-seven years after Trilling's review, the scene I have quoted above seems more like self-parody, as though Orwell's narrative desperately sought its own reduction, its own outrageous descent into the fallacy of believing that only the worst truth about us can be the truth.

Orwell was a dying man as he wrote the book, suffering the wasting away of his body in consumption. D. H. Lawrence, dying the same way, remained a heroic vitalist, as his last poems and stories demonstrate. But Lawrence belonged to literary culture, to the old, high line of transcendental seers. What wanes and dies in *1984* is not the best of George Orwell, not the pamphleteer of *The Lion and the Unicorn* nor the autobiographer of *Homage to Catalonia* nor the essayist of *Shooting an Elephant*. That Orwell lived and died an independent Socialist, hardly Marxist but really a Spanish Anarchist, or an English dissenter and rebel of the line of Cromwell and of Cromwell's celebrators, Milton and Carlyle. *1984* has the singular power, not aesthetic but social, of being the product of an age, and not just of the man who set it down.

ADRIAAN M. DE LANGE

Autobiography:
An Analysis of 'Shooting an Elephant'

Orwell's autobiographical essays include pieces such as 'Such, Such Were the Joys', 'Shooting an Elephant', 'A Hanging', 'How the Poor Die', 'Bookshop Memories', 'Marrakech', 'Confessions of a Book Reviewer' and 'Why I Write'. In these essays Orwell weaves an intricate net of fact, speculation and observation. They are further characterized by the vividness of his descriptions and the controlled, or seemingly controlled, presentation of emotion. 'Shooting an Elephant' is relevant to the present study for two reasons: it was published in 1936 and this study especially concentrates on Orwell's technique after 1936; it is also one of his most famous essays and is generally regarded as representative of his autobiographical approach.

'Shooting an Elephant' must be read against the background of Anglo-Burmese relations in general and Orwell's intense hatred of the imperialist system in particular.[1] During this period (1752–1948) these relations varied from mutual respect to bitter hatred. The years between 1919 and 1930 not only marked the worst period in these relations but were also the period during which Orwell served in the Burma police. Arriving in Burma on 27 November 1922,[2] he was in time to experience the backlash of the dissent that arose after the passing of the Government of India Act in 1919.

In the early years a spirit of goodwill existed between the Burmese and English officials and traders. The communities mixed on a social level

From *The Influence of Political Bias in Selected Essays of George Orwell* pp. 49–60. © 1992 by the Edwin Mellen Press.

and marriages resulted.[3] In 1885 the whole of Burma fell under British rule. It was a logical conclusion that Burma would either be turned into a protectorate or be treated as a separate colony with its own identity. This was not to be—Burma was merely turned into a province of India.[4] This humiliation led to several uprisings which were easily crushed by the police. The growing dissent and dissatisfaction could not, however, be suppressed. The appointment of the Montagu-Chelmsford Commission gave rise to the hope that Burma would not be excluded from consideration for political reform,[5] yet when the Commission recommended a system of reforms for India they did not deem it necessary to include Burma. The Government of India Act, when duly passed by the Parliament of Westminster in 1919, excluded Burma from the reforms that it entailed.

Protests against this decision were heard all over Burma. Feelings ran so high that even the Buddhist priests[6] joined in the protest.[7] Plans to restore good relations by means of education failed when students at the newly formed University of Rangoon called out a strike.[8] Hence the 'sneering yellow faces of young men that met me [Orwell] everywhere'.[9] Orwell began his career in the wake of this unrest and its effect on him was to manifest itself later in his work.

The nation-wide movement for political freedom persisted, forcing the British government to extend the dyarchy reforms to Burma.[10] Liberal Burmese leaders distrusted the government's motives. These reforms caused a division among the liberals, whose own differences caused them to lose power over the peasants. This situation led to the national peasants' revolt in 1930.[11]

The hostility of the people and the reaction of the colonial government left a deep impression on Orwell's mind. The harsh facts of life which he encountered for the first time compelled him to define his own position in terms of the ideals of the Imperialist regime. His attitude towards the system was later articulated in *The Road to Wigan Pier*, and he made no bones about his feelings:

> I was in the Indian Police five years, and by the end of that time I hated the imperialism I was serving with a bitterness which I probably cannot make clear. In the free air of England that kind of thing is not fully intelligible. In order to hate imperialism you have got to be part of it. Seen from the outside the British rule in India appears—indeed, it is—benevolent and even necessary; and so no doubt are the French rule in Morocco and the Dutch rule in Borneo, for people usually govern foreigners better than themselves. But it is not possible to be a part of such a system

without recognizing it as an unjustifiable tyranny. Even the thickest-skinned Anglo-Indian is aware of this. Every "native" face he sees in the street brings home to him this monstrous intrusion ... All over India there are Englishmen who secretly loathe the system of which they are part; and just occasionally, when they are quite certain of being in the right company, their hidden bitterness overflows.[12]

It is in this context that one should read 'Shooting an Elephant'.

The opening paragraph introduces two of the three main motifs—the anti-imperialist feeling of the Burmese and the alienation of the white man in the East. The speaker states that 'in an aimless, petty kind of way anti European feeling was very bitter'[13] and that he is 'hated by large numbers of people—the only time that I have been important enough for this to happen to me'.[14] This paragraph illustrates how 'artfully' Orwell's technique operates. By using emotive words such as 'hated' and 'bitter' Orwell immediately captures his readers' attention. He then 'illustrates' his (generalizing) statement by three incidents: the spitting of betel juice over the European woman's dress, the Burman tripping Orwell up on the football field and the jeering of the young Buddhist priests. The reddish betel juice resembles the colour of blood and in the context of oppression becomes a symbol of the suffering of the oppressed people. The football-episode refers to former times when Burmese and English communities mixed socially. The present state of affairs contrasts sharply with those times. The jeering Buddhist priests are representative of the political involvement of the priests. These examples—drawn as they are from economic, social and religious spheres—emphasize the fact that anti-European feeling influenced all strata of Burmese society.

The fact that the European character is isolated and alone in each of these incidents is significant, as it introduces a major motif in the essay, that of isolation and alienation. This motif has a structural and moral significance: it links the main characters and provides the basic paradigm for what Orwell is trying to convey. Alienation leads to death—either physically or emotionally. The white man is alienated from his Burmese subordinates because of race, religion, language and attitude. The people are alienated from their oppressors because of the unjust treatment they receive. The elephant, the biggest animal in the jungle, is made to do things totally foreign to its nature in an environment alien to its natural habitat. The black Dravidian coolie is alienated from the other Asians because of his race, his religion and the superior attitude of the Burmese. The Buddhist priests are alienated from the true nature of their religion when they become involved in political squabbles.

The sub-theme of violence is manifested in each of these characters, thus adding a structurally unifying device.

The juxtaposition between superiority and inferiority provides the third motif. The following passage not only captures the tension of this juxtaposition in the imperial context, but also emphasizes Orwell's own cynicism:

> And it was at this moment, as I stood there with the rifle in my hands, that I first grasped the hollowness, the futility of the white man's dominion in the East. Here was I, the white man with his gun, standing in front of the unarmed native crowd—seemingly the leading actor of the piece; but in reality I was only an absurd puppet pushed to and fro by the will of those yellow faces behind. I perceived in this moment that when the white man turns tyrant it is his own freedom that he destroys. He becomes a sort of hollow, posing dummy, the conventionalized figure of a sahib. For it is the condition of his rule that he shall spend his life in trying to impress the "natives" and so in every crisis he has got to do what the natives expect of him. He wears a mask, and his face grows to fit it. I had got to shoot the elephant. I had committed myself to doing it when I sent for the rifle. A sahib has got to act like a sahib; he has got to appear resolute, to know his own mind and do definite things.[15]

The implication is that the oppressors regard themselves as superior to those they oppress. Yet this is a paradoxical situation. They do what the oppressed natives expect of them and so lose their freedom of choice—they cannot act as superiors as they would like, but must do what is expected— 'A white man mustn't be frightened in front of "natives"'.[16] The feeling of inferiority is hidden behind the facade of political and military power of the oppressors. As a police officer Orwell sees the result of the pain caused by the inability to handle the authority, the 'wretched prisoners huddling in the stinking cages of the lock-ups, the grey, cowed faces of the long-term convicts, the scarred buttocks of the men who have been flogged by bamboos'.[17] This paradox governs the actions of the men who serve the system. Their power is based on conventional action. Loyalty cannot be demanded—it has to be forced. To lose face is to lose power. That is why the older officials condone Orwell's deed—they have been in the East long enough to realize that 'every white man's life in the East, was one long struggle not to be laughed at'.[18] Orwell had acted according to conventions and was therefore in the right. Hence Orwell's justification to soothe his own conscience—'I often wondered whether any of the others grasped that I had done it solely to avoid looking a fool'.[19]

The theme of superiority vs inferiority is manifested by the juxtaposing of the white man and the Asians, and man and animal.

The opposition between European and Burmese is a major structural device in the essay. The Europeans are 'jeered at from a safe distance'.[20] The police officers are taunted 'whenever it seemed safe to do so'.[21] Orwell himself experiences a feeling of superiority—he feels like driving a 'bayonet into the Buddhist priest's guts'.[22]

Man's control over the elephant is another example of the paradox as the Dravidian coolie, who is supposed to control it, is trampled to death by the elephant. In each of these instances there is no real reason for the feeling of superiority—in fact, it is actually a false feeling of superiority which causes the oppressors to behave in the way they do.

The speaker, Orwell, is the principal actor in the drama. Two of his characteristics are emphasized—his ambivalence and his feeling of inferiority. These aspects are brought to the fore by his dealings with the crowd and the elephant. Orwell is torn between a sense of duty and personal identification. He identifies himself openly with the Burmese: 'For at that time I had already made up my mind that imperialism was an evil thing and the sooner I chucked up my job and got out of it the better. Theoretically—and secretly, of course— I was all for the Burmese and all against their oppressors, the British'.[23] On the other hand he experiences feelings of hatred for the Burmese: 'All that I knew was that I was stuck between hatred of the empire I served and my rage against the evil-spirited little beasts who tried to make my job impossible'.[24] The episode with the elephant brings him to a crisis in his life—a point at which he loses his ability to choose because a choice is forced on him. When he receives a plea for help he has no intention of killing the elephant because the harassed animal reminds him of his own alienation and harassment. He makes an uncertain choice: 'I could watch him for a little while to make sure that he did not turn savage again, and then go home'.[25] This is not to be: the crowd forces him to act as they expect him to, and in doing so, Orwell proves his inferiority:

> It was an immense crowd, two thousand at least and growing every minute ... I looked at the sea of yellow faces above the garish clothes—faces ... all certain that the elephant was going to be shot ... suddenly I realized that I should have to shoot the elephant after all. The people expected it of me and I had got to do it; I could feel their two thousand wills pressing me forward, irresistibly.[26]

As is the case with any individual who has allowed himself to be part of a tyrannical system, Orwell loses his freedom of choice; he has turned 'tyrant and it is his own freedom that he destroys'.[27] Stansky and Abrahams succinctly summarize Orwell's dilemma:

> His sympathies are as strong as his resentments, and they are all for the appointed victim of the ceremony, the elephant who must be sacrificed, and whose death Orwell invests with a dignity and pathos that are in painful contrast to the pettiness of the "natives" who have come to see the show, and of the police officer who is fearful of being laughed at. The death of the elephant, so magnificently and feelingly described, is the preordained conclusion of a ritual that satisfied the "natives", re-affirms Blair in his role as the servant (the victim) of Imperialism, and adds to the burden of self-hatred and guilt he will take away from Burma.[28]

Orwell realizes that the elephant is a symbol of his own state of alienation but is forced to kill it. This adds a sense of pathos to his character. In destroying his fellow outcast, he destroys part of himself. The immediate dramatic action thus assumes symbolic significance.

The crowd acts as a catalyst in Orwell's process of recognition of his alienation. When he feels 'their two thousand wills pressing me forward, irresistibly'[29] he is forced to admit his and his fellow Europeans' inferiority. Note, however, that the vicious circle of oppression encompasses the crowd as well. They become tyrants by wanting the elephant dead and in doing this they lose their ability to think and to make a choice. Knowing full well the worth of a working elephant, they carry on regardless and in destroying the elephant they symbolically destroy part of their own livelihood.

The 'black Dravidian coolie' adds to the paradox. His death provides Orwell with a justification for killing the elephant: 'afterward I was very glad that the coolie had been killed; it put me legally in the right and gave me sufficient pretext for shooting the elephant'.[30] The attitude towards him is the typical attitude held by whites towards Asians; that is why the young men feel that 'it was a damn shame to shoot an elephant for killing a coolie, because an elephant was worth more than any damn Coringhee coolie'.[31] Thus the character of the Indian is instrumental in presenting a division among the Europeans. On the one hand there is the older generation who feels that the honour of the whites has been saved; on the other hand there are the younger men who feel that it was unnecessary to shoot the elephant for a coolie. The effect of the invidious system is obvious—the longer one is part of a tyrannical system, the more freedom one loses. In playing up to the crowd's will, Orwell comes to the recognition that he has completely lost his freedom of choice.

The elephant has many symbolic meanings. He is both a symbol of the oppressor and the oppressed. In turning tyrant he destroys a bamboo hut, kills a cow, inflicts violence on a municipal rubbish van and tramples the Dravidian coolie to death, leaving him 'lying on his belly with arms crucified and head sharply twisted to one side'.[32] As is the case with Orwell, the elephant loses freedom and life when it turns tyrant. The death of the elephant is symbolic of the death of the Imperial regime. When the Burmese strip the elephant's carcass to the bone Orwell seems to imply that the vicious circle continues when the oppressed now becomes the oppressor. The threatening attitude in the first paragraph now turns into a physical deed. The elephant acts as a foil to Orwell, its actions bringing Orwell to a moment of recognition. The elephant also functions as a symbol of death: its horrible death is symbolic of the death of the empire, as well as the deaths of many oppressed under a tyrannical regime. It indicates the death of individual choice within a rigid system in a way which reveals Orwell's artistic prowess, his ability to 'fuse political purpose and artistic purpose into one whole':[33]

> It was obvious that the elephant would never rise again, but he was not dead. He was breathing very rhythmically with long rattling gasps, his great mound of a side painfully rising and falling. His mouth was wide open—I could see far down into caverns of pale pink throat. I waited a long time for him to die, but his breathing did not weaken. Finally I fired my two remaining shots into the spot where I thought his heart must be. The thick blood welled out of him like red velvet, but still he did not die. His body did not even jerk when the shots hit him, the tortured breathing continued without a pause. He was dying, very slowly and in great agony, but in some world remote from me where not even a bullet could damage him further. It seemed dreadful to see the great beast lying there, powerless to move and yet powerless to die, and not even to be able to finish him. I sent back for my small rifle and poured shot after shot into his heart and down his throat. They seemed to make no impression. The tortured gasps continued as steadily as the ticking of a clock.[34]

The elephant fulfills a major structural function in the essay. It is the focal point of the sub-theme of violence. The characters are all linked through this theme—the Dravidian coolie is trampled to death, Orwell kills

TECHNICAL COLLEGE OF THE LOWCOUNTRY
LEARNING RESOURCES CENTER
POST OFFICE BOX 1288
BEAUFORT, SOUTH CAROLINA 29901-1288

the elephant, the crowd strips the carcass of the elephant. Within the context the implicit meaning of the violence motif is that violence is a product of an Imperialist system.

The rifle and the betel juice are also symbols of violence. The rifle is also a symbol of power. It is used in an ironical sense—the 'beautiful German thing'[35] is instrumental in causing an agonizing death. Initially, Orwell is faced with a problem. He has the power in his hands: he can use it against the elephant, or against the crowd. Regardless of the consequences the fact remains that he has the power in his hands; what is important is what he chooses to do with the power. Yet he is not free to exercise the authority vested in him according to his own initiative. The conventional attitude corrupts his choice and the gun is used to kill the elephant. The betel juice is a symbol of violence and suffering and resembles the blood of the oppressed Burmese and the elephant.

Part of the success of 'Shooting an Elephant' can be ascribed to its vivid description of events and scenes. However, most of the success should, to my mind, be ascribed to Orwell's skill in evoking and manipulating his readers' emotions. The truths about imperialism at grassroots level become all the more horrifying because he succeeds in presenting his own awareness of reality in such a poignant but carefully controlled manner. He uses his familiar technique of capturing his readers' attention and persuading them to accept his point of view by skillfully 'perverting' words and symbols. It is one of the most successful examples in which Orwell succeeds almost fully to 'fuse political purpose and artistic purpose into one whole'.[36]

'Shooting an Elephant' was written in 1936 when Orwell's viewpoint had already been defined. He was already writing 'against totalitarianism and for democratic Socialism'.[37] He shows a deliberate didactic and moral intention: '["Shooting an Elephant" is] an artefact consciously shaped to point a moral'.[38] It is a parable of the emptiness of imperial domination. It is a clear indication of the direction which Orwell's thinking would take, towards becoming a 'real rebel'[39] fighting an unjust system.

Notes

1. Maung Htin Aung, 'George Orwell and Burma', *The World of George Orwell*, ed. Miriam Gross (London: Weidenfeld and Nicholson, 1971), p. 20.

2. *Ibid.*, p. 20.

3. *Ibid.*, p. 22.

4. *Ibid.*, p. 23.

5. *Ibid.*, p. 23.

6. The fact that the Buddhist priests became involved in the political struggle is significant. Buddhism is normally a pacific religion, concentrating on spiritual rather than physical action.

7. Aung, p. 23.

8. *Ibid.*, p. 23.

9. Orwell, 'Shooting an Elephant', *CEJL* I, p. 265.

10. The dyarchy system, in accord with the Montagu-Chelmsford proposals, was a system whereby Indians were offered representation and a say in government. However, important areas of government, such as finance, were still restricted.

11. Aung, p. 27.

12. Orwell, *The Road to Wigan Pier* (Harmondsworth: Penguin, 1980), pp. 126–27.

13. 'Shooting an Elephant', p. 265.

14. *Ibid.*, p. 265.

15. *Ibid.*, p. 269.

16. *Ibid.*, p. 270.

17. *Ibid.*, p. 266.

18. *Ibid.*, p. 270.

19. *Ibid.*, p. 272.

20. *Ibid.*, p. 265.

21. *Ibid.*, p. 265.

22. *Ibid.*, p. 266.

23. *Ibid.*, p. 266.

24. *Ibid.*, p. 261.

25. *Ibid.*, p. 269.

26. *Ibid.*, p. 269.

27. *Ibid.*, p. 269.

28. P. Stansky and W. Abrahams, *The Unknown Orwell* (London: Granada, 1981), p. 183.

29. 'Shooting an Elephant', p. 269.

30. *Ibid.*, p. 272.

31. *Ibid.*, p. 272.

32. *Ibid.*, p. 268.

33. 'Why I Write', *CEJL* I, p. 29.

34. 'Shooting an Elephant', pp. 271–72.

35. *Ibid.*, p. 271.

36. 'Why I Write', p. 29.

37. Ibid., p. 28.

38. J.R. Hammond, *A George Orwell Companion* (London: MacMillan, 1982), p. 214.

39. Cyril Connolly once described Orwell as 'a real rebel'. See C. Connolly, *Enemies of Promise* (Harmondsworth: Penguin, 1961), p. 178.

Bibliography

A. Books by Orwell

Orwell, Sonia and Angus, I., eds. *The Collected Essays, Journalism and Letters of George Orwell*, Vol. I–IV. Harmondsworth: Penguin, 1982.

Orwell, G. *Down and Out in Paris and London*. Harmondsworth: Penguin, 1979.

———. *Burmese Days*. Harmondsworth: Penguin, 1979.

———. *Keep the Aspidistra Flying*. Harmondsworth: Penguin, 1981.

———. *The Road to Wigan Pier*. Harmondsworth: Penguin, 1980.

———. *Homage to Catalonia*. Harmondsworth: Penguin, 1979.

————. *Coming Up for Air*. Harmondsworth: Penguin, 1979.

————. *Animal Farm*. Harmondsworth: Penguin, 1979.

————. *Nineteen Eighty-Four*. Harmondsworth: Penguin, 1979.

————. *Nineteen Eight four*. With a Critical Introduction and Annotations by Bernard Crick. Oxford: Clarendon Press, 1984.

B. Books about Orwell

Alldrit, K. *The Making of George Orwell: An Essay in Literary History*. London: Edward Arnold, 1969.

Atkins, J. *George Orwell: A Literary Study*. London: Calder and Boyars, 1971.

Aung, M.H. 'George Orwell and Burma'. *The World of George Orwell*, ed. Miriam Gross. London: Weidenfeld and Nicholson, 1971, pp. 19–30.

Brander, L. *George Orwell*. London: Longmans, 1956.

Crick, B. *George Orwell: A Life*. Harmondsworth: Penguin, 1980.

Fyvel, T.R. *George Orwell: A Personal Memoir*. London: Hutchinson, 1982.

Gloversmith, F., ed. 'Changing Things: Orwell and Auden'. *Class, Culture and Social Change: A New Hew of the 1930's*, ed. F. Gloversmith. Sussex: The Harvester Press, 1980, pp. 101–141.

Gross, Miriam, ed. *The World of George Orwell*. London: Weidenfeld and Nicholson, 1971.

Hammond, J. R. *A George Orwell Companion*. London: MacMillan, 1982.

Hartley, R. 'Orwell: Political Criticism and Fictional Vision'. 1936. *The Sociology of Literature*, Vol. 2. *Practices of Literature and Politics*, ed. F. Barker. University of Sussex, 1979, pp. 232–244.

Hollis, C. *A Study of George Orwell: The Man and His Works*. London: Hollis and Carter, 1956.

Hope, F. 'Schooldays'. *The World of George Orwell*, ed. Miriam Gross. London: Weidenfeld and Nicholson, 1971, pp. 9–18.

Hunter, Lynette. *George Orwell: The Search for a Voice*. Milton Keynes: Open University Press, 1984.

Kubal, D.L. *Outside the Whale: George Orwell's Art and Politics*. Notre Dame: University of Notre Dame Press, 1972.

Meyers, J. *A Reader's Guide to George Orwell*. London: Thames and Hudson, 1975(a).

————. *George Orwell: An Annotated Bibliography of Criticism*. New York: Garland, 1977.

————, ed. *George Orwell: The Critical Heritage*. London: Routledge and Kegan Paul, 1975(b).

Oxley, B.T. *George Orwell*. London: Evans Brothers, 1967.

Rees, R. *George Orwell: Fugitive from the Camp of Victory*. Carbondale: Southern Illinois University Press, 1961.

Stansky, P. and Abrahams, W. *Orwell: The Transformation*. London: Granada, 1981(a).

————. *The Unknown Orwell*. London: Granada, 1981(b).

Thomas, E.M. *Orwell*. Edinburgh: Oliver and Boyd, 1965.

Wain, J. 'George Orwell as a Writer of Polemic'. *George Orwell: A Collection of Critical Essays*, ed. R. Williams. Englewood Cliffs: Prentice Hall, 1974, pp. 89–102.

————. 'In the Thirties'. *The World of George Orwell*, ed. Miriam Gross. London: Weidenfeld and Nicholson, 1977, pp. 75–93.

Williams, R. *George Orwell: A Collection of Critical Essays*. Englewood Cliffs: Prentice Hall, 1974.

————. *Orwell*. London: Fontana, 1979.

Woodcock, G. *The Crystal Spirit: A Study of George Orwell*. London: Jonathan Cape, 1967.

Zwerdling, A. *Orwell and the Left*. New Haven: Yale University Press, 1974.

C. Articles about Orwell

Auden, W.H. 'W.H. Auden on George Orwell'. *Spectator* (16 January 1975), pp. 86–87.

Bal, S.S. 'The Spanish Civil War and Orwell's Ethics of Commitment'. *Commonwealth Quarterly* 3, XI (1979), pp. 68–84.

Crowcroft, P. 'Politics and Writing: The Orwell Analysis'. *New Republic* (3 January 1955), pp. 17–18.

Dooley, D.J. 'The Limitations of George Orwell'. *University of Toronto Quarterly* 28 (1958–59), pp. 291–300.

Fixler, M. 'George Orwell and the Instrument of Language'. *Iowa English Yearbook* Fall 1964), pp. 46–54.

Freedman, C. 'Writing, Ideology and Politics: Orwell's "Politics and the English Language" and English Composition'. *College English* 43:4 (April 1981) pp. 327–340.

Fyvel, T.R. 'A Case for George Orwell'. *Twentieth Century* 160 (September 1956), pp. 254–257.

Glicksburg, C. 'The Literary Contribution of George Orwell'. *Arizona Quarterly* 10 (Autumn 1954), pp. 234–245.

Harris H.J. 'Orwell's Essays and 1984'. *Twentieth Century Literature* IV (January 1959), pp. 154–161.

Hoggart, R. 'George Orwell and *The Road to Wigan Pier*'. *Critical Quarterly* 7 (1965), pp. 72–85.

Hunter, J. 'Orwell's Prose: Discovery, Communion, Separation'. *Sewanee Review* 87 (1979), pp. 436–454.

Husain, S.W. 'The Essays of George Orwell'. *The Aligarh Journal of English Studies* 9:1 (1984), pp. 90–106.

Ingle, S.J. 'The Politics of George Orwell: A Reappraisal', *Queen's Quarterly*, 80 (1973), pp. 22–23.

King, C. 'The Politics of George Orwell'. *University of Toronto Quarterly* 26 (1956), pp. 79–91.

Lang, B. 'Politics and the Art of Decency: Orwell's Medium'. *South Atlantic Quarterly* 75 (1976), pp. 422–433.

Leavis, Q.D. 'The Literary Life Respectable: Mr George Orwell'. *Scrutiny* 9 (September 1940), pp. 173–176.

Mander, J. 'George Orwell's Politics'. *Contemporary Review* 197 (January and February 1960), pp. 32–36 and pp. 113–119.

Meyers, J. 'Review Article: George Orwell, the Honorary Proletarian,' *Philological Quarterly* 48:4 (1969), pp. 526–549.

Rossi, J.P. 'Orwell's Road to Socialism'. *Four Quarters* 28 (1978), pp. 3–10.

Rowse, A.L. 'The Eccentric Idealist.' *Times Literary Supplement* (14 September 1956), p. 539.

Shapiro, Marjorie. 'George Orwell's Criticism'. *Connecticut Review* 6:2 (1973), pp. 70–75.

Smith, M. 'George Orwell, War and Politics in the 1930's'. *Literature and History: A New Journal for The Humanities* 6 (1979), pp. 219–234.

Tibbets, Anne M. 'What did Orwell Think About the English Language?' *College Composition and Communication* 29 (1978), pp. 162–166.

Voorhees, R.J. 'Orwell's Secular Crusade'. *Commonweal* 61 (28 January 1955), pp. 448–451.

Wain, J. 'Orwell and the Intelligentsia'. *Encounter* 2 (September 1968), pp. 78–80.

———. 'Orwell'. *The Spectator* (19 November 1954), pp. 630–634.

Warncke, W. 'George Orwell's Critical Approach to Literature'. *Southern Humanities Review* 2 (1968), pp. 484–498.

———. 'George Orwell's Dickens'. *South Atlantic Quarterly* 69 (1970), pp. 373–381.

Watson, G. 'Orwell and the Spectrum of European Politics'. *Journal of European Studies* 1(1971), pp. 191–97.

Wolf, H. 'George Orwell and the Problematics of Non-Fiction'. *Critical Quarterly* 27:2 (1985), pp. 23–30.

Woodcock, G. 'George Orwell, 19th Century Liberal'. *Politics* (December 1946), pp. 384–385.

D. General Works

Baker, Frances *et. al. The Sociology of Literature: Practices of Literature and Politics*. Essex: University Essex Press, 1979.

Branson, Noreen and Heinemann, Margot. *Britain in the Nineteen Thirties*. London: Weidenfeld and Nicolson, 1971.

Chapman, F. Review: *New Writing*, ed. J. Lehmann. *Criterion* XVI, lxii (Oct. 1936), pp. 162–165.

Clark, J. *et. al.*, eds. *Culture and Crisis in Britain in the Thirties*. London: Lawrence and Wishart, 1979.

Corbett, T.G.P. 'Boy Scouts'. *Encyclopaedia Britannica, Vol.* 4 (1971), p. 48.

Cunningham, V. 'Neutral?: 1930's Writers, and Taking 1930's Sides'. *Class, Culture and Social Change: A New View of the 1930's*, ed. F. Gloversmith. Sussex: The Harvester Press, 1980, pp. 45–69.

———. *British Writers of the Thirties*. Oxford: Oxford University Press, 1988.

Dickens, C. *Nicholas Nickleby*. London: British Books, n.d.

Glicksburg, C. *Literature and Society*. The Hague: Martinus Nijhoff, 1972.

———. *The Literature of Commitment*. Lewisburg: Bucknell University Press, 1976.

Gloversmith, F., ed. *Class, Culture and Social Change. A New View of the 1930's*. Sussex: The Harvester Press, 1980.

Hynes, S. *The Auden Generation: Literature and Politics in England in the 1930's*. London: The Bodley Head, 1976.

Kettle, A. 'W.H. Auden: Poetry and Politics in the Thirties'. *Culture and Crisis in Britain in the Thirties*, ed. J. Clark *et. al.* London: Lawrence and Wishart, 1979, pp. 83–102.

Klugmann, J. 'The Crisis in the Thirties: A View From the Left'. *Culture and Crisis in Britain in the Thirties*, ed. J. Clark *et. al.* London: Lawrence and Wishart, 1979, pp. 13–36.

Lucas, J., ed. *The 1930's. A Challenge to Orthodoxy*. Sussex: The Harvester Press, 1978.

Macmillan, H. *Winds of Change, 1914–1939*. London: Macmillan, 1966.

Mander, J. *The Writer and Commitment*. London: Secker and Warburg, 1961.

Reid, Betty. 'The Left Book Club in the Thirties'. *Culture and Crisis in Britain in the Thirties*. London: Lawrence Wishart, 1979, pp. 193–208.

Stevenson, J. and Cook, C. *The Slump: Society and Politics during the Depression*. London: Jonathan Cape, 1977.

Taylor, A.J.P. *English History 1914–45*. Oxford University Press, 1965.

Unstead, R.J. *Britain in the Twentieth Century*. London: A and C Black, 1966.

Upward, E. 'Sketch for a Marxist Interpretation of Literature'. *The Mind in Chains: Socialism and the Cultural Revolution*, ed. C. Day Lewis. London: Frederick Muller, 1937, pp. 41–55.

Widdowson, P. 'Between the Acts? English Fiction in the Thirties'. *Culture and Crisis in Britain in the Thirties*, ed. J. Clark, *et. al.* London: Lawrence and Wishart, 1979, pp. 133–164.

Woodcock, G. *The Writer and Politics*. London: The Porcupine Press, 1948.

Woolf, Virginia. 'The Leaning Tower'. Folios *of New Wining* (Autumn 1940), pp. 11–33.

ROGER FOWLER

Versions of Realism

In Chapters 5 to 9 I will discuss some stylistic features of the seven books which were published between 1933 and 1939. Orwell's productivity in this period was astonishing: one book a year, each taking a few months to write, despite other commitments, recurrent serious illness, poverty, several changes of home base, a research trip to the North of England, fighting in the Spanish Civil War ... Each book seems to have been written straight out, with no overlapping: if the pace seems frantic, there was the gain of concentrated focus, a condition which will be appreciated by any writer who has to grapple with a number of simultaneous projects.

Orwell frequently revalued his books with hindsight reflections, with a tendency to *de*value them.[1] Critics also practise a kind of retrospection. Their vantage-point is the high territory of *Animal Farm* (1945) and *Nineteen Eighty-Four* (1949) which have of course enjoyed a phenomenally greater acclaim than the 'early' books. From this perspective, the seven books written and published in the 1930s might be seen as hastily-written, ragged, pot-boilers, inferior to the 'masterpieces' and interesting primarily as anticipating, in theme and/or in style, the two most popular books. Now it seems to me valid to find in the 1930s works numerous foreshadowings, both in ideas and in techniques, of the two major books; to regard some aspects of them as stages in the working-out of what we know were Orwell's

From *The Language of George Orwell*: pp. 60–86. © 1995 by Roger Fowler.

preoccupations in his last years. However, this should not lead to the dismissal of the early fiction and documentary writings as try-outs by an apprentice. As a matter of fact, each of the early books was a distinct piece of writing, usually relating to some specific section of experience in Orwell's own life, or phase in the development of his political and artistic thinking. Each has its own models, and strategies of composition, and these are quite various: they deserve an attempt at understanding in their own terms. To grant the first seven books this minimal respect is not to deny that they have faults: they have been criticised, variously, for flat characterisation, uncertainty of point of view, unmotivated stylistic shifts and narrative transitions, and intrusive commentary. However, it is by no means the case that all these uncertainties of technique afflict all the early books. Every one of them has been acclaimed by different critics and reviewers at some time during its history; and all have remained in print since popular editions were published after Orwell's death. There is a strong tradition of appreciative literary criticism which, quite justifiably, finds reasons to admire Orwell's early fictional and documentary output as a whole.[2]

Four aspects of the language of the 1930s books will be examined. In this chapter I will demonstrate, largely with reference to *Down and Out in Paris and London*, *The Road to Wigan Pier*, *Burmese Days* and *Coming Up for Air*, three interlinked styles of 'realistic' writing, which I will call **descriptive realism**, **naturalism** (or 'sordid realism'), and **surrealism** (or 'hyperrealism'). In Chapter 6 the subject will be 'voices of the other', Orwell's representation of modes of speech which differ from standard English, and the importance of stylistic and social heteroglossia in his work. In Chapter 7 I will look at another set of topics: literary strategies relating to description and figurative language, and will develop the discussion of 'voices of the other' (heteroglossia). Chapter 8 will examine the linguistic construction of narrative point of view, a subject which becomes of fundamental importance in *Animal Farm* (Chapter 9) and *Nineteen Eighty-Four* (Chapter 10).

Let us remind ourselves of the dates and sequence of the books concerned:

- *Down and Out in Paris and London*, 1933
- *Burmese Days*, 1934
- *A Clergyman's Daughter*, 1935
- *Keep the Aspidistra Flying*, 1936
- *The Road to Wigan Pier*, 1937
- *Homage to Catalonia*, 1938
- *Coming Up for Air*, 1939

Then, after a gap occupied by collections of essays, by journalism and by BBC work, there followed *Animal Farm* (1945); finally, in his Jura and hospital days, he wrote *Nineteen Eighty-Four* (1949).

Though each has an individual occasion and technique, the books of the 1930s may be divided for the purposes of stylistic discussion into two groups. Four of them, *Burmese Days*, *Clergyman's Daughter*, *Aspidistra* and *Coming Up for Air*, are novels more or less strictly speaking: they are fictionalised narratives told in the third person, or in one case, *Conning Up for Air*, a first-person narration in which the speaker is a character and not an Orwell-toned narrator.

The other three (*Down and Out*, *Wigan Pier* and *Catalonia*) are mixed genres, part-autobiography, part-documentary or reportage, part-commentary or general essay. In all of them Orwell figures directly, but in various guises and speaking in different voices. All three versions of 'Orwell', however, can be best seen as involving variants of the 'personal voice' of the previous chapter, that personal voice by which the man Blair constructed himself as the writer George Orwell, an observer of, and commentator on, his life and times.

Each of these three books makes very specific demands of its reader, who must adjust his or her expectations to each text: no pre-existing generic model will fit. There is no familiar form to bring to these works, unlike the case of, for example, *Burmese Days*, where the reader will not be let down if s/he brings a foreknowledge of the 'colonial novel' of the Kipling (or even Burgess) tradition, or more specifically Forster's *A Passage to India* (1924). Each of the three books must be read—to use a phrase which seems necessary but surely abhorrent to Orwell as a piece of pretentious academic jargon— *sui generis*, one of a kind. No single generic label and assumptions will fit any of them properly: *Down and Out* is an anonymised fragment of personal autobiography, has a slight narrative continuity but digresses to documentary and commentary. When Orwell has some general points to make, he boldly breaks off from the narrative and starts up again in a first-person essayistic style: ch. 22 opens 'For what they are worth I want to give my opinions about the life of a Paris *plongeur*' (p. 117); ch. 32, 'I want to put in some notes, as short as possible, on London slang and swearing' (p. 170); ch. 36, 'I want to set down some general remarks about tramps' (p. 203). *Wigan Pier*, which was commissioned as a report rather than a story, is also of mixed genre. It has a fictionalised personal opening, a mass of documentation (including photographs, though these were not taken in the areas he visited)[3], and passages in a plain realistic style; but as we have seen, Part Two of *Wigan Pier* shifts abruptly and stridently to a polemical and abusive style. *Homage to Catalonia* is a narrative account of Orwell's experiences in the Spanish Civil

War, but also contains set descriptive passages and elements of travelogue, and is interrupted by political analyses and documentary quotations (especially chs. 5 and 11). He declares:

> If you are not interested in the horrors of party politics, please skip; I am trying to keep the political parts of this narrative in separate chapters for precisely that purpose. (*Catalonia*, p. 46)

'Artistic' integration is not prominently on the agenda. None of these three books is strongly driven or unified by story, none is consistently essay, or description, or analysis; each mixes all these, and other ingredients, in various proportions.

The seven books published in the 1930s encompass a variety of genres, and three of them, *Down and Out*, *Wigan Pier* and *Catalonia*, settle to no recognisable prior form. Relatedly, they manifest a remarkable variety of *stylistic* techniques between them, and individually, each includes a range of styles. The juxtaposition of distinct styles within one work may be called **heteroglossia**: it is a feature of Orwell's writing in all his books except *Animal Farm*, and its artistic and political significance will be discussed in Chapter 10 in relation to *Nineteen Eighty-Four*. In the present and the following two chapters we will identify some of the elements of the heteroglossic mix.

The Three 'Realisms': Brief Characterisation

The first thing to acknowledge is that the three versions of realism are not watertight distinct styles but overlapping stylistic models: it is not possible to find absolutely clear instances, to say that one style starts here in the text and ends there, to be replaced by some other clear style, say 'demotic' or 'lyrical'. The three styles of realism (as generally with 'styles') are 'models' in the sense introduced in Chapter 4 (p. above). Key features or cues—which may be just single words or phrases, or individual phonetic or metaphoric usages, symbols, etc.—encourage the reader to experience a part of the text as a particular kind of representation of the world. The reader's previous literary and other linguistic experience, including in this case familiarity with the writer's usual practices, brings the models to a reading of the text, and they are activated by the liaison of the pre-existing model and the textual cues.

Descriptive realism is a realism of physical particularity, a focus on what he called 'solid objects and scraps of useless information' (p. 19 above). This 'descriptive realism' is less obviously literary than the more sensationalist 'sordid realism', but no less crafted. It is an illusion of clarity and precision created by certain linguistic techniques including focus on detail or 'microscopism'; the enumeration of facts; and a preoccupation with textures, spatial dimensions and other material considerations. Orwell's work has been much admired for the concreteness and memorability of his descriptions of settings and places. His ideal of prose as clear as a window pane comes to mind, but as we will see at the end of this chapter, description is not readily separable from the narrator's views and values, so the clarity is often not perfect.

Naturalism has later nineteenth-century literary origins[4] and consists of a focus on suffering and on physical squalor in people and places. Extremes of sensation are evoked: dirt, smell, noise, light and dark, heat and cold, violent movement, crowding, confinement, physical contact (sensations to which Orwell seems to have had powerful personal aversions). The style is hyperbolic, and relies to a considerable extent on metaphor, evocative adjectives and intensifying phrases; the tone is generally negative or condemnatory, a tendency which meshes well with Orwell's dominant discontent and anger.

Surrealism in Orwell's writing is, as I have tried to suggest by the alternative term 'hyperrealism', a stage beyond naturalism. In hyperrealism the assault on the senses is intensified and diversified, and there are odd juxtapositions of images suggesting a more discordant world, one more difficult to figure out, than the real world. Metaphors and similes, often unusual and opaque, are common. Sensory experience is presented in terms of a fictional or alien world: in the passages to be examined below, there are evocations of hell, or a lunar landscape. Symbolism is constantly hinted, though usually in an imprecise way. Surrealism is usually achieved through descriptions of sights and scenes, but once, in a Joycean chapter of *A Clergyman's Daughter*, Orwell tries for the only time a surrealistic effect based on a disorienting medley of voices (see Chapter 6, fourth section).

In Chapter 7 we will examine a fourth style of descriptive writing which could not be called 'realistic', the picturesque, the highly visual and colourful evocation of unusual, striking, scenes and landscape, often exotic. The picturesque is prominent in *Burmese Days* and found in passages of *Homage to Catalonia*; it is a style which Orwell, with hindsight, confessed to rather than admired. There is a less spectacular, more rural, variant which I have called pastoral, well-illustrated in *Coming Up for Air* but occurring at romantic moments elsewhere.

Both the 'descriptive' and the 'sordid' models of realism persist throughout Orwell's writings up to and including his final novel, *Nineteen Eighty-Four*. In the early works there are prominent 'set pieces' of description in one or the other mode, but sometimes they are tendencies rather than utterly distinct, and are often interwoven, or just cued by some significant detail. 'Surrealism' or 'hyperrealism' is not simply an indulgence of Orwell's early, experimental, work, but has a specific function in *Nineteen Eighty-Four* as communicating Winston Smith's dreaming and hallucinatory states (Chapter 10, pp. 192–3).

Descriptive Realism and the Sense of 'Place'

Orwell's writing has frequently been praised for the precision and memorability of his descriptions of settings and locations, particularly those that convey the minutiae of English life; for example, J. R. Hammond: 'his undoubted talent lay in the power to evoke a setting with such clarity that the picture remains in the mind long after the book has been laid aside'.[5] Hammond may here be recalling a comment of Orwell on Dickens that he quotes elsewhere:

> Much that he wrote is extremely factual, and in the power of evoking visual images he has probably never been equalled. When Dickens has once described something you see it for the rest of your life. (*CEJL*, I, 485)

Details such as the following, from the opening pages of *Coming Up for Air*, abound in Orwell:

> Down below, out of the little square of bathroom window, I could see the ten yards by five of grass, with a privet hedge round it and a bare patch in the middle, that we call the back garden. There's the same back garden, same privets, and same grass, behind every house in Ellesmere Road. Only difference—where there are no kids there's no bare patch in the middle ...
>   Our dining-room, like the other dining-rooms in Ellesmere Road, is a poky little place, fourteen feet by twelve, or maybe it's twelve by ten, and the Japanese oak sideboard, with the two empty decanters and the silver egg-stand that Hilda's mother gave us for a wedding present, doesn't leave much room. (*Coming Up for Air*, pp. 7, 10)

These two fragments, inserted in George Bowling's account of a morning at his house, contribute, with other jigsaw pieces, to an overall description of the spiritless modern housing estate where he and his family live. Because the description is given in bits, the details remain prominent: a few nouns list the salient points, and because they are few in number and in very brief passages, they are highlighted: 'grass', 'privet', 'bare patch', 'Japanese oak sideboard', 'the two empty decanters and the silver egg-stand'. There is in fact space for extra detail to be mentioned and not lost: the bathroom window is not simply a viewing point on the garden, it is a 'little square'; the sideboard is 'Japanese oak'. The dimensions, both of the garden and of the dining-room, are specified, as is very common in Orwell.

Orwell's finest descriptions are of settings that typify the life of a traditional, even vanished, England; they are often *remembered* by the narrator, not just observed, and for this reason are charged with a kind of evocative power. *Coming Up for Air* contains a chain of nostalgic passages in which the hero and narrator George Bowling recalls his childhood impressions of his family's home and shop (has father was an animal feed merchant):

> The very first thing I remember is the smell of sainfoin chaff. You went up the stone passage that led from the kitchen to the shop, and the smell of sainfoin got stronger all the way. Mother had fixed a wooden gate in the doorway to prevent Joe and myself ... from getting into the shop. I can still remember standing there clutching the bars, and the smell of sainfoin mixed up with the damp plastery smell that belonged to the passage. It wasn't till years later that I somehow managed to crash the gate and get into the shop when nobody was there. A mouse that had been having a go at one of the meal-bins suddenly plopped out and ran between my feet. It was quite white with meal. (*Coming Up for Air*, pp. 35–6)

Note the use of smells to prompt memory; the simple details that nevertheless give an image and a texture: 'the stone passage', 'a wooden gate'; the clear focus on a single mouse 'quite white with meal'. The child George progresses to the shop:

> And the shop itself, with the huge scales and the wooden measures and the tin shovel, and the white lettering on the window, and the bullfinch in its cage—which you couldn't see very well even from the pavement, because the window was always dusty—all these things dropped into place one by one, like bits of a jigsaw puzzle. (ibid, p. 36)

The jigsaw metaphor (which I borrowed above) is instructive. Knowledge, here the boy's mental map of his home surroundings, is a whole picture which is constituted from 'bits' of sensory experience which become integrated as they snap into place: they cease to be isolated fragments, but acquire meaning when they are understood as functioning in relation to one another. This is as good a theory of the way readers integrate and interpret textual description as it is of the way children make sense of the bits of the world.[6] We recover the individual 'bits' from the text; in Orwell, these are characteristically given in very simple and concrete noun phrases (hence the feeling of visual precision):

> the shop, the huge scales, the wooden measures, the tin shovel, the white lettering on the window, the bullfinch in its cage, the pavement, the windows ... always dusty.

The scales, measures and shovel are the implements for scooping, weighing and serving for an old-fashioned 'corn and seed merchant' like George's father; the white applied lettering is characteristic of pre-war shop fronts; the window is dusty, not through any slovenliness but because the goods in which the shop deals are dusty, dry animal feeds stocked in bulk. Orwell highlights the separate components—which are therefore distinct as they are read and remembered—and the reader makes the connections as s/he reconstructs the fictional world which the boy is remembering.[7] From a few spare references to a coherent set of physical objects, each mentioned with precision, we build a picture of an old-fashioned shop, and an atmosphere. The fact that we know that the scene is remembered by the narrator with affectionate nostalgia helps us to imagine this atmosphere, without Orwell having to mention explicitly the feeling by any adjectives or adverbs of attitude and evaluation. The plain, concrete yet suggestive style dominates this section of *Coming Up for Air*, and is carried very effectively in some quite sensitive sections, for example, the description of the kitchen and his mother's work within it (pp. 48–9).

An additional small point which might be noticed is that each of the descriptions quoted so far contains one reference to something slightly odd or puzzling: the 'silver egg-stand' and 'the bullfinch in its cage'. These slight incongruities complicate the tone somewhat: the grotesque egg-stand hints at George's hostility to his mother-in-law, while the pet bullfinch domesticises a commercial setting (it is presumably an advertisement for the bird-seed that George's father sells). Both references, slightly off-beat, may act as short-cuts to retrieve the setting from our memory store.

Interiors, settings and scenes are described in this lucid and economical but suggestive way throughout Orwell's writings. I would like to quote two more examples here, two interiors from Orwell's first true novel, *Burmese Days* (1934), famed for the landscape descriptions discussed in Chapter 7 below. There is a shading here into other kinds of writing, judgemental in the first, and symbolic in the second. First, the basic account of the 'white man's Club' in colonised Kyauktada, Burma:

Inside, the Club was a teak-walled place smelling of earth-oil, and consisting of only four rooms, one of which contained a forlorn 'library' of five hundred mildewed novels, and another an old and mangy billiards table—this, however, seldom used, for during most of the year hordes of flying beetles came buzzing round the lamps and littered themselves over the cloth. There was also a card-room and a 'lounge' which looked towards the river, over a wide veranda; but at this time of day all the verandas were curtained with green bamboo chicks. The lounge was an unhomelike room, with coconut matting on the floor, and wicker chairs and tables which were littered with shiny illustrated papers. For ornament there were a number of 'Bonzo' pictures, and the dusty skulls of sambhur. A punkah, lazily flapping, shook dust into the tepid air. (*Burmese Days*, p. 19)

The second passage describes the bedroom in the quarters of John Flory, the central protagonist in *Burmese Days*:

The bedroom was a large square room with white plaster walls, open doorways and no ceiling, but only rafters in which sparrows nested. There was no furniture except the big four-poster bed, with its furled mosquito net like a canopy, and a wicker table and chair and a small mirror; also some rough bookshelves containing several hundred books, all mildewed by many rainy seasons and riddled by silver fish. A *tuktoo* clung to the wall, flat and motionless like a heraldic dragon. Beyond the veranda eaves the light rained down like glistening white oil. Some doves in a bamboo thicket kept up a dull droning noise, curiously appropriate to the heat—a sleepy sound, but with the sleepiness of chloroform rather than a lullaby. (ibid, pp. 47–8)

As the intricate and well-devised narrative of the novel unfolds, quite a lot of action occurs in these two locations, particularly at the Club; and the basic function of these two passages is to map out in an introductory way the structure and contents of the settings. As is common in Orwell's descriptions of places, the style is basically nominal: a framework of nouns listing the main features of the rooms and what was contained in them—four rooms, billiard-table, lamps, card-room, lounge, veranda, bamboo chicks, coconut matting, wicker chairs and tables, papers, pictures, skulls, punkah, white plaster walls, open doorways, etc. The verbs introducing these nouns might not be noticed: they are largely 'was' and 'were', plus 'contain' in both passages;

significant is the avoidance of any more informative verbs, or decorative ones: even simple locative verbs like 'stood', or 'placed', are absent, and there is a marked scarcity of prepositions indicating spatial relationships between the objects listed, only 'towards' and 'beyond'. Just enough information is given to allow readers to understand the use of these spaces in future scenes: the four rooms of the Club are carefully distinguished, so that we can construct how, later, the English with their sexual and political tensions occupy parts of this building in their various role-playings and crises.

But the sparse description means also sparseness of the rooms and objects described: Flory's bedroom, it is hinted, is under-furnished by British standards; the Club is tatty and institutional; there is nothing personal, nothing luxurious. Some simple negative words carry a "large weight of meaning: '*only* four rooms', '*open* doorways', '*no* ceiling', '*only* rafters', '*no* furniture'. In the description of the Club, a string of adjectives indicate seediness and neglect: 'forlorn', 'mildewed', 'old and mangy', 'littered', 'unhomelike', 'dusty', 'tepid'. Both places are infested, with sparrows, flying beetles, silver fish, a 'tuktoo'. These locations are both described and judged, and they are judged negatively: they symbolise the dehumanisation of the English in Burma, and are fitting settings for the inadequacies of social and sexual relationship which their situation brings about, and particularly for the racism which is enacted in the book. In describing the Club, Orwell lays the ground for a critique of it and its members; this typical mixture of description and evaluation will be discussed in the final section of the present chapter.

The second passage, the description of Flory's bedroom, moves from a matter-of-fact account of the room to an evocation of a mood symbolised by the light and the sound of the Burmese natural world. Orwell's correlation of the characters' feelings and the sensations of landscape and climate in *Burmese Days* will be discussed in Chapter 7.

Naturalism and Surrealism in
DOWN AND OUT IN PARIS AND LONDON

Down and Out has its sources in Orwell's personal travels of 1927–9: his voluntary tramping in the East End of London, followed by eighteen months trying to live as a writer in Paris, where he became genuinely destitute and worked as a *plongeur* or dishwasher.[8] Orwell vouched for the authenticity of the book: 'nearly all the incidents described there actually happened, though they have been rearranged' (*Wigan Pier*, p. 133). The English and French experiences have been transposed. The book starts in a poor quarter of Paris with depictions of a hotel and bar and its neighbourhood, and of various eccentrics (his term) who live at or frequent the hotel and bistro. By Chapter

3 the narrator has lost his money; he teams up with Boris, a Russian waiter, to search for work, and the next several chapters follow their adventures and financial decline until they secure work at a hotel. Boris is a caricature, a Dickensian grotesque; their hunt for a job, a picaresque farce. The structure so far is rambling and anecdotal, a series of comic or pathetic incidents, and curious tales narrated by the 'eccentrics'.

Chapter 10 has the narrator and Boris employed at the 'Hôtel X', and here begins a section of some sixty pages depicting the hotel and restaurant world seen from below. This sequence can be regarded as the imaginative centre of the book. Orwell devotes great descriptive and poetic energy to presenting the squalid conditions of the kitchens; the power hierarchy in the work force, with the lowest grade, the *plongeurs* (at which level Orwell was employed) being essentially slaves; the cheating of, and contempt for, customers. In his review, C. Day Lewis commented 'if you wish to eat a meal in a big hotel without acute nausea, you had better skip pp. 107–109'.[9] Here is art as political writing. There are a number of often-quoted set pieces, including recurrent treatments of a motif that clearly preoccupied Orwell: his vision (from a position of privilege) of labour and working life as a descent into hell; there is a version of inferno at his first entrance into the Hôtel X:

> He led me down a winding staircase into a narrow passage, deep underground, and so low that I had to stoop in places. It was stiflingly hot and very dark, with only dim, yellow bulbs several yards apart. There seemed to be miles of dark labyrinthine passages—actually, I suppose, a few hundred yards in all—that reminded one queerly of the lower decks of a liner; there were the same heat and cramped space and warm reek of food, and a humming, whirring noise (it came from the kitchen furnaces) just like the whir of engines. We passed doorways which let out sometimes a shouting of oaths, sometimes the red glare of a fire, once a shuddering draught from an ice chamber. (*Down and Out*, p. 54)

The narrator moves from the Hôtel X to a pretentious but filthy and disorganised restaurant; the squalor and chaos are again portrayed in detail. He escapes by borrowing the money to return to England, but before he relates his return he offers a chapter of 'opinions about the life of a Paris *plongeur*' (Ch. 22).

The book continues with a rambling account of life among tramps and beggars in London (which in Orwell's real life was a voluntary descent undertaken before his trip to Paris). The procedure and structure are similar to the first part: Orwell puts his narrator in association with two low-life characters, Bozo the 'screever' or pavement artist, and Paddy the tramp, and takes the reader from location to location, describing lodging houses and 'spikes' ('casual wards' for the homeless) with a documentary detail that foreshadows *Wigan Pier*. He ends with an essay on the social and economic conditions of tramps. This is a direct treatment of one aspect of the theme of the book (destitution), voiced in the form of a commentary. Critics have expressed their dissatisfaction with this essay, treating it as a deviation from a predominantly fictional mode. But the narrative fiction—the low-life stories peopled with Dickensian oddities—is itself only an instrument, as Orwell clearly announced in the first chapter:

> I am trying to describe the people in our quarter, not for the mere curiosity, but because they are all part of the story. Poverty is what I am writing about, and I had my first contact with poverty in this slum. The slum, with its dirt and its queer lives, was first an object-lesson in poverty, and then the background of my own experiences. It is for that reason that I try to give some idea of what life was like there. (*Down and Out*, p. 5)

The dominant mode of representation in the first part of *Down and Out* is naturalistic: 'sordid realism'. Significantly, Orwell invokes Zola, whom we know (note 4) he much admired: 'I wish I could be Zola for a little while, just to describe that dinner hour' (ibid, p. 64; peak demand at the hotel, frenzied activity in the kitchen). The point is not whether Orwell emulated Zola's style in detail, but that his descriptive model is in general terms naturalistic in the Zola mode, and therefore literary in character.

The opening description of the street and the hotel where the narrator lived is a characteristic evocation of 'noise and dirt', the keynotes of Orwell's representation in the Paris section:

> The Rue du Coq d'Or, Paris, seven in the morning. A succession of furious, choking yells from the street. Madame Monce, who kept the little hotel opposite mine, had come out on to the pavement to address a lodger on the third floor. Her bare feet were stuck into sabots and her grey hair was streaming down.
> *Madame Monce*: '*Salope! Salope!* How many times have I told you not to squash bugs on the wallpaper? Do you think you've bought the hotel, eh? Why can't you throw them out of the window like everyone else? *Putain! Salope!*' ... Quarrels, and the desolate cries of street hawkers, and the shouts of children chasing orange-peel

over the cobbles, and at night loud singing and the sour reek of the refuse-carts, made up the atmosphere of the street.

It was a very narrow street—a ravine of tall, leprous houses, lurching towards one another in queer attitudes, as though they had all been frozen in the act of collapse ... My hotel was called the Hotel des Trois Moineaux. It was a dark, rickety warren of five storeys, cut up by wooden partitions into forty rooms. The rooms were small and inveterately dirty, for there was no maid, and Madame F., the *patronne*, had no time to do any sweeping. The walls were as thin as matchwood, and to hide the cracks they had been covered with layer after layer of pink paper, which had come loose and housed innumerable bugs. Near the ceiling long lines of bugs marched all day like columns of soldiers, and at night came down ravenously hungry, so that one had to get up every few hours and kill them in hecatombs. Sometimes when the bugs got too bad one used to burn sulphur and drive them into the next room; whereupon the lodger next door would retort by having his room sulphured, and drive the bugs back. It was a dirty place, but homelike, for Madame F. and her husband were good sorts. The rent of the rooms varied between thirty and fifty francs a week. (ibid, pp. 1–2)

The 'realism' here is of a very literary kind. The verbless opening sentence 'The Rue du Coq d'Or ...' is like the title of a picture, or a scene-setting opening stage-direction: Orwell signals that he is to embark on a word-painting of 'the atmosphere of the street'. A second verbless sentence follows, conveying an impression rather than a narrative report of an event; further on, the sentence beginning 'Quarrels ...', though finite (culminating in a verb that completes it), is dominated by a string of noun phrases which offer a series of discrete sensory impressions. We saw in the previous chapter that the list or series is a favourite stylistic device of Orwell's. It is here used to suggest a crowding of sensory stimuli; we will encounter some more spectacular lists later.

Three other simple linguistic strategies dominate this impressionistic technique of 'sordid realism'. The first is a set of nouns and verbs, in a colloquial register, designating unpleasant, intrusive or low-life objects, sensations and actions:[10]

yells, bare feet, squash bugs, throw [bugs] out of the window, quarrels, cries, shouts, orange-peel, singing, reek, refuse-carts, cracks, bugs (x 4), kill, burn sulphur.

The second strategy is effected through the adjectives, and is highly typical of Orwell: the passage is suffused by adjectives offering consistently negative judgements; none severe in itself, but together producing an overwhelmingly gloomy effect:

> furious, choking, bare, grey, desolate, loud, sour, narrow, leprous, queer, dark, rickety, small, dirty, thin, loose, too bad, dirty.

Once again this is, apart from 'desolate' and 'leprous', a vernacular register, part of Orwell's way of maintaining contact with 'demotic speech'. And the oppressive negativity foreshadows the gloom of such later books as *Aspidistra* and *Nineteen Eighty-Four*. Only at the end are positive evaluations offered: 'homelike', 'good sorts'.

A third feature of this version of naturalism is a general heightening of sensation carried by some of the adjectives which suggest some extreme state of affairs, or at least a high level of energy output or sensation (for example 'furious', 'choking', 'loud', 'tall'), and by intensifiers:

> very narrow, inveterately, as thin as, layer after layer, innumerable, long, all day, ravenously, every few hours, too bad.

We can begin to see in this passage how Orwell's style tends toward hyperbole, even exaggeration and stridency. Later, in the set descriptive passages on hotel kitchen life, his use of these linguistic resources results in sensationalism or surrealism rather than naturalism, as we will see.

This realism is done in one of Orwell's mixed styles. Part of the vocabulary is 'low'; the tone is urgent as if the speaking voice wishes to break through. There may be seeds of the descriptive realism of *Wigan Pier*: the bugs on the pink paper are observed microscopically, the rents of the lodgings are stated in a matter-of-fact way, but without the foregrounded precision of the room dimensions and family budgets of *Wigan Pier*. But the painterly opening sentence, the traces of a high-register vocabulary ('sabots', 'leprous', 'hecatombs'), and the high-profile metaphors, encase the realism in a literary frame. There are two set-piece metaphors, the first extensive and complex, but ostentatious and laboured:

> a very narrow street—a ravine of tall, leprous houses, lurching towards one another in queer attitudes, as though they had all been frozen in the act of collapse.

The first part of the complex metaphor, 'ravine', invokes landscape to picture the geometry of the street; that visual field is then replaced by an image drawn from human disease to convey the texture of rotten, broken plaster; 'lurching' makes the houses lean and jerk like drunks; 'frozen' arrests the lurching motion, but in this sensorily confusing context the normal suggestions of ice, coldness, hardness are irrelevant or not activated—the final part of the metaphor remains dead because the context does not motivate it. The second set metaphor is more unified:

> long lines of bugs marched all day like columns of soldiers

The image is visually precise, not dissipated like the previous one; and the military metaphoric vehicle evokes purpose and threat. But it is presented comically: the bugs are mocked by the disproportionately elevated classicism 'hecatombs' and by the farce of smoking them backwards and forwards from room to room. The unexpected learned word 'hecatomb', which stands out in the vernacular context, is a typical Orwell strategy: from time to time he drops in a strikingly erudite word which many readers will have to look up (I did: a hecatomb was a Greek or Roman ceremonial sacrifice of 100 oxen). Orwell's extreme stylistic self-consciousness and his respect for the colloquial would rule out mere display of cleverness: the aim seems to be comic here, while elsewhere a learned polysyllable seems to serve to unsettle the style, to keep the reader alert.

The 'naturalistic' style of the opening, then, is far from 'documentary'. It is decorative, hyperbolic, and whimsical in tone. This is also a literary set piece, a passage of atmospheric writing which prefigures the Zolaesque kitchen descriptions at the centre of the book; it differs from them in its interweaving of distaste and humour. One of these set pieces has been excerpted earlier; I will extend the quotation here:

> He led me down a winding staircase into a narrow passage, deep underground, and so low that I had to stoop in places. It was stiflingly hot and very dark, with only dim, yellow bulbs several yards apart. There seemed to be miles of dark labyrinthine passages—actually, I suppose, a few hundred yards in all—that reminded one queerly of the lower decks of a liner; there were the same heat and cramped space and warm reek of food, and a humming, whirring noise (it came from the kitchen furnaces) just like the whir of engines. We passed doorways which let out sometimes a shouting of oaths, sometimes the red glare of a fire, once a shuddering draught from an ice chamber. As we went along, something struck me violently in the back. It was a hundred-pound block of ice, carried by a blue-aproned porter.

After him came a boy with a great slab of veal on his shoulder, his cheek pressed into the damp, spongy flesh. They shoved me aside with a cry of '*Sauve-toi, idiot!*' and rushed on. On the wall, under one of the lights, someone had written in a very neat hand: "Sooner will you find a cloudless sky in winter, than a woman at the Hôtel X. who has her maidenhead." It seemed a queer sort of place. (*Down and Out*, pp. 54–5)

Some elements of the style of the first passage are intensified here: naturalism is raised to hyperrealism. There is, for example, the crowding and diversity of violent and unpleasant sensations, hurled at the reader in rapid lists of noun phrases: 'heat and cramped space and warm reek of food, and a humming, whirring noise', 'sometimes a shouting of oaths, sometimes the red glare of a fire, once—a shuddering draught from an ice chamber'. There is the heightening of impression through constant intensifiers: 'narrow', 'deep', 'so low', 'stiflingly hot', 'very dark'. The extremes of heat, cold, noise, confinement and darkness hold the passage together as one of Orwell's literary visions of hell,[11] quite explicit on the next page as he moves to describe the kitchen:

The kitchen was like nothing I had ever seen or imagined—a stifling, low-ceilinged inferno of a cellar, red-lit from the fires, and deafening with oaths and the clanging of pots and pans.

Remarkably, this highly picturesque and impressionistic writing, with a strong literary heritage in images of hell, is achieved with a very ordinary vocabulary. The vocabulary is neutral (e.g. 'low', 'stoop', 'cramped', 'staircase', 'passage', 'doorways') or vernacular ('shoved', 'queer'). Much of it is native in origin rather than Latin or French.

There is little figurative language, certainly none of the ostentatious metaphors or similes found elsewhere in Orwell. Much of the vocabulary is of one or two syllables only; often a whole clause or sentence is constructed in this mainly monosyllabic mode:

there were the same heat and cramped space and warm reek of food ... After him came a boy with a great slab of veal on his shoulder, his cheek pressed into the damp, spongy flesh.

There is one foregrounded classical polysyllabic word, 'labyrinthine', but its meaning and its connotations of the Minotaur are entirely appropriate in the context.[12]

The relationship between language and context, and what the context does to our perception of style, is important here.[13] A piece of language—a sentence, a paragraph, a text—has certain objective and describable structural characteristics: its words may be short or long, native or foreign, concrete or abstract, vernacular or technical, and so on; they are arranged in a certain syntax, an ordering of words and phrases. But a description of the objective features of a text's language does not predict what significance they may have for the writer and for readers within different contexts of discourse. Similar linguistic characteristics may have—will have—different social and rhetorical meanings depending on the nature of the text as a whole, its cultural context and the expectations of its readers. To take the sentence about the boy with the slab of veal, its language is objectively 'simple' in a number of ways which could be exactly stated. In the context of a literary inferno, however, the sentence carries complicated and rather sinister connotations: the anonymous boy is a diabolical helper like the 'twelve cooks [who] skipped to and fro' at the 'furnaces' on the next page; the unconcerned intimacy of his living face and the dead flesh is not only gruesome but also surreal. Suppose, however, that the context were different: Orwell might perhaps have described work at an abattoir. In that context, the sentence about the boy carrying the veal might be experienced very differently, as a plain, matter-of-fact account of a routine act of work, unpleasant in itself but without the connotations suggested by the context of the diabolical kitchen.

This example suggests that the *language* of literary naturalism and its hyperreal extension may not be markedly different from that of the descriptive realism for which Orwell is praised, and that is the case at least for *Down and Out*. The plain and vernacular basis for the descriptive style is also present in the more elevated styles. I will simply illustrate this fact with a passage from *Down and Out*, reserving a more detailed treatment of descriptive realism for the discussion of *Wigan Pier*, below. This is Orwell's first description of conditions in a common lodging house:

> [T]he boy led me up a rickety unlighted staircase to a bedroom. It had a sweetish reek of paregoric and foul linen; the windows seemed to be tight shut, and the air was almost suffocating at first. There was a candle burning, and I saw that the room measured fifteen feet square by eight high, and had eight beds in it. Already six lodgers were in bed, queer lumpy shapes with all their own clothes, even their boots, piled on top of them. Someone was coughing in a loathsome manner in one corner.
>
> When I got into the bed I found that it was as hard as a board, and as for the pillow, it was a mere hard cylinder like a block

of wood. It was rather worse than sleeping on a table, because the bed was not six feet long, and very narrow, and the mattress was convex, so that one had to hold on to avoid falling out. The sheets stank so horribly of sweat that I could not bear them near my nose. Also, the bedclothes only consisted of the sheets and a cotton counterpane, so that though stuffy it was none too warm. Several noises recurred throughout the night. About once in an hour the man on my left—a sailor, I think—woke up, swore vilely, and lighted a cigarette ... [other noises] ... Once when [the man in the corner] struck a match I saw that he was a very old man, with a grey, sunken face like that of a corpse, and he was wearing his trousers wrapped round his head as a nightcap, a thing which for some reason disgusted me very much. (*Down and Out*, pp. 131–2)

Like the other passages discussed, this one conveys a range of sensory impressions, with a strong emphasis on their effect on the narrator—here, a consistent and powerful sense of physical disgust, unrelieved by any comedy or symbolism such as is found in the other extracts. We will see below that 'realistic' representation in Orwell is very much something experienced in the senses and feelings rather than coldly observed and recorded. There is always a very emotive tone: involvement and opinion are never far away when Orwell writes of the life of the poor. The impression of realism coexisting with the thread of judgement and feeling comes from an insistence on particularity of reference: here, the measurements of the room, the count of eight beds and six lodgers in them, the bed 'not six feet long', the texture and geometry of objects—'lumpy shapes', 'hard as a board', 'cylinder', 'narrow', 'convex', 'sunken face', and so on. Orwell is also fond of material arrangements that the reader has to work at to visualise: 'his trousers wrapped round his head as a nightcap', a precise, grotesque and defamiliarising image.[14]

Naturalism in HOMAGE TO CATALONIA

In the next section of this chapter I will discuss some heightened versions of 'realistic' writing, and the way they carry social and political judgement. But before moving on from the subject of naturalism or 'sordid realism', it is appropriate to refer to its place in the third of the 'mixed genre' books that Orwell wrote in the 1930s, *Homage to Catalonia* (1938). In December 1936, Orwell 'had come to Spain with some notion of writing newspaper articles, but I had joined the militia almost immediately, because at that time and in that atmosphere it seemed the only conceivable thing to do' (*Catalonia*, p. 8).

Catalonia is his record of the time and the atmosphere (a word which recurs in the book), of his very physical experiences of warfare in the trenches and of violent turmoil in Barcelona; and his discussion of the politics of the various parties involved in the Spanish Civil War, and of British responses to the War.

Orwell was conscious that Spain, like Wigan, Paris, Burma and the London of the destitute, was unknown territory to his middle-class English reader. In this book, Spain in civil war has to be communicated physically to those who have not had his privilege of direct experience, and discussed politically for those who may be misled by foreign commentators who have not observed directly. We are concerned with the former aspect of the work, the communication of material conditions and atmosphere. He writes:

> I wish I could convey to you the atmosphere of that time. I hope
> I have done so, a little, in the earlier chapters of this book. It is all
> bound up in my mind with the winter cold, the ragged uniforms
> of militiamen, the oval Spanish faces, the morse-like tapping of
> machine-guns, the smells of urine and rotting bread, the tinny
> taste of bean-stews wolfed hurriedly out of unclean pannikins.
> (*Catalonia*, p. 103)

These phrases are shorthands or mnemonics for scenes and topics that are detailed earlier in the book. Orwell conveys the squalid physical experience of the trenches, the filth and cold and deprivation, in considerable detail; also the devastation of the areas around the front, and of the villages and buildings touched by the War. Here is one such piece of naturalistic description:

> [Alcubierre had] ... the peculiar squalid misery of the Aragonese
> villages. They are built like fortresses, a mass of mean little
> houses of mud and stone huddling round the church, and even
> in spring you see hardly a flower anywhere; the houses have no
> gardens, only back-yards where ragged fowls skate over the beds
> of mule-dung. It was vile weather, with alternate mist and rain.
> The narrow earth roads had been churned into a sea of mud, in
> places two feet deep, through which the lorries struggled with
> racing wheels and the peasants led their clumsy carts which were
> pulled by strings of mules, sometimes as many as six in a string,
> always pulling tandem. The constant come-and-go of troops
> had reduced the village to a state of unspeakable filth. It did not
> possess and never had possessed such a thing as a lavatory or
> a drain of any kind, and there was not a square yard anywhere

where you could tread without watching your step. The church had long been used as a latrine; so had all the fields for a quarter of a mile around. I never think of my first two months at war without thinking of wintry stubble fields whose edges are crusted with dung. (Ibid., p. 19)

The hallmarks of naturalism are here as they are in many passages of the book: references to mundane or unpleasant things, 'mud', 'mule-dung', 'lavatory', 'drain', 'latrine', 'dung'; negative adjectives, 'squalid', 'mean little', 'ragged', 'vile', 'clumsy', etc.; an almost exaggerated judgement as in 'peculiar', 'a mass of', 'even', 'unspeakable'. This kind of naturalism is a prominent style in the early parts of *Homage to Catalonia*: the accounts of life in the trenches offer a strong and repulsive physical evocation, with great particularity, and are a strength of a book that has been much admired.

Realism, Judgement and Symbolism in THE ROAD TO WIGAN PIER

Although the passages from *Down and Out* and *Catalonia* just quoted are naturalistic in technique, heightened in tone, and convey, as so often in Orwell, repulsion, they are at least 'concrete' and 'objective' in their detailing of shape, texture, measurement and the narrator's sensory perceptions. In relation to this concreteness, we may recall Orwell's later reflection that 'So long as I remain alive and well I shall continue to ... love the surface of the earth, and to take pleasure in solid objects' (cf. Chapter 3, p. 19 above). In *Wigan Pier* there are more passages of naturalistic description of this kind: based in objective observation but emphasising squalor and his response to it:

There were generally four of us in the bedroom, and a beastly place it was, with that defiled impermanent look of rooms that were not serving their rightful purpose ... We were therefore sleeping in what was still recognisably a drawing-room. Hanging from the ceiling there was a heavy glass chandelier on which the dust was so thick that it was like fur. And covering most of one wall there was a huge hideous piece of junk, something between a sideboard and a hall-stand, with lots of carving and little drawers and strips of looking-glass, and there was a once-gaudy carpet ringed by the slop-pails of years, and two gilt chairs with burst seats, and one of those old-fashioned horsehair armchairs which you slide off when you try to sit on them. The room had been turned into a bedroom by thrusting four squalid beds in among this other wreckage. (*Wigan Pier*, p. 5)

The precision of reference that is the foundation of any realistic style is so obvious as to need little comment: the little drawers and strips of mirror, etc., help the reader to visualise the nameless piece of Victorian furniture; the simile of dust 'like fur' is precisely evocative for anyone who has entered a long-neglected attic or cellar; the rings on the carpet suggest a careful observer who makes his survey at eye-level and ceiling, and then *looks downward* to complete his survey. But, like the previous passage, this is by no means straightforward description. It retains the sordid component of naturalism (dust, slop-pail, etc.), and it is framed in a suffusion of value judgement in words from the negative end of Orwell's demotic vocabulary: 'beastly', 'defiled', 'hideous', 'junk', 'squalid', 'wreckage'.

The origin of *Wigan Pier* was a commission from the publisher Victor Gollancz to report on the conditions of poverty and unemployment in the North. Orwell spent two months visiting Wigan, Barnsley, and Sheffield, two months of intensive observation of industrial, mining, and domestic conditions and of local political activity. He gathered a mass of observations, some of which are recorded in documentary fashion in *Wigan Pier*: on unemployment figures, for example:

> Take the figures for Wigan, which is typical enough of the industrial and mining districts. The number of insured workers is round about 36 000 (26 000 men and 10 000 women). Of these, the number unemployed at the beginning of 1936 was about 10 000. But this was in winter when the mines were working full-time; in summer it would probably be 12 000. Multiply by three, as above, and you get 30 000 or 36 000. The total population of Wigan is a little under 81 000; so that at any moment more than one person in three out of the whole population—not merely the registered workers—is either drawing or living on the dole. (*Wigan Pier*, p. 68)

Elsewhere in the book he reproduces his notes on individual houses, with dimensions and inventories of furniture (ibid, pp. 44–8, 59–60), gives examples of household budgets (p. 83), tabulates the rates of unemployment benefit (pp. 68–9), and so on. He explains in more or less factual terms the procedures of mining using a mechanical coal-cutter (pp. 27–8), describes a caravan-dwellers' colony with some precision (pp. 54–5), gives a general characterisation of workers' housing (p. 45).

Although the passages quoted show that Orwell *could* write in a plain, referential, style, the realism of the book is hardly documentary overall. His political conscience was too demanding for the plain style, requiring a rhetoric of outrage which could not be kept wader restraint until the polemical Part Two. Even passages of straightforward reportage are generally framed with authorial judgement, and the judgemental frame is more typically Orwell in style than the document or description within the frame. Often Orwell *precedes* a description with a pointed negative evaluation, so that it is bound to be read in terms of those values; for example, his chapter on housing begins:

> As you walk through the industrial towns you lose yourself in labyrinths of little brick houses blackened by smoke, festering in planless chaos round miry alleys and little cindered yards where there are stinking dust-bins and lines of grimy washing and half-ruinous WCs. (*Wigan Pier*, p. 45)

This is the style of sordid realism, driven by Orwellian guilt about the condition of the poor; he then particularises, but the detail is of course smeared by the preceding judgement:

> The interiors of these houses are always very much the same, though the number of rooms varies between two or [sic] five. All have an almost exactly similar living-room, ten or fifteen feet square, with an open kitchen range; in the larger ones there is a scullery as well, in the smaller ones the sink and copper are in the living-room. At the back there is the yard ... (*Wigan Pier*, p. 45)

We read a text in terms of what we have already experienced; and we read a part of a text in terms of what has gone before. This is true of the book as a whole, not merely individual passages such as the one just quoted. The sensationally squalid opening chapter, a devastating naturalistic account of Orwell's lodging above a tripe shop, gives immediate notice that the book is not going to convey a material reality calmly while leaving readers to make up their own minds, but that it will voice its author's outrage and shame at Northern working-class life in no uncertain terms (hence the polemical Part Two, which I briefly characterised in the preceding chapter, is well expected from the beginning). A celebrated passage from the first chapter is in principle 'realistic' in its microscopic detail, but communicates primarily an oratorical expression of disgust:

in the middle of the room was the big kitchen table at which the family and all the lodgers ate. I never saw this table completely uncovered, but I saw its various wrappings at different times. At the bottom was a layer of old newspaper stained by Worcester Sauce; above that a sheet of sticky white oil-cloth; above that a green serge cloth; above that a coarse linen cloth, never changed and seldom taken off. Generally the crumbs from breakfast were still on the table at supper. I used to get to know individual crumbs by sight and watch their progress up and down the table from day to day. (*Wigan Pier*, p. 7)

The opening chapter of *Wigan Pier* (so resented by generations of Wigan readers!) has plenty of objective reference, plenty of linguistic precision, but the overall effect is one of sordid realism, and this sets the keynote of the book: it is hardly the spotless window pane of documentary; the pane is etched by authorial feeling, and we cannot see the scene except through his emotions.

The chapter also contains another noted image: it has a high visual precision of a quality Orwell often achieves, but it is not descriptive realism because the passage is shot through with expression of pathos, guilt and distaste:

The train bore me away, through the monstrous scenery of slag-heaps, chimneys, piled scrap-iron, foul canals, paths of cindery mud criss-crossed by the prints of clogs. This was March, but the weather had been horribly cold and everywhere there were mounds of blackened snow. As we moved slowly through the outskirts of the town we passed row after row of little grey slum houses running at right angles to the embankment. At the back of one of the houses a young woman was kneeling on the stones, poking a stick up the leaden waste-pipe which ran from the sink inside and which I suppose was blocked. I had time to see everything about her—her sacking apron, her clumsy clogs, her arms reddened by the cold. She looked up as the train passed, and I was almost near enough to catch her eye. She had a round pale face, the usual exhausted face of the slum girl who is twenty-five and looks forty, thanks to miscarriages and drudgery; and it wore, for the second in which I saw it, the most desolate, hopeless expression I have, ever seen ... She knew well enough what was happening to her—understood as well as I did how dreadful a destiny it was to be kneeling there in the bitter cold, on the slimy stones of a slum backyard, poking a stick up a foul drain-pipe. (*Wigan Pier*, pp. 16–17)

What we have here, despite its clarity of detail, is not description but symbolism: the 'slum girl' (an interesting category in itself) and everything about her stand for the degradation and hopelessness Orwell perceives in this Northern town. As for Orwell himself, he is enclosed in the train, and escaping; there is something of the voyeur's eye about his vision. His confidence about her typicality is patronising.

The first part of *Wigan Pier* begins, as we have seen, with a naturalistic description of the tripe-shop lodging; it ends with surreal landscapes of Wigan and Sheffield. The slag-heaps of Wigan are presented as a 'lunar landscape' (his phrase):

The canal path was a mixture of cinders and frozen mud, criss-crossed by the imprints of innumerable clogs, and all around, as far as the slag-heaps in the distance, stretched the 'flashes'—pools of stagnant water that had seeped into the hollows caused by the subsidence of ancient pits. It was horribly cold. The 'flashes' were covered with ice the colour of raw umber, the bargemen were muffled to the eyes in sacks, the lock gates wore beards of ice. It seemed a world from which vegetation had been banished; nothing existed except smoke, shale, ice, mud, ashes and foul water. (*Wigan Pier*, p. 95)

And then Sheffield:

At night, when you cannot see the hideous shapes of the houses and the blackness of everything, a town like Sheffield assumes a kind of sinister magnificence. Sometimes the drifts of smoke are rosy with sulphur, and serrated flames, like circular saws, squeeze themselves out from beneath the cowls of the foundry chimneys. Through the open doors of foundries you see fiery serpents of iron being hauled to and fro by red-lit boys, and you hear the whizz and thump of steam hammers and the scream of iron under the blow. (*Wigan Pier*, p. 96)

Orwell professes to be showing the 'ugliness' (his word) of these industrial scenes, but the descriptions (which are much more extended than my quotations, totalling nearly three pages), dense with metaphors and allusions, achieve a conventional literary beauty. In fact the sources are literary, notably Dickens's surrealist evocation of 'Coketown' in *Hard Times*:

> It was a town of red brick, or of brick that would have been red if the smoke and ashes had allowed it; but, as matters stood it was a town of unnatural red and black like the painted face of a savage. It was a town of machinery and tall chimneys, out of which interminable serpents of smoke trailed themselves for ever and ever, and never got uncoiled. It had a black canal in it, and a river that ran purple with ill-smelling dye, and vast piles of building full of windows where there was a rattling and a trembling all day long, and where the piston of the steam-engine worked monotonously up and down, like the head of an elephant in a state of melancholy madness.[15]

The 'serpents' metaphor seems to indicate Orwell's specific indebtedness to this passage; indeed the stylistic influence of Dickens was considerable and various, and we will see another aspect of it in the next chapter. But the point of the present comparison is simply that, in his descriptive writing, even treating a concrete material subject such as an industrial town, Orwell is definitely a literary rather than a documentary writer.

Notes

1. See 'Why I write', *CEJL*, I, pp. 23–30; Letter to Henry Miller, *CEJL*, I, pp. 257–9.

2. Characteristic critical responses to Orwell's work are to be found in J. Meyers (ed.) *George Orwell: The Critical Heritage*, (London: Routledge and Kegan Paul, 1975). See also J. R. Hammond, *A George Orwell Companion* (London: Macmillan, 1982).

3. The photographs are not reproduced in the Penguin edition, but may be found in the Secker & Warburg edition of the complete novels, vol. 5 (1986).

4. The main influence on Orwell seems to have been the French novelist Emile Zola, whom he much admired. In 1940 he included Zola in a list of eleven 'writers I care most about and never grow tired of' (*CEJL*, II, 39). In 1932, with *Down and Out* recently finished, he tried to persuade Chatto & Windus to allow him to translate Zola (*CEJL*, I, 102). A book review of 1936 uses Zola as a standard of comparison, and produces a characteristic Orwellian simile in which the organicism of Zola is opposed to mechanical composition:

> The scenes of violence Zola describes in *Germinal* and *La Debacle* are supposed to symbolize capitalist corruption, best they are also scenes. At his best, Zola is not synthetic. He works under a sense of compulsion, and not like an amateur cook following the instructions on a packet of Crestona cake-flour. (*CEJL*, I, 279)

5. J. R. Hammond, *A George Orwell Companion* (London: Macmillan, 1982) p. 40; cf. pp. 36–7, 99; and p. 83 for the quotation from Orwell on Dickens.

6. An illuminating, if difficult, account of the way readers produce a coherent, integrated model of the content of a text on the basis of textual cues (which give incomplete information) and their existing knowledge of the world is given in R. de Eeaugrande and W. Dressler, *Introduction to Text Linguistics* (London: Longman, 1981) ch. 5.

7. The integration of separate components of a text depends on the reader bringing to bear whatever background knowledge s/he possesses from experience of the real, or other fictional, worlds. The question must be raised as to how accessible this particular world is to a modern reader. Clearly to Orwell and his narrator the shop was already old-fashioned by the late 1930s. I was born in 1938, the year before *Coming Up for Air* was published, and, brought up in a rural area, can just about remember this kind of shop.

8. See B. Crick, *George Orwell: A Life* (London: Secker & Warburg, 1980) ch. 6. Orwell's own account of the tramping, and of the interest in unemployment, poverty and 'working-class conditions' which led him to it, is well worth reading: see *Wigan Pier*, ch. See also 'The Spike', 1931 (*CEJL*, I, pp. 58–66); and the preface to the 1935 French edition of the *Down and Out*, translated by J. Meyers, *George Orwell: The Critical Heritage* (London: Routledge & Kegan Paul, 1975) pp. 39–40.

9. Quoted in J. Meyers (ed.) *George Orwell: The Critical Heritage* (London: Routledge & Kegan Paul, 1975), p. 42.

10. A simple practical suggestion: photocopies of the text and a highlighting pen are invaluable tools for revealing the kinds of lexical pattern studied here, which are otherwise difficult to perceive in an ordinary reading.

11. This passage, like many others in Orwell, is oppressively claustrophobic. Cf. the discussion of his descent of a coal-mine in chapter 2 of *Wigan Pier*, and the many references to the dimensions of small rooms. Orwell was himself exceptionally tall and long-limbed for his generation.

12. 'Labyrinth' recurs in Orwell; cf. *Wigan Pier*, p. 45, quoted on p. 83, 'labyrinthine streets', *A Clergyman's Daughter*, p. 130; 'the labyrinthine world of doublethink', 'unseen labyrinth', 'the labyrinth of London', *Nineteen Eighty-Four*, pp. 36, 39, 74.

13. This theoretical point is discussed in more detail in R. Fowler, *Linguistic Criticism* (Oxford: Oxford University Press, 1986) ch. 11.

14. 'Defamiliarisation', in the theories of the Russian formalists, is the use of literary devices which shake readers out of automatic habits of thought. See V. Shklovsky, 'Art as Technique' [1917] in L. T. Lemon and M. J. Reis (eds) *Russian Formalist Criticism* (Lincoln: University of Nebraska Press, 1965). There is considerable discussion of the linguistics of defamiliarisation in R. Fowler, *Linguistic Criticism* (note 13).

15. Charles Dickens, *Hard Times* ed. by David Craig, (London: Penguin, 1985) p. 65.

ADRIAN WANNER

The Underground Man as Big Brother: Dostoevsky's and Orwell's Anti-Utopia

"I admit that two times two makes four is an excellent thing, but if we are going to praise everything, two times two makes five is sometimes also a very charming little thing."

—Dostoevsky, Notes from Underground

"You are a slow learner, Winston," said O'Brien gently.

"How can I help it" he blubbered. "How can I help seeing what is in front of my eyes? Two and two are four."

"Sometimes, Winston. Sometimes they are five.... "

—Orwell, Nineteen Eighty-Four

Dostoevsky's *Notes from Underground* and Orwell's *Nineteen Eighty-Four* are perhaps the two most popular and seminal examples of anti-utopian literature ever written. Dostoevsky's novella has been called "probably the most important single source of the modern dystopia" (Morson 130). Its hero, the anonymous "underground man," has acquired the status of a literary archetype, a symbol of alienation in an oppressively normative world. Orwell's novel serves as a popular dystopian icon even for people who never read it, but for whom the adjective "Orwellian" designates anything perceived as ominous or threatening in modern civilization. Both Dostoevsky's and Orwell's text have been exposed to a confusing variety of divergent interpretations, ranging from

From *Utopian Studies* Vol. 8, No. 1 (1997): pp. 77–88. © 1997 Society for Utopian Studies.

dissections of the author's psychopathology to theological laments over the evils of human nature to existentialist declarations of faith in human dignity against the odds of an adverse world. While many of those readings can be stimulating in their own way, sometimes critics have tended to lose sight of the satirical and parodistic element in both works, which suggests a common origin of the two texts in the genre of political satire.[1]

Do these parallels allow us to postulate a direct connection between Dostoevsky and Orwell? Although we know that Orwell was familiar with *Notes from Underground*,[2] Dostoevsky does not loom large in his critical writings. The four-volume edition of Orwell's collected essays, journalism and letters contains only one reference to the Russian novelist. Dostoevsky's name comes up in a passage of the 1940 essay "Inside the Whale," where Orwell laments the tendency of the English intelligentsia to ignore "the places where things are actually happening," such as Soviet Russia: "The Russian Revolution, for instance, all but vanishes from the English consciousness between the death of Lenin and the Ukraine famine—about ten years. Throughout those years Russia means Tolstoy, Dostoievski and exiled counts driving taxi-cabs" (*CEJL* 1:508). In dismissing Dostoevsky as part of a cluster of cliches denoting an outdated Russia, it did not seem to occur to Orwell that Dostoevsky's writings could be mined for insights about the current Russian situation. In particular, he seemed to overlook the fact that his critique of Soviet Communism was foreshadowed by Dostoevsky's hostility toward the left-wing radicals of his own time.

If it has to remain doubtful whether a direct connection between Dostoevsky and Orwell can be established, an indirect connection exists beyond doubt through Yevgeny Zamyatin's novel *We*. Zamyatin's dystopia forms, as it were, the connecting link in the genealogical tree leading from Dostoevsky to Orwell. As a Russian novelist, Zamyatin was of course well acquainted with Dostoevsky's oeuvre, and his book contains a whole network of allusions both to *Notes from Underground* and the Legend of the Grand Inquisitor in *The Brothers Karamazov* (see on this Morson 131–133). Orwell read Zamyatin's novel in French translation while he was working on *Nineteen Eighty-Four*, and devoted a sympathetic review to it (*CEJL* 4:72–75). Since then, it has become a critical commonplace to identify Zamyatin's *We* and Orwell's *Nineteen Eighty-Four* together with Huxley's *Brave New World* (which was perhaps also inspired by Zamyatin) as the three classic dystopias of our century. Together with Dostoevsky's "ur-dystopia," they articulate the by now familiar angst over the obliteration of individual freedom and human personality in the machinery of a totalitarian system of thought control. In this perspective, Zamyatin's Benefactor, Huxley's World Controller, and Orwell's torturer O'Brien are all descendants of Dostoevsky's Grand Inquisitor.

The parallels between *Nineteen Eighty-Four* and Dostoevsky's Legend of the Grand Inquisitor were first noticed by Orwell's publisher, Fredric Warburg, who wrote in a memorandum to his production and promotion staff that "Orwell goes down to the depths in a way which reminds me of Dostoievsky. O'Brien is his Grand Inquisitor, and he leaves Winston, and the reader, without hope" (quoted in Crick 396). Philip Rahv, in his review of *Nineteen Eighty-Four* in *Partisan Review*, also mentioned the parallels between O'Brien and the Grand Inquisitor, but at the same time pointed to a crucial difference between the two: Dostoevsky's dictator (as well as Zamyatin's and Huxley's) claims to have an ulterior philanthropic motivation for his repressive system—the happiness of his subjects. Orwell's O'Brien, however, dispenses altogether with philanthropy; for him, power becomes an aim in itself ("the object of power is power"). Rahv found this blunt admission closer to the truth, although the Grand Inquisitor's self-delusion about the beneficial purpose of his terror seemed to him more psychologically plausible (see Philip Rahv, "The Unfuture of Utopia" [1949], in Howe 181–185).

Whatever we think of Rahv's assessment, it seems evident that Orwell's dystopia is of a different character than those of his predecessors. His party rulers have abandoned the utopian ideal of universal happiness altogether, although they still may pay lip service to it for propaganda purposes. Dostoevsky's, Zamyatin's and Huxley's dystopian societies, in contrast, represent not abandoned, but realized utopias. On their own terms, their dictators have been quite successful in creating a "happy" society, which has even led some readers to actually embrace their arguments.[3] Conversely, the notion of an abandoned, or betrayed, utopia put forth by Orwell, or rather by his fictional character Emmanuel Goldstein who is modelled on Trotsky, leaves the possibility of a true utopia open. Goldstein's "book" is quite explicit on this account. At times, his arguments sound like a straightforward expression of nineteenth-century utopian optimism: "From the moment when the machine first made its appearance it was clear to all thinking people that the need for human drudgery, and therefore to a great extent for human inequality, had disappeared. If the machine were used deliberately for that end, hunger, overwork, dirt, illiteracy, and disease could be eliminated within a few generations.... But by the fourth decade of the twentieth century all the main currents of political thought were authoritarian. *The earthly paradise had been discredited at exactly the moment when it became realizable*" (*NE* 156, 168, italics added). While Dostoevsky and his successors Zamyatin and Huxley problematized the notion of a rational, scientific utopia by suggesting that its realization would lead inevitably to a dystopian society, this passage promotes the idea of a machine-generated utopia as both realizable and desirable. Of course, it is not Orwell himself who expresses this opinion, but the shadowy

Goldstein (or perhaps even O'Brien, who claims to have co-authored the book allegedly written by Goldstein). What was Orwell's own attitude toward the socialist "earthly paradise?" In trying to clarify this question, it will be useful to compare *Nineteen Eighty-Four* with its ancestor *Notes from Underground*, Dostoevsky's seminal anti-utopia.

Dostoevsky's main satirical target in *Notes from Underground* was the utopian optimism of Nikolay Chernyshevsky's novel *What Is to Be Done?* (1863), which had an enormous impact on several generations of Russian radicals, including Lenin. *Notes from Underground* is replete with concrete references and allusions to Chernyshevsky's book (for a thorough discussion of *Notes from Underground* as a parody of *What Is to Be Done?*, see Frank, passim). Dostoevsky found Chernyshevsky's vision of a society based on scientific positivism and enlightened self-interest distasteful. His underground man displays the twisted psychology of a character both affected by and revolting against the implications of philosophical materialism. An apt image for positivist thinking and the finality of the laws of nature is provided by the formula "two times two makes four," which recurs as a leitmotiv throughout the first half of the text. Driven by his urge for irrational freedom, the underground man rejects this formula, even though he is aware of the absurdity of his revolt: "... you might as well accept it, you can't do anything about it, because two times two is a law of mathematics. Just try refuting it.... Good God! but what do I care about the laws of nature and arithmetic, when, for some reason, I dislike those laws and the fact that two times two makes four?" (*NU* 12). In particular, the underground man rejects the project of a utopian society based on mathematical calculations à la Bentham or Fourier, where "all human actions will... be tabulated according to these laws, mathematically, like tables of logarithms up to 108,000 and entered in a table" (*NU* 22). As he points out, such a world will lead to the elimination of free will: "Bah, gentlemen, what sort of free will is left when we come to tables and arithmetic, when it will all be a case of two times two makes four? Two times two makes four even without my will" (*NU* 28). Ultimately, he declares, "two times two makes four... is no longer life, but is the beginning of death" (*NU* 30). The build-up of obsessive references finally leads to a grotesque personification, where the abstract mathematical formula acquires the feature of an obnoxious human character: "Granted that man does nothing but seek that two times two makes four, that he sails the oceans, sacrifices his life in the quest, but to succeed, really to find it—he is somehow afraid, I assure you.... Two times two makes four seems to me simply a piece of insolence. Two times two makes four is a fop standing with arms akimbo barring your path and spitting" (*NU* 30). Cornered by the iron-clad finality of positivism, the underground man can only respond by "spitting back," so to speak, and to declare that "two times two makes five is sometimes also a very charming little thing." This gesture of spite is the mathematical equivalent of sticking out one's tongue at the Crystal Palace, Chernyshevsky's symbol of the scientifically induced happy future of mankind inspired by the edifice erected for the Great Exhibition of 1851 in London, which Dostoevsky treated with revulsion and scorn in his *Winter Notes of Summer Impressions*.

The world of Zamyatin's *We* is just such a Crystal Palace, where people live in fully transparent glass cubes (blinds are lowered only during sex hour) in an existence of mathematically calculated and regimented bliss. In what looks like a direct reference to the underground man, the engineer D-503, the narrator of *We*, also invokes the formula "two times two makes four": "The multiplication table is wiser and more absolute than the ancient God: it never errs. And there are no happier figures than those which live according to the harmonious, eternal laws of the multiplication table. No hesitations, no delusions. There is only one truth, and only one true way; this truth is two times two, and the true way—four. And would it not be an absurdity if these happily, ideally multiplied twos began to think of some nonsensical freedom—i.e., clearly, to error?" (66–67). The wisdom of the multiplication table even inspires the poets of the "One State." D-503 is led to his reflections while pondering over a sonnet called "Happiness," which prompts him to remark: "I think I will not be mistaken if I say that it is a poem of rare and profound beauty of thought. Here are its first four lines:

> Eternally enamored two times two,
> Eternally united in the passionate four,
> Most ardent lovers in the world—
> Inseparable two times two....

And so on—about the wise, eternal bliss of the multiplication table" (66). Anything that does not fit into this simplistic framework, such as imaginary numbers or non-Euclidean geometry, let alone the more complex emotions of the human soul, seem to D-503 a threat to his sanity. Conveniently relieved of his "soul" by a state-ordered lobotomy at the end of the book, he expresses confidence in the victory of the state over an insurrection of primitivist rebels, because "Reason must prevail" (232).

Orwell's Winston Smith, as has been noticed many times, shares some essential features with Zamyatin's D-503: both are mid-level intellectuals in the service of a totalitarian state, both keep a secret diary and become rebels through an erotic relationship with a dissident woman, and both are successfully brought back to the fold at the end through the drastic intervention of the state security organs. Despite these parallels, however, it is curious to note that Orwell's use of mathematical imagery is the exact opposite of Dostoevsky's and Zamyatin's. In *Nineteen Eighty-Four*, it is not the dystopian state that clings to the iron laws of mathematical formulas and epistemological positivism, but the dissident rebel Winston Smith. As he explains in his diary: "Freedom is the freedom to say that two plus two make four. If that is granted, all else follows" (69). The formula becomes something like a secret battle cry for Winston. Shortly before his arrest, the sight of a sturdy "prole" woman prompts him to fantasize about a future revolution: "Out of those mighty loins a race of conscious beings must one day come. You were the dead; theirs was the future. But you could share in that future if you kept alive the mind as they kept alive the body, and passed on the secret doctrine that two plus two makes four" (182). It is not surprising that the party authorities, who read Winston's diary and seem to be able to guess any of his thoughts, make the refutation of this formula a major focus of their "reeducation" program in the torture chambers of the Ministry of Love. By means of electric shocks, Winston is forced to acknowledge that two plus two can make five if the party wishes so. The treatment is so successful that at the end Winston actually sees five fingers when his torturer O'Brien holds up his hand with the thumb concealed.

Orwell's use of the formula "$2+2=5$" inverts the relationship of reason and madness laid out by his predecessors. In Dostoevsky's and Zamyatin's dystopian dictatorships of reason, madness becomes a strategy of resistance. The underground man declares that in a world which reduces humans to the role of a "piano key," "man would purposely go mad in order to be rid of reason and have his own way!" (*NU* 28). In the world of *Nineteen Eighty-Four*, conversely, it is the representative of state power, O'Brien, who seems insane. While he is lecturing Winston in the Ministry of Love, his face bears the expression of a "lunatic enthusiasm" (211). His eyes, we are told, are animated by a "mad gleam" (216). Many of his views and patterns of behavior seem reminiscent of those of the underground man. He rejects scientific positivism and sensory evidence in favor of an epistemology that seems oddly postmodern in its denial of objective truth. As he makes clear, the narrative of history has no grounding in reality and can be rewritten at will by those in power. Even the laws of nature—the positivist's pet and the underground man's bete noire—turn out to be a mere human construct and are therefore open to manipulation: "We control matter because we control the mind. Reality is inside the skull.... You must get rid of those nineteenth-century ideas about the laws of nature. We make the laws of nature" (218). Another nineteenth-century idea which both the underground man and O'Brien treat with scorn is "the stupid hedonistic Utopias that the old reformers imagined" (220). O'Brien's ideal society is not based on scientifically maximized happiness, but, quite to the contrary, on maximized suffering: "If you want a picture of the future, imagine a boot stamping on a human face—forever" (220). Sadism, the perverse pleasure derived from the infliction of suffering, is a key psychological feature shared by both O'Brien and the underground man. The latter's treatment of the prostitute Liza resembles O'Brien's "reeducation" of Winston. The moralizing sermon with which the underground man seemingly tries to "reform" the poor woman is in reality a mere exercise of power, an attempt to completely humiliate and dominate his victim: "l felt for some time that I was turning her soul inside out and breaking her heart, and the more I was convinced of it, the more I wanted to gain my end as quickly and as forcefully as possible. The game, the game attracted me; yet it was not merely the game" (*NU* 91, translation slightly adjusted). O'Brien uses similar terms when he explains to Winston that "we convert [the heretic], we capture his inner mind, we reshape him.... We shall squeeze you empty, and then we shall fill you with ourselves" (210–11).[4]

It does perhaps not seem altogether facetious then to suggest that the dystopian society of *Nineteen Eighty-Four* has been created by a bunch of "underground men" who left their basement dwellings to assume dictatorial power. By acting out his sadistic fantasies of total domination, O'Brien overcomes the alienation caused by the clash of human freedom with positivist determinism. In his recent study of the "abject hero," Michael André Bernstein has pointed out that in the underground man's "*ressentiment*, for all its shabbiness and self-loathing, there is a potential for extraordinary violence and a rage whose ferocity has been repeatedly mobilized by political movements" (27). This observation is certainly borne out by the example of 20th-century totalitarianism, which provided the primary inspiration for the dystopia of *Nineteen Eighty-Four*. An almost paradigmatic specimen of an underground man in the role of Big Brother can be found in Adolf Hitler, the frustrated artist and bohemian low-life who turned his *ressentiment* into a power tool and instrument of political charisma. In his review of *Mein Kampf*, Orwell seemed to suggest a likeness of Hitler to some of his own literary anti-heroes, when he declared, rather shockingly, perhaps: "l have never been able to dislike Hitler.... There is something deeply appealing about him. One feels it again when one sees his photographs.... It is a pathetic dog-like face, the face of a man suffering under intolerable wrongs. ... The initial personal cause of his grievance against the universe can only be guessed at" (*CEJL* 2:28).

In one respect, to be sure, the modern totalitarian functionary represented by O'Brien is the opposite of the underground man: he does not resent at all being a "piano key"—on the contrary, his sense of purpose and self-assurance derives directly from the awareness of being a minuscule part of a larger whole with which his self merges like the individual atman with the universal brahma. As he explains to Winston: "Alone—free—the human being is always defeated. It must be so, because every human being is doomed to die, which is the greatest of all failures. But if he can make complete, utter submission, if he can escape from his identity, if he can merge himself in the Party so that he is the Party, then he is all-powerful and immortal" (*NE* 218). By becoming a cog in a totalitarian machine of terror, the underground man has finally found happiness.

Unlike Chernyshevsky's utopia of the Crystal Palace with its Enlightenment belief in the power of reason and human perfectibility, Orwell's totalitarian state has its roots in the Counter-Enlightenment. Exactly because it takes into account man's irrational side, modern totalitarianism constitutes, according to Orwell, a more psychologically plausible system than nineteenth-century scientific utopianism. In his review of Hitler's *Mein Kampf*, Orwell stated that "Fascism and Nazism are psychologically far sounder than any hedonistic conception of life. The same is probably true of Stalin's militarized version of Socialism. All three of the great dictators have enhanced their power by imposing intolerable burdens on their peoples. Whereas Socialism, and even capitalism in a more grudging way, have said to people 'I offer you a good time,' Hitler has said to them 'I offer you struggle, danger and death,' and as a result a whole nation flings itself at his feet" (*CEJL* 2:14). Orwell made a similar point in his review of Zamyatin's *We*, which he found superior to Huxley's *Brave New World* because of its "intuitive grasp of the irrational side of totalitarianism—human sacrifice, cruelty as an end in itself, the worship of a Leader who is credited with divine attributes ..." (*CEJL* 4:75). Although Orwell makes no reference to him, it was Dostoevsky who provided in his fiction the first full-fledged prophecy of the modern totalitarian mind and its irrational will to power, notably in the Legend of the Grand Inquisitor with his cult of "miracle, mystery and authority." The specter of the irrational demagogue is raised also in *Notes from Underground* when the underground man predicts that "a gentleman with an ignoble, or rather with a reactionary and ironical, countenance" will arise and suggest to "kick over all that rationalism at one blow." All that would not matter, adds the narrator, "but what is annoying is that after all he would be sure to find followers—such is the nature of man" (*NU* 23).

Despite their common role as rebellious individualists, Dostoevsky's underground man and Orwell's Winston Smith seem to occupy diametrically opposed positions in the ideological spectrum. Whereas the underground man revolts against the dictatorship of reason (2+2=4) in the name of irrational freedom (2+2=5), Winston Smith revolts against irrationalism (2+2=5) in the name of reason (2+2=4). If Winston Smith represents the Enlightenment, the underground man represents the Counter-Enlightenment. Does that make polar opposites of Dostoevsky and Orwell? In pondering this question, it is helpful to keep in mind that *Notes from Underground* and *Nineteen Eighty-Four* are works of literature, not political treatises. Although both Dostoevsky and Orwell intended to deliver a political message, they did so indirectly. Both the underground man and Winston Smith do express their author's opinion, but it is important to realize that they are also flawed characters. In particular, both of them are prone to sadomasochistic behavior, which indicates that they have been corrupted by the system they are fighting against (for a cogent discussion of Winston Smith as a flawed hero, see James Connors, "Do It to Julia," in Kuppig 224–241). The underground man's ostentatious irrationalism is a last-ditch defense against the reductionism of a totally rational and utilitarian view of human nature. Surely, this does not make of Dostoevsky an apostle of madness and chaotic destruction for its own sake, although the text could be and has been misread in this way. Similarly, Winston Smith's embrace of positivist truisms has to be understood as a reaction against the "controlled insanity" of the totalitarian society in which he lives. It is a desperate attempt to gain firm ground in a world that has become completely illusionary. To be sure, resorting to an empty tautology like "2+2=4" hardly seems a promising strategy, and the book ends indeed with Winston's utter defeat. It needs to be pointed out that neither Dostoevsky nor Orwell affirm irrationality or positivism for their own sake, but in a dialectical relationship to the other: as *ultima ratio* in the struggle against a system which fetishizes the snug rationality of "2+2=4" or the irrational "doublethink" of "2+2=5."[5]

It is interesting to observe that Dostoevsky's and Orwell's anti-utopias, although seemingly coming from opposite directions, yield similar results: both hypertrophied rationalism and totalitarian irrationalism lead to the disappearance of the human personality. The end result is indistinguishable. The dystopian world of *Nineteen Eighty-Four* applies equally to Stalin's and Hitler's regimes, which could be characterized as perverted outgrowths of Enlightenment and Counter-Enlightenment ideals. In a larger sense, both Dostoevsky and Orwell see human autonomy threatened by the forces of modernity who tend to make the individual into a mere "piano key." Although they were both in a way children of the Enlightenment, Dostoevsky and Orwell shared a common suspicion of numbers, the myth of progress and the idea of science as salvation. Real-life versions of the mathematical madness parodied by Dostoevsky and Orwell can be found both in Soviet and Chinese Communist production quotas and in the "scientific management" principles of Taylorism.

In his mature novels, particularly *The Possessed*, Dostoevsky tirelessly attacked the politics of utopian social engineering as an alley leading to insanity and destruction. Any ideal of a secular utopia could for him only result in a de-humanizing "anthill." Like Alexander Solzhenitsyn, Dostoevsky probably would have interpreted the Stalinist Gulag as the logical outcome of a "godless" utopian ideology. Orwell's position, in comparison, seems more ambivalent. Is *Nineteen Eighty-Four* an attack on the very idea of socialism, as Orwell's detractors on the left and his admirers on the right have claimed, or is it a spirited defense of true socialism against its Stalinist distortions? The wide range of divergent opinions on this topic is perhaps an indicator of a certain vagueness and inconsistency in Orwell's own position. To be sure, Orwell himself insisted that his novel was not intended as an attack on socialism, of which he claimed to be a supporter, but as a "show-up of the perversions to which a centralized economy is liable and which have already been partly realised in Communism and Fascism" (see Orwell's well-known statement published in *Life* and the *New York Times Book Review* in 1949 [*CEJL* 4:502]). While it is quite clear indeed what Orwell rejects in his book, it seems less clear what he advocates. Does the crushing defeat of Winston Smith with his belief in common sense and the "spirit of man" indicate Orwell's own pessimism and despair with human nature? Or is it a defiant assertion of humanistic values *ex negativo*?[6]

The only character in *Nineteen Eighty-Four* with a positive attitude toward socialist utopianism, as we have seen, is Emmanuel Goldstein. Although the function of Goldstein's book consists in providing the reader with a description and analysis of the world of 1984 from a more knowledgeable source than Winston Smith, it would be naive to simply identify his point of view with Orwell's. Within the fictional universe of the novel, Goldstein's status is uncertain: like Big Brother, he may have been invented by the Party. More importantly, Goldstein's book is a parody of Trotsky's *The Revolution Betrayed*, and we know that Orwell had ambivalent feelings toward its author. He explicitly rejected "the usual Trotskyist claim that Stalin is a mere crook who has perverted the Revolution to his own ends, and that things would somehow have been different if Lenin had lived or Trotsky had remained in power" ("James Burnham and the Managerial Revolution" [1946], *CEJL* 4:168).

With Goldstein's utopian beliefs in a bright socialist future discredited, the only repositories of positive values in the book remain Winston Smith and his lover Julia. The values they represent—private concerns, family life, nature—have a conservative rather than revolutionary tinge (not surprisingly, Orwell has been taken to task by feminist critics for his patriarchal views on gender).[7] Significantly, Winston raises his glass to toast "to the past" rather than to the future. In this implicit traditionalism lies another common element between Orwell and Dostoevsky, the former utopian socialist who turned into a political conservative. The theme of memory plays a crucial role for both authors. Both Dostoevsky and Orwell regard the capacity to remember as the key feature that constitutes the uniqueness of human personality, and erasure of memory denotes for both of them the ultimate dehumanization. Winston Smith unsuccessfully tries to establish a link with the past, with which he is intermittently and tenuously connected through flashes of memory of his mother. This seems strangely reminiscent of Dostoevsky's Alyosha Karamazov, whose memories of his mother, which he lost at an early age, accompany him all his life "like spots of light out of darkness, like a corner torn out of a huge picture, which was all faded and disappeared except that fragment" (*BK* 13). The pictorial circumstances in which Alyosha remembers his mother, a "still summer evening" illuminated with the "slanting rays of the setting sun," reoccur in Winston Smith's vision of his mother. The memory of her "large eyes" leads him to dream about "standing on short springy turf, on a summer evening when the slanting rays of the sun gilded the ground. The landscape that he was looking at recurred so often in his dreams that he was never fully certain whether or not he had seen it in the real world. In his waking thoughts he called it the Golden Country" (*NE* 29).

In their encyclopedic investigation of utopian thought in the Western world Frank and Fritzie Manuel have observed that "in the background of many a dystopia there is a secret utopia" (6). The cluster of maternal memories, idyllic nature and slanting rays of the sun denotes for both Dostoevsky and Orwell a picture of utopian yearning. Inspired by Claude Lorrain's painting "Acis and Galathea" which he saw in Dresden, Dostoevsky incorporated images of the Golden Age in several of his novels (see Stavrogin's dream in *The Possessed* and Versilov's vision in *A Raw Youth*). As Edward Wasiolek has noted with regard to Dostoevsky's "Dream of a Ridiculous Man," the Golden Age was for him a "dialectical concept" oscillating between sacrament and blasphemy (145). A dangerous delusion when advocated by atheist socialists, it could acquire a positive meaning when seen as the fulfillment of his own millenarian hopes. We know that Dostoevsky planned to incorporate a positive Christian message in his *Notes from Underground*, but was prevented from doing so by tsarist censorship (see Dostoevsky's letter to his brother quoted in Dostoevskii 5: 375). While he was adamant in his rejection of atheist utopianism, however, Dostoevsky seemed less secure in his faith in the possibility of a Christian utopian kingdom. The vision of ecstatic life on earth promoted by the Elder Zosima in *The Brothers Karamazov* perhaps comes closest to this ideal of a "Golden Age," but on the whole, Dostoevsky's utopian streak is shot through with bouts of anti-utopian scepticism. As Gary Saul Morson put it in his study of Dostoevsky's utopianism: "The author of two of the most influential anti-utopias in European literature, *Notes from*

Underground and *The Possessed*, remained uncertain whether he wished to deny not only the desirability of Western socialism, but also the possibility of any kingdom of God on earth" (36–37).

As an avowed agnostic, Orwell had little patience for religious messianism, which may account for the little attention he paid to Dostoevsky. The non-religious Freudian and existentialist appropriation of the Russian author in the twentieth century did not do much either to endear him to Orwell. Although in a way affected by those movements, Orwell did not care much for complex theories or abstract philosophical schemes, preferring to stick to his pet notions of "decency" and "common sense." One can only regret this lack of interest. In spite of important differences, in studying Dostoevsky more closely, Orwell would have discovered an author whose anti-utopian forebodings closely resembled his own totalitarian nightmare. Both Dostoevsky and Orwell were propelled by an emotional yearning for "brotherhood" which made them resent capitalist exploitation as well as radical dogmatism. Both authors had a populist streak, but harbored ambivalent feelings toward the peasants and the "proles." From an initial commitment to socialist ideas, their political views evolved to what has been described as an "odd tangle of conservative and radical strands" (Zwerdling 113). In 1947, Orwell wrote: "Our activities as Socialists only have meaning if we assume that Socialism can be established, but if we stop to consider what probably *will* happen, then we must admit, I think, that the chances are against us" (*CEJL* 4: 370). Ultimately, Dostoevsky's wavering attitude toward the possibility of a "kingdom of God on earth" seems to foreshadow Orwell's own pessimistic attitude toward the possibility of a socialist utopia.

Notes

1. For a discussion of *Notes from Underground* as a "Swiftian satire," see Frank, 316 ff. The satirical element in *Nineteen Eighty-Four* was first commented on by V.S. Pritchett in his 1949 review of the book (reprinted in Kuppig 151–157). For a more recent view, see Bernard Crick, "*Nineteen Eighty-Four*: Satire or Prophecy?" in Jensen 7–21.

2. See Orwell's "How Long Is a Short Story?" *Manchester Evening News* (7 September 1944) mentioned in Steinhoff, 246.

3. D.H. Lawrence, for example, praised the Grand Inquisitor as a "great, wise ruler" in his 1930 introduction (see *BK* 829–836). Huxley himself was ambivalent about his *Brave New World*. Although the book was meant to be a dystopia, Huxley later incorporated some of its techniques of mind control (hypnopaedia, drugs) in his positive utopia, *Island*.

4. For an interpretation of O'Brien's behavior from the point of view of game theory, see Patai 220–238.

5. The formula "2+2=5" was actually used in Stalinist Russia as an exhortation to fulfill the Five-Year Plan in four years. See Eugene Lyon's account quoted in Steinhoff, 172.

6. Both opinions have been extensively argued in recent monographs on Orwell. For the first point of view, see, for example, Rai, for the second, Gottlieb.

7. In addition to Patai's book, see also Leslie Tentler, "'I'm Not Literary, Dear': George Orwell on Women and the Family," in Jensen 47–63.

References

Bernstein, Michael André. *Bitter Carnival: Ressentiment and the Abject Hero*. Princeton: Princeton UP, 1992.

Crick, Bernard. *George Orwell: A Life*. Boston: Little, Brown and Company, 1980.

Dostoevskii, F.M. *Polnoe Sobranie Sochinenii. Vol. 5: Povesti i Rasskazy 1862–1866*. Leningrad: Nauka, 1973.

Dostoevsky, Fyodor. *Notes from Underground and The Grand Inquisitor*. Trans. Ralph E. Matlaw. NY: E.P. Dutton, 1960. Cited in text as *NU*.

———. *The Brothers Karamazov*. Trans. Constance Garnett. Ed. Ralph E. Matlaw. NY: Norton, 1976. Cited in text as *BK*.

Frank, Joseph. *Dostoevsky: The Stir of Liberation, 1860–1865*. Princeton: Princeton UP, 1986.

Gottlieb, Erika. *The Orwell Conundrum: A Cry of Despair or Faith in the Spirit of Man?* Ottawa: Carleton UP, 1992.

Howe, Irving, ed. *Orwell's Nineteen Eighty-Four: Text, Sources, Criticism*. NY: Harcourt, Brace & World, Inc., 1963.

Jensen, Ejner J., ed. *The Future of 'Nineteen Eighty-Four.'* Ann Arbor: U of Michigan P, 1984.

Kuppig, C.J., ed. *Nineteen Eighty-Four to 1984: A Companion to the Classic Novel of Our Time*. NY: Carroll & Graf Publishers, 1984.

Manuel, Frank E. and Fritzie P. Manuel. *Utopian Thought in the Western World*. Cambridge: Harvard UP, 1979.

Morson, Gary Saul. *The Boundaries of Genre: Dostoevsky's 'Diary of a Writer' and the Traditions of Literary Utopia*. Evanston: Northwestern UP, 1981.

Orwell, George. *Nineteen Eighty-Four*. NY: Penguin Books, 1983. Cited in text as *NE*.

———. *The Collected Essays, Journalism and Letters of George Orwell*. Ed. Sonia Orwell and Ian Angus. 4 vols. NY: Harcourt, Brace & World, Inc., 1968. Cited in text as *CEJL*.

Patai, Daphne. *The Orwell Mystique: A Study in Male Ideology*. Amherst: U of Massachusetts P. 1984.

Rai, Alok. *Orwell and the Politics of Despair: A Critical Study of the Writings of George Orwell*. Cambridge: Cambridge UP, 1988.

Steinhoff, William. *George Orwell and the Origins of '1984.'* Ann Arbor: U of Michigan P, 1975.

Wasiolek, Edward. *Dostoevsky: The Major Fiction*. Cambridge: M.I.T. Press, 1964.

Zamyatin, Yevgeny. *We*. Trans. Mina Ginsburg. NY: Avon Books, 1987.

Zwerdling, Alex. *Orwell and the Left*. New Haven: Yale UP, 1974.

PATRICIA RAE

Orwell's Heart of Darkness:
The Road to Wigan Pier
as Modernist Anthropology

*Critics have charged that Orwell's complaints about the dirt
and smell of working-class houses in* The Road to Wigan Pier
*inadvertently show that he was contemptuous of the class he claimed
to serve. This essay disputes that assessment, arguing that Orwell's
study is an admirable example of "modernist anthropology," a genre
whose goal is to give an uncensored account of an ethnographer's
difficulties in the field. Unlike the self-fashioned father of this
genre, Malinowski, who sacrificed Conradian irony for the sake
of "anthropological authority," Orwell courageously portrays the
prejudices of his fieldworker-persona, hoping to expose a form of
hypocrisy typical of left-wing middle-class domestic ethnographers
in the 1930s. Orwell's text emulates Conrad's* Heart of Darkness,
*both in its rich portrait of an unreliable investigator, whose horrified
reactions to an alien environment signify a parallel journey into the
"darkness" of his own heart, and in its complex ideological analysis
of the phenomenon of self censorship.*

Woe unto you, scribes and Pharisees, hypocrites! for ye make
clean the outside of the cup and of the platter, but within they are
full of extortion and excess.
  Woe unto you, scribes and Pharisees, hypocrites! for ye are like

From *Prose Studies* 22, no. 2 (April 1999): pp. 71–102. © 1999 by Frank Cass & Co. Ltd.

unto whited sepulchres, which indeed appear beautiful outward, but are within full of dead men's bones, and of all uncleanness.

Matt. 23: 25, 27

George Orwell's controversial 1937 study of mining life in the north of England, *The Road to Wigan Pier*, is widely regarded as the text that proved him a hypocrite, an ostensibly sympathetic observer of the working class, critical of the snobbery of his own class yet "trapped ... by the mental habits he claim[ed] to discard."[1] It is the work in which Orwell, despite avowing a socialist agenda, complains excessively about the filth of his subjects' habits and habitations, the site of his infamous pronouncement that "the lower classes smell."[2] In an influential early study of Orwell, echoed by many others, Tom Hopkinson pronounced it his "worst book," charging that Orwell's "preoccupation with himself and his own experience" in Wigan "prevented his enlarging that experience by sympathetic understanding of others."[3] This sentiment has been echoed by many feminist critics, from Storm Jameson to Daphne Patai and Beatrix Campbell, who see the worst aspect of the book as its self-indulgent posturing before the specter of Wigan's impoverished women.[4] I intend here to respond to such judgments by arguing that *The Road to Wigan Pier* is an exercise in "modernist anthropology," a genre that ironizes the reactions of the fieldworker in order to foreground the difficulty of attaining an objective and genuinely sympathetic understanding of alien cultures.[5] Its offending attributes, I argue, are not inadvertent, but calculated to dramatize flaws typical of domestic ethnographers in 1930s Britain. Like its modernist intertext,[6] *Heart of Darkness*, it is an expose of the "scribes and Pharisees" of twentieth-century ethnography, writers gripped by fear of contamination by their subjects and simultaneously intent on hiding the "uncleanness" of their own minds and hearts.

II

James Clifford provides the opening for a revaluation of Orwell's project in his 1986 reassessment of the work of the Polish father of modernist anthropology, Bronislaw Malinowski. Historians of anthropology, Clifford observes, generally agree that Malinowski's report on his fieldwork in the Trobriand Islands, *Argonauts of the Western Pacific* (1922), begins the "modernist epoch" in anthropology.[7] *Argonauts* is a vivid example of "participant-observation": an eye-witness account of a foreign culture aimed at correcting both the misconceptions of its distant audience and the generalizations of deductive anthropology. What makes it "modernist," from the perspective of contemporary theorists of anthropology, is its apparent effort to dramatize the Nietzschean principle that every such observer is embedded in a culturally constructed linguistic system—that he is "in a state of culture while looking at culture."[8] To put it in terms borrowed from another definer of "modernist" modes of representation, William James, it appears to portray not just the "facts" of the culture under investigation, but a fieldworker's "pure experience" of those facts: it is an example of the undivided and unedited perceptual field James defined for "radical empiricism."[9] "Radically empirical" writing, whether that of a modernist novelist or memoirist or anthropologist, offers personal "experience" as the only legitimate ground for truth-claims. It admits nothing as "fact" "except what can be experienced at some definite time by some experient."[10] More importantly, this authoritative "experience" is one in which the self and the world interact, or remain undivided. The radical empiricist does not aim to eradicate "subjective" feelings from "objective" facts: "[T]here is no self-splitting" of his experience "into consciousness and what the consciousness is 'of.'" In effect, this programme amounts to a policy of full disclosure: radical empiricism, James says, disallows anything not directly experienced, but must "not *exclude* ... any element that is directly experienced."[11]

Malinowski paved the way for his reputation as "modernist anthropologist," says Clifford, when he declared his intention to "be the Conrad"[12] of anthropology, carrying a copy of *Heart of Darkness* with him into the field. Malinowski's goal in striving to emulate Conrad appears to have been to be a radical empiricist: to give as full and honest account of his "experience" in the Trobriands as Conrad had given of Marlow's in the Congo. He set out, that is, not to hide any of the reactions or prejudices produced by his own cultural position, no matter how inhumane. Malinowski had endorsed the method of "radical empiricism" while writing a dissertation in the philosophy of science at the Jagellonian University. Deriving its account of the method from James's close associate, Ernst Mach, the dissertation offered a "sustained critique of any philosophy of science which fails to take account of the observer and his position relative to the object of observation."[13] As Robert Thornton has argued, there appears to be a direct line between this perspective and the representational practice he subsequently claims to deploy in *Argonauts of the Western Pacific*.[14] There, he vows to foreground the "customs, beliefs and prejudices" into which he, as observer, has been acculturated; he aims to be honest about these even when they have hindered his best efforts to get "into real touch with the natives...."[15]

Clifford, however, is sceptical about this "modernist" construction of Malinowski and *Argonauts of the Western Pacific*. He contends that the ethnographer's commitment to making an unexpurgated record of his experience ceded to the more self-serving project of fashioning himself as an "Anthropologist-hero": an "authoritative" persona, free of distorting biases, and absorbed in "sympathetic understanding of the Other."[16] The occasion for this reassessment was the publication of the field diary for *Argonauts of the Western Pacific* in 1967, which revealed *for the first time* that the fieldworker Malinowski had been deeply alienated from his Trobriand subjects, harbouring the ugliest of sentiments towards them. The unedited Malinowksi refers to the Trobrianders as "niggers," and desperately wishes to be free of "the atmosphere created by foreign bodies."[17] For Clifford, the important lesson to be learned from the diary is that *Argonauts of the Western Pacific* is no *unexpurgated* record—no full and complete rendering of "pure experience," as radical empiricism requires—but rather an exercise in self-censorship. Among the most significant of the remarks cut from the final text was one borrowed directly from *Heart of Darkness*. With Kurtz's infamous remarks echoing in his ears, Malinowksi confesses to himself that "At moments I was furious with [the islanders], particularly because after I gave them their portions of tobacco they all went away. On the whole my feelings toward the natives are decidedly tending to 'Exterminate the brutes.'"[18]

In a move replicating Marlow's editing of the report Kurtz had prepared for the "Society for the Suppression of Savage Customs,"[19] Malinowksi cut out the offending phrase from the final draft of *Argonauts*. His goal in doing so, in this example and many others, argues Clifford, was to establish "anthropological authority": an appearance of both scientific objectivity and compassion. Whatever Malinowski's insights into the alienating cultural prejudices of fieldworkers, it seems, he was not willing to expose *all* of his own; far from embracing the fulsome representations typical of "radical empiricism," he attempted to *divide* "pure experience" into subjective and objective components, erasing the most offensive of the former. As he himself describes his practice, it is necessary to transform "the *brute* material" gathered in the field into the "*authoritative* presentation of the results," or, deploying a key metaphor, to "clean up" the "dust of little bits of information" and expose the "final ideals of knowledge."[20] For Clifford, this self-censorship—not any commitment to "modernist" radical empiricism—was Malinowksi's true legacy to twentieth-century anthropology. By following both his instructions and his example, ethnographers have created a body of literature that systematically both minimizes the emotional responses of the fieldworker and exaggerates his cognitive abilities. This tendency has meant that there has not yet been full-blown modernist irony in ethnographic literature. "Anthropology," Clifford concludes, "*still awaits its Conrad.*"[21]

My goal here is to demonstrate that anthropology *has* had its Conrad—in Orwell. *The Road to Wigan Pier* is Orwell's *Heart of Darkness*: first, in Clifford's sense—it is a bluntly honest portrait of a fieldworker's responses—and second, in a meta-anthropological sense, because it shares *Heart of Darkness*'s perspective on the general syndrome of ethnographic hypocrisy. Though the words Marlow excises from Kurtz's report to the Society for the Suppression of Savage Customs belong literally to Kurtz, Conrad encourages readers to view Kurtz as a *representative* voice: the inner voice of all colonialist adventurers, including Marlow himself, who come unhinged when confronting the Other. When Marlow predicts to Kurtz "You will be lost … utterly lost,"[22] he is predicting his culture's suppression of the truth about such encounters, a conspiracy in which he himself participates when he edits Kurtz's report. Orwell's text teaches the same lesson: it, too, is a parable about the kind of "whitewashing" (or what Orwell called "voluntary self-censorship"[23]) that occurs when adventurers report their experiences of exploring a "foreign" culture. Since the inspiration for its fieldworker-persona was a community of British ethnographers in the 1930s who emulated Malinowski, it also anticipates Clifford's critique of the discipline fifty years later.

III

The Road to Wigan Pier is divided into two parts: Part One, an apparently straightforward account of what Orwell witnessed in Wigan, and Part Two, a polemical essay incorporating both autobiography and provocative advice to writers and activists on the Left. Despite the many efforts to find an appropriate generic classification for the book, only Philip Toynbee has suggested the ethnographic monograph.[24] The matter deserves more consideration, for Part One of the book, in particular, clearly has much in common with contemporaneous ethnographic studies of British working-class culture whose purpose was to counter middle-class misconceptions with the evidence of participant-observation, and through that exercise to provoke social change.

One of the most striking affinities between *The Road to Wigan Pier* and the productions of contemporaneous ethnographers is its treatment of the British working class as a foreign culture—its characterization of the northern mining community as a second, colonized "nation" or "race" within Britain.[25] Orwell repeatedly emphasizes the blackness of the miners' skins and their "Christy-Minstrel faces" (32), calling them "negroes" (33). He describes his trip north in terms more commonly applied to journeys south: as the adventure of a "civilized man venturing … among savages" (101). In Part Two of his study, he traces his appreciation of the parallel between British worker and colonial subject back to his return from a disillusioning stint with the Indian Imperial Police in Burma (1922–27), the impetus behind all his subsequent investigations into domestic poverty:

I felt that I had got to escape not merely from imperialism but from every form of man's dominion over man. I wanted to submerge myself, to get right down among the oppressed, to be one of them and on their side against their tyrants.... It was in this way that my thoughts turned towards the English working class. It was the first time that I had ever been really aware of the working class, and to begin with it was only because they supplied an analogy. *They were the symbolic victims of injustice, playing the same part in England as the Burmese played in Burma.* (138–9; my italics)

Orwell's perception of the analogy between British worker and colonial subject was far from original. The insight that the working class constituted a foreign country within Britain went back at least as far as 1845, with Disraeli's declaration that Britain contained "two nations," Rich and Poor.[26] As Judith Walkowitz has recently related,[27] during the latter part of the nineteenth century, middle-class male explorers, journeying with horrified fascination into London's slums, adopted the language of imperialism to describe the urban poor. Henry Mayhew, for example, in his massive 1861 study *London Labour and the London Poor*, described the "moral and intellectual change" demanded by his investigation as "so great, that it seems as if we were in a new land, and among another race." In 1883, George Sims wrote in a similar vein about his journey through "a dark continent that is within easy walking distance of the General Post Office." These privileged investigators, confident in their scientific capabilities, viewed their goal as developing a comprehensive knowledge of this alien space, or, as Charles Booth put it in his sociological study *East London* (1889), as "shedding light" on the "darkness" of this "terra incognita."[28] In the 1930s, two closely related cultural enterprises reactivated the analogy between domestic and foreign underclasses, both explicitly, in their own discourse, and implicitly, in their lofty scientific ambitions. One was the British documentary movement spearheaded by John Grierson. This movement, as Marsha Bryant has recently argued, was governed by a "colonizer/colonized binarism" in two senses: literally, in that many of the first British documentaries were produced for the Empire Marketing Board, and philosophically, in the documentarists' presumption about their cultural superiority over their subjects.[29] Reflecting on the task of documenting the lives of Britain's industrial workers, as well as those of the inhabitants of jungles and igloos, Grierson wrote: "We have taken our cameras to the more difficult territory. We have set up our tripods among the Yahoos themselves...."[30] Bryant describes the effects of this attitude in the 1933 Grierson documentary "Industrial Britain," a film that "unintentionally exposes its own imperialist vision, prompting the viewer to see its objectified images of coal miners and steelworkers as the colonial within, as 'material' in the service of empire."[31] The second forum for the analogy between workers and colonials in the 1930s was the burgeoning field of domestic anthropology itself, which often worked in close alliance with documentary photographers and filmmakers. Some of the key figures in this field came to it fresh from fieldwork abroad, and regarded their project as one of applying to British subjects the same investigative rigor they had applied to foreign, ones. Malinowksi had by this time taken up a post at London University, from which he served as advisor to such efforts.[32] Among other activities, he consulted on the largest project in domestic social anthropology in 1930s Britain: Mass-Observation. Officially launched by Charles Madge, Humphrey Jennings, and Tom Harrisson (who himself came to the project fresh from completing an ethnographic study of Malekula) in the same year Orwell's study appeared, and centered in the industrial town of Bolton, in the same Lancashire district as Wigan, the movement announced its aims as being to produce an "anthropology of our own people" conducted with all the rigor of ethnographic inquiry "in Africa or Australia."[33]

While writing up his field-notes from Wigan during 1936 and 1937, Orwell corresponded with at least two participants in, and advocates of, the effort to import the ethnographic techniques deployed abroad. One was the social anthropologist Geoffrey Gorer, an associate of Harrisson's who, as Orwell reminds him in a May 1936 letter, had recently written of the importance of "studying our own customs from an anthropological point of view."[34] The other was James Hanley, proletarian novelist turned ethnographer, and author of a 1937 study of the life of a Welsh mining community, *Grey Children*. In his study of the miners, Hanley recommended the project of domestic ethnography to any curious anthropologist tired of travelling too far afield: "Some enterprising anthropologist, perhaps a little tired of those continuous travels to survey the African native and his village, might well travel down to a mining district, any mining district will do. Providing he has the impartial eye, and the steady one, there is no reason why he should not surprise us all by something quite original when his survey is finished."[35]

Orwell appears to have taken seriously the project of representing Wigan as if it were an African village, or at least a village in the British colonies. As we shall see, however, there was a key difference between the parallel developed in his text and the one inhabiting the productions of many of his predecessors and contemporaries. As his account of his first perception of the analogy indicates, he deployed the analogy neither in the celebratory fashion of Grierson, nor with the unselfconscious scientism of a Booth, Harrisson, or

Hanley, but rather with a view to *critiquing* the parallel relationships between colonizer and colonized, middle-class *voyeur* and working man (or woman). Ultimately, as we shall see, his goal was to criticize "colonialist" attitudes implicit in the ethnographic exercise itself.[36]

For as much as he shared with it, Orwell was also set on *challenging* domestic ethnographic discourse in the 1930s, which was dominated by the principles and example set by Malinowski.[37] At the centre of this challenge lay a position consistent with what we might call, in a sense indebted to Clifford Geertz, Orwell's "anti-anti-modernism."[38] Throughout the decade, Orwell resisted the hostility to modernist aesthetics emerging among "committed" writers on the Left, the growing sense that modernist experiments were elitist, escapist, and socially irresponsible.[39] One form of "anti-modernism" officially endorsed by the Communist Party, and supported by writers on the Left in Britain, Communist and non-Communist alike, was a hostility to the kind of "impressionist" writing that effaced tough social realities by focusing on the consciousness of the bourgeois observer.[40] The Malinowskian domestic anthropology of Orwell's contemporaries, like the socialist realism officially sanctioned by the Soviet regime, eschewed excessive emphasis on the inner life of the observer—on what Christopher Caudwell, championing socialist realism, called the "flux of perplexed agony" enjoyed by bourgeois centres of consciousness, or what Storm Jameson, speaking for anthropology, dismissed as the "spiritual writhings" of the fieldworker.[41] The goal of the middle-class investigator in a mining town, as Hanley put it in the passage already cited, was to cultivate an "impartial" and "steady" eye.[42] Or, as Jameson explains, writing in the influential journal of domestic anthropology, *Fact*, "The first thing a socialist writer has to realize is that there is no value in the emotions ... started in him by the sight, smell, and touch of poverty. The emotions are no doubt unavoidable. There is no need to record them. Let him go and pour them down the drain." For Jameson, *The Road to Wigan Pier* epitomized a lapse into a self-indulgent focus on the observer's reaction, rather than on the external conditions he observes. Of Orwell's accounts of his encounters with Wigan's women, in particular, some of the most self-conscious and emotionally charged episodes in the narrative, she complains, "Too much of [Orwell's] energy runs away in an intense interest in and curiosity about his feelings. 'What things I am seeing for the first time! What smells I am enduring! There is the woman raking ashes with her hands and here I am watching her!'"[43] Jameson views Orwell's interest in the fieldworker's emotional responses to his data as being at odds with his duty to present social "fact." For Orwell (rather as for Adorno, in the roughly contemporaneous German Marxist debate on the subject),[44] these responses are *part* of social "fact," a part we ignore at our peril.

It is vital to note that these injunctions against personal feeling in anthropology and socialist realism in the 1930s applied exclusively to the inner life of the observer: the narrators of ethnographic reports and realist novels were to transcend themselves *in order to enter into the inner lives* of their working class subjects. "Getting beneath the skin"[45] of people on the other side of the class divide, as Montague Slater called it, was seen as vital to fostering the solidarity that socialist change requires. Without representing something of the inner lives of his subjects, Ralph Fox argued, the socialist realist novelist could not convince his readers of the obstacles presented by physical and economic reality: that is, he could not present an instructive image of the dialectic between individual aspirations and material conditions.[46] Or, as Jameson also explained, an "objective" account of a butcher, "however full, accurate, and exciting, will be nothing better than a blurred photograph" if it does not somehow capture "the inner life of the men and women [represented]...."[47] Theoretically, then, for both novelist and ethnographer the isolated protagonist of impressionist fiction, the Marlow or Dowell who typically proclaims his ignorance of the "hearts of men,"[48] was to be rejected in place of an ostensibly omniscient narrator perfectly capable of knowing the frustration and despair experienced by society's victims. Hanley summarizes the policy in a scene recounted in *Grey Children* where he takes pains to read the feelings behind an unemployed miner's tone of voice: he reassures the miner that I'll understand your feelings very well indeed. And if we all understood each other, life might be very different."[49]

The anti-modernist attitudes I have identified, and which I am suggesting Orwell challenges in *The Road to Wigan Pier*, shaped the founding principles of Mass-Observation. James Buzard has recently argued that the discourse of Mass-Observation was continuous with that of modernist fiction.[50] With Samuel Hynes, he sees an analogy between one of the movement's earliest productions, *May 12th*, a study summarizing the experiences of hundreds of Britons on Coronation Day, 1937, and modernist day-books like Woolf's *Mrs. Dalloway* and Joyce's *Ulysses*. While this claim has its merits, it is based largely on an observation of only one of two major kinds of project undertaken by the movement: the study of the contributions of a "Volunteer Panel" who submitted personal diaries recording their activities, thoughts, and feelings on an appointed day. The movement's other major project falls in line with the kinds of domestic ethnographic study of which I have been speaking. This was the creation of an army of (mostly) middle-class ethnographic "Observers," who would watch and record the habits of working-class citizens at work and leisure, attempting where possible to discern the feelings and motivations behind their behavior.[51] It may have Harrisson's ethnographic training, or perhaps the direct influence of Malinowksi, that shaped the instructions that went out to would-be Observers in the founding pamphlet of Mass-Observation, instructions that reflect what Clifford has seen as Malinowski's concern with establishing "anthropological authority." The pamphlet stresses that these Observers are to avoid at all cost the appearance of "subjective bias." They are not to "mix up fact and interpretation of fact." They are to get rid of "feelings" that, among other things, "interfere in the choice of facts."[52]

Chief among the preventative measures the Observers were to take was providing Mass-Observation's editors with autobiographical "reports on self," reports that would alert the editors to potential biases in the descriptions submitted. As the manifesto explains,

> Everything will depend on the reliability of ... [the] Observer ... Feelings will interfere in the choice of facts and method of approach, especially through the unconscious omission of certain facts. It is seldom that there is any chance of knowing what personal bias is likely to have affected the findings of scientists; but in the case of the Observers, we aim at having sufficient cross-references about them to indicate the probable nature of bias in each individual. We want the Observers themselves to give us these cross-references, and if possible to have them corroborated by someone else. To write objective reports comes naturally to some, to others calls for a process of self-schooling. The first task of an Observer is to write an objective report on himself.[53]

Under the scrupulous eye of the editors, the reports submitted by the Observers were to be sifted and shaped into unbiased, objective, records of how working people go about the business of modern life.[54] Significantly, the movement's inaugural pamphlet prefaces its statement of commitment to such a product with an implicit *complaint* about the literary practices recently deployed to record the experience of modern life, a complaint particularly about the flight into interiority characteristic of modernist impressionist fiction:

> [R]evolutionary inventions have been especially numerous during the past hundred years. The steam railway, the spinning jenny, electric power, photography, have had so great an impact on mental and physical behaviour that we are barely conscious of it. *Those who have attempted to convey an impression of what this impact has been like have been reduced to abandoning all coherence and realism, and have fled in the direction of the interior life or the*

abstract form. Some reminiscences and diaries, some realistic novels, have provided a fragmentary picture, but always from a personal angle or from the angle of romance. A description in scientific terms of the changes in modes of living during the nineteenth century is unachieved. A similar description for our own day is practically unattempted.[55]

Mass-observation, in other words, eschewed the alienated narrative stance of impressionism for the purportedly omniscient stance of socialist realism. The "fascination" of the observers' reports, the pamphlet concludes, "is akin to that of the realistic novel, with the added interest of being fact and not fiction."[56]

In formulating a program for ethnographic observers to achieve self-transcendence, a program which reinstates the Cartesian division into subject and object rejected by radical empiricism, Harrisson and Madge appear to have assumed that acts of self-examination can be conducted from a perspective that is *itself* free of bias. This assumption, along with the conviction that society's interests were best served by eliminating the biases of the ethnographic observer, was a major target of Orwell's "anti-anti-modernism," and an object of parody in *The Road to Wigan Pier*, Part Two.

IV

Orwell's attitude toward the anti-modernist anthropological project in the 1930s mirrored the "paradox,"[57] or hypocritical inconsistency, that Raymond Williams and others have complained about in his work: he was both supportive of the quest for sympathetic identification across class lines and resistant to the pose of self-transcendence that typically accompanied it. On the one hand, he did much to affirm the anti-modernist project of "getting beneath the skin" of the Other—or as he put it, of "breaking down the solitude in which the human being lives."[58] On the other, he celebrated the kind of literature that seemed to reinforce the idea of human solitude: fiction that foregrounded the feelings, fears, and prejudices of its bourgeois observer. The two tendencies come together in *The Road to Wigan Pier*, where he draws from the strategies of impressionist fiction to recount an effort at sympathetic identification that *fails*.

The most striking evidence of Orwell's support for the project of "getting beneath the skin" of citizens of another class was his famous masquerade "down and out" in Paris and London between 1928 and 1930. Disguising himself as a tramp in order to occupy the Other's subject-position was a strategy he shared with many other domestic anthropologists in the

1930s, including the Mass-Observers,[59] and he concludes his account of that adventure, *Down and Out in Paris and London* (1933), with a vow to continue seeking to understand *"what really goes on in the souls* of *plongeurs* and tramps and Embankment sleepers."[60] His commitment to the project of understanding suffering "from the inside"[61] is also reflected in his well-known 1931 account of a hanging he witnessed while a policeman in Burma:

> It is curious, but till that moment I had never realised what it means to destroy a healthy, conscious man. When I saw the prisoner step aside to avoid the puddle, I saw the mystery, the unspeakable wrongness, of cutting a life short when it is in full tide. This man was not dying, *he was alive just as we were alive.* All the organs of his body were working—bowels digesting food, skin renewing itself, nails growing, tissues forming—all toiling away in solemn foolery. His nails would still be growing when he stood on the drop, when he was falling through the air with a tenth of a second to live.[62]

This intense moment of sympathetic identification had marked a turning-point in Orwell's career, rendering him hostile to Britain's imperialist enterprise and determined to understand the inner lives of its casualties, both abroad and at home. The first step towards comprehending another person's inner life, he suggests here, and in other essays of the early 1930s,[63] is to identify with that person's *body*, or to imagine his or her *somatic* sensations—a strategy *The Road to Wigan Pier* suggests sometimes proves more than a squeamish ethnographer can bear.

But at the same time as Orwell was seeking self-transcendence through role-playing, and praising writers like Jack Hilton for successfully conveying the feeling of poverty "from the inside," he was formulating a powerful defense of the kind of modernist fiction that foregrounds the inner life *of its alienated bourgeois narrator*. In the same year that Karl Radek denounced Joyce's emphasis on the subjectivity of his narrators at the All-Union Congress of Soviet Writers, Orwell effusively praised *Ulysses* to his friend Brenda Salkeld, remarking on the almost paralyzing inferiority complex it gave him as a writer.[64] The essence of his admiration for Joyce, and for Henry Miller, was a perception of the courage it takes to offer unexpurgated descriptions of the dancer thoughts and feelings of human beings. As he explained in a November 1935 review of *Tropic of Cancer*, Miller's detailed portrayal of his protagonist's brutal sexual desires is necessary because "Man ... is rather like a Yahoo and needs to be reminded of it from time to time": Miller, he says, has been uncommonly brave in daring to dramatize "facts well known to everybody but never mentioned in print."[65] The ultimate value of this kind of honesty, he was later to note, is in their power to make the reader confront previously unacknowledged parts of himself:

> [Joyce] dared—for it is a matter of *daring* just as much of technique—to expose the imbecilities of the inner mind.... Here is a whole world of stuff which you have lived with since childhood, stuff which you supposed to be of its nature incommunicable, and somebody has managed to communicate it.... When you read certain passages in *Ulysses* you feel that Joyce's mind and your mind are one, that he knows all about you though he has never heard your name, that there exists some world outside time and space in which you and he are together....[66]

The courage of such "emotionally sincere"[67] writing is also a central theme in the polemical essay addressed to Leftist writers in Part Two of *The Road to Wigan Pier*. There, Orwell singles out for special praise the work of Somerset Maugham and George Saintsbury, which portrays "without humbug" (120) middle-class attitudes towards the working-class, and openly describes middle-class squeamishness at a perception of working-class dirt and smell: "Most people are a little shy of putting that kind of thing on paper. But what Saintsbury is saying here is what any little worm with a fairly safe five hundred a year *thinks*, and therefore in a way one must admire him for saying it. *It takes a lot of guts to be openly such a skunk as that*" (124; last italics mine). In the context of his other remarks on the value of honest renderings of prejudice, Orwell's praise for Maugham and Saintsbury suggests a mitigating intention behind the infamous expressions of snobbery in his text. The offending utterances in *The Road to Wigan Pier*, particularly its remarks about working-class hygiene, are *meant* to offend, and to educate through their familiarity.

Despite the obvious relevance of Maugham's and Saintsbury's texts for Orwell's, however, the most suggestive intertext for the ironic psychological drama in *The Road to Wigan Pier* is Conrad's *Heart of Darkness*.[68] Orwell's decision to represent the trip to Wigan as a journey into the *"filthy heart* of [British] civilization" (16; my italics) is but one clue to this. During the months he was translating his Wigan diary into a book, he was actively defending Conrad from detractors on the left;[69] that defense surfaces in Part Two, where he disputes Prince Dmitri Mirsky's accusation that the novelist was "no less imperialist than Kipling" (168). Two things may have motivated his allegiance to Conrad during this period, and prompted him to echo *Heart of Darkness* in his tale. The first may have been to introduce a *critique* into the intertwined discourses of classism and colonialism often invoked uncritically by domestic anthropologists and documentarists. This would have seemed a compelling project, given his own perception of the parallel indignities suffered by colonial and British worker on his return from Burma; he remarks in Part Two of his study that many on the British Left were quicker to recognize foreign oppression than its equivalent at home.[70] His invocation of Marlow's journey in recounting his own, then, may have been designed to mirror his audience's darkness back to them in the shape of an evil they already recognized and repudiated.[71] The second motivation for invoking Conrad's text may have been an interest in exploring the phenomenon of hypocrisy in both foreign and domestic contexts. While Orwell was in the process of writing up his fieldnotes, his friend, anthropologist Geoffrey Gorer wrote him a letter pointing out that the parallel between domestic and colonial situations extended to the hypocrisies of middle-class Britons and Burmese sahib-log.[72] And, as I have been suggesting, following Clifford, the main interest of Marlow's story is not so much the prejudices he and others harbor toward their subjects as his determination to lie about them: not so much the fact that colonizers' hearts are "dark" as the fact society pretends they are "white." The following reading of Orwell's text will suggest that it was just this kind of hypocrisy Orwell hoped his readers would come to recognize, and correct, in themselves.

V

The central formal device *The Road to Wigan Pier* shares with *Heart of Darkness* is a dramatic protagonist, or naive narrator: following Raymond Williams, I shall call him "Orwell."[73] "Orwell" is both an individual and a type, a representation of Orwell himself and a portrait of the kind of middle-class Leftist Orwell would have expected to find in large numbers among his readers, which eventually included many Mass-Observers.[74] His goals typify those of the Malinowskian ethnographer writing for a middle-class audience: he aims to counter misconceptions about the working class with the evidence of participant-observation; to empathize deeply with his subjects; to draw his readers into the experience; to establish his own authority with empathy and self-awareness. But the story here is one about the *failure* of that project. If "Orwell's" aim is to investigate the habits and inner lives of a dark-skinned Other—to be an "emissary of light"[75] into Wigan's darkness— the book's main interest is in the epistemological difficulties he experiences in the attempt, aptly characterized by Marlow's description of travelling down the Congo through the fog:

> Now and then a boat from the shore gave one momentary contact with reality. It was paddled by black fellows. You could

see from afar the white of their eyeballs glistening. They shouted, sang; their bodies streamed with perspiration; they had faces like grotesque masks—these chaps; but they had bone, muscle, a wild vitality, an intense energy of movement, that was as natural and true as the surf along their coast. They wanted no excuse for being there. They were a great comfort to look at. *For a time I would feel I belonged still to a world of straight-forward facts; but the feeling would not last long. Something would turn up to scare it away.*[76]

Like Marlow's glimpses of his subjects through the mist, "Orwell's" investigation into the lives of those who dwell in the "filthy heart" of England is a search for "straight-forward facts" frequently disrupted by unbidden feelings. Like Marlow's journey, too, it is a quest for the truth about an external darkness—in this case, about the community of "black fellows" toiling deep in the coal mines—that ultimately reverses the direction of the investigator's light, into the darkness of his own soul. When Marlow recalls reaching his furthest point of navigation, he says that the experience "seemed to throw a kind of light on everything about me—*and into my thoughts.*"[77] Commenting similarly on the vision at the end of a mine shaft—the head of a "glittering river of coal"—"Orwell" recalls that "You cannot see very far because the fog of coal dust *throws back the beam of your lamp* ..." (19; my italics).

"Orwell's" goal in recounting his trip to Wigan in Part One is to dispel the "widespread illusions" (35) that have distorted middle-class readers' understanding of the working class. Like Marlow, who envisions getting at the truth as a matter of "penetrating deeper and deeper" into the fog,[78] "Orwell" imagines himself piercing through surface-truths to uncover the grim realities hidden beneath. One concrete model for this procedure is his journey into the interior of a working-class house, where the furnishings in the outer rooms obscure the squalor behind the scenes:

One thing that is very noticeable is that the worst squalors are never downstairs. You might visit quite a number of houses, even among the poorest of the unemployed, and bring away a wrong impression. These people, you might reflect, cannot be so badly off if they still have a fair amount of furniture and crockery. But it is in the rooms upstairs that the gauntness of poverty really discloses itself. (55)

The journey from parlour to back room is emblematic of an effort to shatter comfortable ideological truths, to bring the reader face to face with the truth about the workers' lives. Behind all "Orwell's" efforts to expose the truth below the surface is the Marxian base/super-structure model of society. The world where the coal is dug and the coal-miners' families dwell in their slums, he says, is "a sort of world apart which one can quite easily go through life without ever hearing about," yet it is the "absolute necessary counterpart" of the "world above," where the privileged classes eat their ices and write their novels (29).

Though he devotes some energy to correcting middle-class assumptions about the miners' hours and wages, the most memorable (and carefully analyzed) of the "wrong impressions" that "Orwell" discredits are those about what his subjects *feel*. To the dehumanizing perception of miners "skipping round the pit props almost like dogs," for example, he responds that "it is quite a mistake to think that they enjoy it": "I have talked about this to scores of miners and they all admit that the 'travelling' is hard work ... comparable, perhaps, to climbing a smallish mountain before and after your day's work" (26). In the passage that offended Storm Jameson, to which I shall be returning, he issues a similar challenge to middle-class perceptions of working-class women:

> At the back of one of the houses a young woman was kneeling on the stones, poking a stick up the leaden waste-pipe which ran from the sink inside and which I suppose was blocked. I had time to see everything about her—her sacking apron, her clumsy clogs, her arms reddened by the cold. She looked up as the train passed, and I was almost near enough to catch her eye. She had a round pale face, the usual exhausted face of the slum girl who is twenty-five and looks forty, thanks to miscarriages and drudgery; and it wore, for the second in which I saw it, the most desolate, hopeless expression I have ever seen. It struck me then that *we are mistaken when we say that 'It isn't the same for them as it would be for us, and that people bred in the slums can imagine nothing but the slums. For what I saw in her face was not the ignorant suffering of an animal.* She knew well enough what was happening to her—*understood as well as I did how dreadful a destiny it was to be kneeling there in the bitter cold, on the slimy stones of a slum backyard, poking a stick up a food drain-pipe.* (15; my italics)

Again the speaker meets his middle-class readers on the surface—invoking the common presumption that "It isn't the same for them as it would be for us"— and again he plunges them through it, emphasizing the continuity between her inner life, his, and theirs. The destiny of kneeling on slimy stones, "poking a stick up a foul drain-pipe," is to be, momentarily at least, shared.

But such efforts at empathy never last long. "Orwell" is repeatedly being distracted from his purpose by the grime encrusting skin, furnishings, and food: recoiling from a slice of bread-and-butter "intimately" and "lingeringly" marked by his landlord Mr Brooker's thumb (6); from the same thumb planted "well over the rim" of a full chamber-pot (10); from a marmalade jar that is an "unspeakable mass of stickiness and dirt" (13); from "some dreadful slimy thing among the coal dust"—a "chewed quid of tobacco" (20–21). "As you walk through the industrial towns," he complains. with typical excess, "you lose yourself in labyrinths of little brick houses blackened by smoke, festering in planless chaos round miry alleys and little cindered yards where there are slinking dustbins and lines of grimy washing and half-ruinous wcs" (46). "Orwell's" disgust with his subjects' lack of hygiene—"the dominant and essential thing," he says, about their world (54)—steadily erodes his sympathy for their plight. "Even if you live in a back to back house and have four children and a total income of thirty-two and sixpence a week from the PAC," he grumbles, "there is no *need* to have unemptied chamber-pots standing about in your living room" (55). In the deeply embedded value system of this modernist narrator, "cleanliness" and "decency" go hand in hand.[79]

"Orwell's" disruptive obsession with dirt and smell is a classic case of what Mary Douglas has labeled "pollution behaviour": "the reaction which condemns any object or idea likely to confuse or contradict cherished classifications." In this scheme, "uncleanliness or dirt is that which must not be included if a pattern is to be maintained."[80] The fear of ingesting another person's saliva or dung, in particular—"Orwell's" dread of chewed fluids of tobacco and dirty thumbs—is a desire to protect the *body's* boundaries, universal symbol, Douglas argues, for boundaries in general.[81] Orwell had dramatized a similar pollution fear in *Burmese Days*, where an English colonizer's fear of violation by the colonized plays out as a desire to keep the Englishmen's Club clean, or free of "slime": the sour racist, Ellis, dubs a Burmese membership candidate "Very Slimy," and wages a no-holds-barred effort to keep him out.[82] The obsession with dirt in *The Road to Wigan Pier* reflects the lower/upper-middle-class Englishman's fear of violation by a "lower class" in his own country, but, for reasons already mentioned, it is meant to echo colonialist discourse. It is both a response to a literal feature of Wigan and a metaphor for the feelings of a class whose integrity is threatened, not just by this ethnographic exercise, but by the goal of a classless society it is meant to serve.[83]

Functioning both literally and symbolically, "Orwell's" "pollution fear" disturbs the practise of somatic identification we have seen in the narrator of "A Hanging," for his act of imagining himself into the body of the Other occasions a sense of physical intimacy, which in turn introduces a fear of contamination. Consider, for example, another one of the meditations on women whose emphasis on the speaker's tortured feelings displeased Storm Jameson: "One woman's face stays by me, a worn skull-like face on which was a look of intolerable misery and degradation. I gathered that in that dreadful pigsty, struggling to keep her large brood of children clean, *she felt as I should, feel if I were coated all over with dung*" (53; my italics). The key clause in this description is the last one, where "Orwell" reaches for an analogy for the woman's psychological and somatic experience: "*she felt as I should feel if ...*" I would suggest that the analogy chosen (being "*coated all over with dung*") is intended not only as a description of the feelings of the woman but also for the experience of empathizing with the woman, for the feeling that comes of imagining his body identical with hers. Something similar happens in the portrait of a woman cited earlier, where the speaker shares the destiny of "poking a stick up a foul drain-pipe"; in his case, the action may be a crude metaphor for the act of sympathetic or somatic identification itself, which feels like befoulment. Both portraits dramatize the dilemma facing an ethnographer of "Orwell's" class, which he describes at length in Part Two: the requirement of empathy demands the renunciation of a much cherished class distinction, on which the speaker's very sense of self depends. As he explains,

> The fact that has got to be faced is that to abolish class-distinctions means abolishing a part of yourself. Here am I, a typical member of the middle class. It is easy for me to say that I want to get rid of class-distinctions, but nearly everything I think and do is a result of class-distinctions. All my notions—notions of good and evil, of pleasant and unpleasant, of funny and serious, of ugly and beautiful—are essentially *middle-class* notions; my taste in books and food and clothes, my sense of honour, my table manners, my turns of speech, my accent, even the characteristic movements of my body, are the products of a special kind of upbringing and a special niche about halfway up the social hierarchy ... [T]o get outside the class-racket I have got to suppress not merely my private snobbishness, but most of my other tastes and prejudices as well. I have got to alter myself so completely that at the end I should hardly be recognized as the same person. (149–50)

Orwell views his fellow "left-wingers" as holding on tenaciously to class-difference, even when they express their deepest sympathies for victims on the other side of the class divide. Orwell's descriptions of the women dramatize this stubbornness. They do not efface the women's feelings unselfconsciously, but expose the inadequacies of an observer who hypocritically presumes to occupy their subject-position: a middle-class Leftist male who, in disingenuously denying a difference between himself and them, metaphorically "colonizes" their bodies.

Like Conrad, Orwell underscores his protagonist's increasing alienation from his subjects with a shift from metonymic to metaphoric discourse. In a move belying his other efforts to dispel dehumanizing animal metaphors, for example, and mirroring Marlow's increasing need to deny the black men's humanity, he transforms the literal blackbeetles swarming on Mr Brooker's tripe into a figure for the beleaguered masses, "creeping round and round ... in an endless muddle of slovened [*sic*] jobs and mean grievances" (14),[84] and perhaps inspiring Kurtzian thoughts of "extermination." The mines and foundries, too, acquire symbolic resonance: like the infernal scenes Marlow witnesses on the bank of the Congo, they are scenes from hell, inhabited by spectres of attenuated humanity (99).[85] By the end of Part One, "Orwell's" sensitivities leave him as "cut off from the comprehension of his surroundings"[86] as is Marlow, his best efforts at objective reportage and sympathetic identification foiled by deeply conditioned class prejudices. Indeed, his obsession with the miners' dirtiness leads him to the kind of alienated and incurious frame of mind typical of Marlow, and of white colonists in general, the mind-set to which dark bodies are indistinguishable: "You can hardly tell by the look of them," he says, "whether they are young or old. They may be any age up to sixty or even sixty five, but when they are black and naked they all look alike" (20).[87]

If "Orwell's" metaphorical tendency points to his failure in two of the Malinowskian ethnographer's tasks, objectivity and sympathy, it also underscores his failure in a third: the task of "setting his readers down" in the environment he describes. The key trope establishing the irony here is catachresis: the kind of strained metaphor that foregrounds the *distance* between the things it equates. The metaphors he uses to put his readers into the miners' shoes are consistently catachretical, accentuating rather than dissolving class differences.[88] He draws an unlikely comparison, for example, between the experiences of traveling down into the mines and descending into the London Tube, and an even more absurd one between the projects of digging coal and "scooping the central layer from a Neapolitan ice" (26). The bleak northern landscape under snow resembles, not the rippling muscle to which D.H. Lawrence compared it, but "a white dress with black piping running across it" (16), metonym for the social world sustained by the miners' labor. Rather like Marlow's comparison between his ragged steamboat and a Huntley and Palmer biscuit tin,[89] "Orwell's" catachretical metaphors imply a *relationship* between the miners' world and the world "at home"—the relationship of superstructure to economic base—but no *identity* between them. They thus represent a profound challenge to the sentimental humanism of colleagues like Hanley, which, like colonialism, too often fails to respect the difference of the Other.

VI

Part Two of *The Road to Wigan Pier* continues this dramatization of its narrator's limitations. What at the outset promises to be a kind of Mass-Observer "report on self," providing an objective perspective on the prejudices marring the book's first half,[90] quickly reveals itself to be a parody of such efforts.[91] After a catalog of the educational and economic experiences that explain "Orwell's" discomfort with the physical proximity with the "lower classes" (116–26), we encounter the startling claim that his adventure living as a tramp had *cured him* of such queasiness. He *grew up* an "odious little snob" (128), the story goes, a youth who *once* felt squeamish sharing a bottle of beer with a working man, but thanks to his masquerade, *he is not one now*. Not one now? Coming after the overwhelming stench of pollution fear left by Part One, the claim stands out as a self-serving lie, a self-righteous assertion about the virtue of putting oneself in another's shoes. The naive character "Orwell," in other words, does not die at the end of Part One, to be replaced by an authoritative speaker. Rather, the early part of Part Two is his second act: a dramatization of the false claims to objectivity and sympathy Orwell perceives as typical of contemporary socialist ethnographers.

Several theoretical statements in the later part of Part Two (where the unreliable voice of "Orwell" finally fades away) confirm that the lesson to be gleaned from his story is really one about the inescapability of prejudice and the hypocrisy of those who claim otherwise. "Unfortunately you do not solve the class problem by making friends with tramps," Orwell concludes, "At most you get rid of *some* of your own class-prejudice by doing so" (my italics; 143). His motivation in dramatizing both a middle-class socialist fieldworker's prejudices and his blindness to them has been to offer a case study for a syndrome all too common in the community for which he writes:

> Unfortunately it is nowadays the fashion to pretend that the glass
> is penetrable. Of course everyone knows that class-prejudice

exists, but at the same time everyone claims that *he*, in some mysterious way, is exempt from it. Snobbishness is one of those vices which we can discern in everyone else but never in ourselves. Not only the *croyant et pratiquant* Socialist, but every 'intellectual' takes it as a matter of course that *he* at least is outside the class racket; *he*, unlike his neighbours, can see through the absurdity of wealth, ranks, titles, etc. etc. 'I'm not a snob' is nowadays a kind of universal *credo*. (145–6)[92]

Like *Heart of Darkness*, then, *The Road to Wigan Pier* has as its subject the telling of lies, specifically, lies about the cleanliness of the lenses through which the leftist intellectual sees, and the purity of the hearts with which he sympathizes.

As "Orwell's" drama unfolds, moreover, we become aware that in his case, as in Marlow's, the lies are not just personal but cultural, elements of intertwined discourses on knowledge, colonialism, and hygiene. There is a deep affinity between the texts' strategies for critiquing the ideology of these discourses, which amount to questionings of the excessive value ascribed to depth over surface, light over darkness, cleanliness over dirt. At the heart of both critiques is a metaphor offered by Conrad's framing narrator:

> The yarns of seamen have a direct simplicity, the whole meaning of which lies within the shell of a cracked nut. But Marlow was not typical ... to him the meaning of an episode was not inside like a kernel but outside, enveloping the tale which brought it out *only as a glow brings out a haze, in the likeness of one of those misty halos that, sometimes, are made visible by the spectral illumination of moonshine.*[93]

The primary opposition here is the one between depth and surface, between the "inside" of a tale and the "outside." In the context of Marlow's aforementioned valorization of depths and surfaces, the "inside" of a tale corresponds to the "facts" it strains to disclose. But the narrator has also taken to heart Marlow's verdict about the difficulty of such insight, particularly as it applies to the "inner lives" of others—the conviction that, in the end, "we live, as we dream, alone." His perception of Marlow, accordingly, is of one who inverts the initial goal of his reportage. Marlow now sees the value of a report on foreign travel as being not "inside," with disclosed "facts," but "outside," in the mist of culturally conditioned prejudices obscuring the traveler's vision; he regards the point of his "tale" as being the revelation of prejudice, the illumination (not the elimination) of the "haze" by an inquiring light.

As I have been describing it, the drama enacted by "Orwell" culminates in the same inversion of aesthetic values as Marlow's, figured in the same metaphors: what begins as a quest for the "inside" (complete with warnings to the reader against "sliding over" the surface of the writing (52)) turns out to be a story about the "outside," about the "surface truths" that make "Orwell" an inadequate ethnographer in the eyes of contemporaries like Hanley and Jameson. Orwell openly states that portraying the filter is crucial to successful socialist ethnography: "To get rid of class-distinctions," he asserts, you have got to start by showing "*how one class appears when seen through the eyes of another*" (122; my italics). As I now hope to show, he defends this position with a powerful critique of the ideology behind the presumption that middle-class prejudices are conquerable and working-class subjects "penetrable." Crucial to his critique are the very details that have caused most offense, the text's multivalent symbols of dirt and smell. Orwell uses his speaker's obsession with them to raise some important hygiene questions: Is "dirt," in all its senses, to be eradicated or tolerated? What ideological implications attach to the will to clean it up?

Like the beetles on Mr Brooker's tripe, in other words, the dirt from which "Orwell" recoils has symbolic force. It corresponds to the dark pigmentation of colonial subjects, the "earth" in what Orwell elsewhere calls their "earth-coloured bodies."[94] It is the "dirt" of encroaching difference, and the darkness of the Lukácsian "incognito," hiding the Other like a dark shell.[95] In another sense, suggested by passages like the panoramic descriptions of the industrial towns, it implies a metaphysical mess, a "giant's dust bin" (97), or a dusty wasteland,[96] the chaos of a Nietzschean universe awaiting intellectual housekeeping. Most important, for our purposes, in another strategy shared with *Heart of Darkness*, it corresponds to certain attributes *of the observer himself*, and of the class he represents. "Orwell" is dark, or dirty, by virtue of being an upper-middle-class white British male. Literally—at least to Chinese nostrils—he "smells like a corpse" (133). He is implicated in the "dirty work" (136) of Empire, and the industrial "doing of dirt" that has greyed England's pastoral green (16). "Dirt" adheres *to his own eyes*, the blinding residue of his own culture.[97] He has prejudices that make him a "skunk" in his heart (124). All these varieties of grime are subjected to the narrator's urge to clean, and the book's analysis of the discourse on hygiene discredits all of his attempts as ideological. Indeed, the fact that the book foregrounds its narrator's obsession with cleanliness, in a manner closely paralleling Conrad's ironization of Marlow's quest to "throw a kind of light" on things, may be the single thing most distinguishing it from other ethnographic studies deploying the analogy between worker and colonial subject. It presents the obsession with making things "white," an obsession governing such studies, in a variety of ways, as a serious *problem*.

The essence of *The Road to Wigan Pier*'s critique of cleaning is captured in the Biblical intertext serving as epigraph to the present essay, and also famously involved in *Heart of Darkness*: the allegorical verses on hygiene in Matthew 23. "Orwell" and Marlow are both men who would "make clean the outside of the cup and of the platter," but who are themselves "dirty" within; more precisely, they are men who make an effort to "whiten" themselves and their surroundings in the interest of hiding an ineradicable darkness. Conrad, of course, identifies the "whited sepulchre" with the imperial center of Brussels, the glistening city where the Intended tinkles her ivory piano keys. Orwell's version of the "whited sepulchre" is the postwar British factory, whose sanitary appearance belies its brutal relations of production:

> The typical post-war factory is not a gaunt barrack or an awful chaos of blackness and belching chimneys; it is a glittering white structure of concrete, glass, and steel, surrounded by green lawns and beds of tulips ... Though the ugliness of industrialism is the most obvious thing about it and the thing every newcomer exclaims against, I doubt whether it is centrally important. And perhaps it is not even desirable, industrialism being what it is, that it should learn to disguise itself as something else. As Mr. Aldous Huxley has truly remarked, a dark Satanic mill ought to look like a dark Satanic mill and not like the temple of mysterious and splendid gods. (100)

Orwell's criticism of the efforts to whitewash industrialism, both in the factories and in unnaturally sanitary housing states (67), mirrors the Biblical complaint. "There is always a temptation," he notes, "to think that industrialism is harmless so long as it is clean and orderly" (101), but such efforts obscure the truth about workers like the miner, "a sort of grimy caryatid *upon whose shoulders everything that is not grimy is supported*" (18): In pinpointing the ideological function of glittering white exteriors, moreover, Orwell replicates the paradox governing the play on light and darkness in Conrad's novella: the insight that the "light" we shine into hidden depths is a *blinding* light, that the real "facts" are only to be found in darkness.[98] He insists, counterintuitively, that "the time to go [into the mines] is when the machines are roaring and the air is black with coal dust, and when you can actually see what the miners have to do" (18).

The squeamish character "Orwell" serves to illustrate such ideological "cleaning" in all the arenas suggested by his multivalent "dirt." Whether fussing over the Brooker's dirty dishes, sticky marmalade jars, and crumb-covered tablecloth, or advocating better washing facilities for the miners (33), "Orwell" articulates an ideological impulse to "whiten" an environment whose filth speaks more truly of its plight. His obsession with cleaning also recalls the will to annihilate difference characteristic of colonialist discourse: praising pithead baths, he notes that "within twenty minutes of emerging [from a mine] as black as a Negro," a miner "can be riding off to a football match dressed up to the nines" (33), indistinguishable from the rest of the "white men" on the surface. Still another kind of cleaning applies to the kind of "metaphysical" dirt that irritates the intellect, challenging the cherished theories of socialists, in particular:

> Sometimes I look at a Socialist—the intellectual, tract-writing type of Socialist, with his pullover, his fuzzy hair, and his Marxian quotation—and wonder what the devil his motive really *is*. It is often difficult to believe that it is a love of anybody, especially of the working class, from whom he is of all people the furthest removed. The underlying motive of many Socialists, I believe, is simply a hypertrophied sense of order. The present state of affairs offends them not because it causes misery, still less because it makes freedom impossible, *but because it is untidy*; what they desire, basically, is to reduce the world to something resembling a chess-board. (166; my italics)

To draw again from Douglas, Orwell's interest here (and elsewhere, discussing the attraction of a "glittering Wells-world" (201)) is in the fear of the kind of "grit" that "confuses or contradicts cherished classifications," or that "must not be included if a pattern is to be maintained"; it is about an aversion to "ambiguity or anomaly."[99] The anomalous "grit" threatening middle-class socialists, and dramatized in "Orwell"'s experience of Wigan, is the fact that "if a real working man, a miner dirty from the pit ... suddenly walked into their midst, they would ... [be] embarrassed, angry, and disgusted," inclined to flee, "holding their noses" (163). It is what William James would call the "affectional fact" of "disgustingness,"[100] the undivided complex of the filth witnessed and the sentiments accompanying it. "Orwell" engages in a kind of "cleaning," then, when he attempts to deny his own experience of disgust: when he explains how he has gotten over his fear of sharing "cups and platters" with the down and out, and describes the (suspiciously brief) "ten minutes' job" of *Getting the dirt out of [his] eyelids* (33; my italics) after emerging from a mine. These instances (which fulfill Malinowski's instruction to transform the "dust of little bits of information" into the "final ideals of knowledge") represent efforts to "whitewash" those truths about class-interaction that threaten the socialist programme of class-breaking.

In the end, then, Orwell uses the obsessions of his narrator to suggest that the ethnographer's will to "clean up" habitations and representations is a desire to sweep away "facts": facts, he believes, that must be acknowledged if the Socialist cause is to prevail. He thus takes aim at the hypocritical epistemological presumption of contemporaries and predecessors in the field of ethnography, who have replicated the colonialist error of failing to acknowledge and respect cultural differences.[101] If the practice of denying the cultural differences between middle-class ethnographer and working-class subject continues, Orwell warns, potential middle-class converts to the cause may be driven to Fascism instead.[102] Ironically, he concludes, the self-righteous hypocrisy of Socialist ethnography's "scribes and Pharisees" may be the most alienating "smell" of all—the only one *really* worth eradicating.[103]

It should now be clear why Orwell can be said to have been "the Conrad" of anthropology, in ways Malinowski was not. Where Malinowski merely replicated Marlow's editing of Kurtz, Orwell made a cautionary lesson of such censorship. Where Malinowski's final report "cleans up" the "dust" of his field-diary. Orwell's lets his be, like the illuminated "haze" haloing Marlow's moon. Indeed, it might be argued that *The Road to Wigan Pier* makes its field-diary "dirtier": critics have generally regarded the final product as less sympathetic to its subjects than the notes Orwell took in the field."[104] Noting the parallel between Marlow's editing of Kurtz and Malinowski's of his diary, Robert Thornton has described the practice as one of "extracting information from the moral community in which it was written":

> Just as Kurtz's text could only reveal the beauty of the 'exotic immensity ruled by an august Benevolence' once it had been separated from the context of Kurtz's own moral failure, ethnography becomes academic when it is transformed by the rhetoric of classifying sciences. It conceals its context of creation and the moral condition of its author.[105]

Clearly, it was Orwell's goal in *The Road to Wigan Pier* to *reinsert* the ethnographic text into the "moral community" from which it was habitually removed—to *foreground* the "moral condition" of its Kurtzian author. Whatever other shortcomings the text might have, it is far from being guilty of unselfconscious hypocrisy. Its commitment to the unexpurgated descriptions of radical empiricism makes it deserving of a special place, not just in the history of twentieth-century ethnography, but also in recent revisionary histories uncovering the progressive political potential of literary modernism.[106]

Notes

1. Frank Gloversmith, "Changing Things: Orwell and Auden," in Frank Gloversmith (ed.), *Class, Culture, and Social Change* (Sussex: Harvester; New Jersey: Humanities, 1980). 117. Victor Gollancz characterizes Orwell as both "a frightful snob" and a "genuine hater of every form of snobbery" in his Foreword to the first edition of *The Road to Wigan Pier* (London: Gollancz, 1937); rpt. in *George Orwell: The Critical Heritage*, ed. Jeffrey Meyers (London: Routledge & Kegan Paul, 1975), 91–9; at 95. Raymond Williams has called this the "paradox" theory of Orwell: see *George Orwell* (Glasgow: Collies, 1971), 89. Other adherents to the view include Ethel Mannin, "Sense and a Lot of Nonsense," *The New Leader*, 12 March 1937, 5; and Richard Hoggart, Introduction to *The Road to Wigan Pier* (Harmondsworth: Penguin, 1989), ix. Subsequent references to *The Road to Wigan Pier* are to the latter edition and will appear in parentheses in the text.

2. *The Road to Wigan Pier*, 119. For examples of such complaints, see Harry Pollitt, Review of *The Road to Wigan Pier* in *The Daily Worker*, 17 March 1937, cited by Valentine Cunningham, *British Writers of the Thirties* (Oxford: Oxford University Press, 1989), 245: Philip Toynbee, Review of *The Road to Wigan Pier* in *Encounter* (August 1959), 81–2; rpt. in Meyers (ed.), *George Orwell: The Critical Heritage*, 115–18; and Alok Rai, *Orwell and the Politics of Despair: A Critical Study of the Writings of George Orwell* (Cambridge: Cambridge University Press, 1988), 71.

3. Tom Hopkinson, *George Orwell* (London: Longman's Green, 1953), 21. Hopkinson's was the first full-length study of Orwell's work, and set the tone for many others. Raymond Williams also characterizes Orwell as failing in sympathetic understanding; see *George Orwell*, 89.

4. In Storm Jameson, "Documents," *Fact* (July 1937), 9–11; Daphne Patai, *The Orwell Mystique: A Study in Male Ideology* (Amherst: University of Massachusetts Press, 1984), see especially 71–72; and Beatrix Campbell, *Wigan Pier Revisited: Power and Politics in the 80s* (London: Virago, 1984).

5. See Marc Manganaro (ed.), *Modernist Anthropology: From Fieldwork to Text* (Princeton: Princeton University Press, 1990). For the distinctively ironic quality of modernist anthropology, see ibid., Manganaro, "Textual Play, Power, and Cultural Critique: An Orientation to Modernist Anthropology," 3–47, especially 20; and Arnold Krupat, "Irony in Anthropology: The Work of Franz Boas," 133–45, especially 136.

6. The invocation of modernist literary texts is another defining feature of modernist anthropology. See Manganaro, "Textual Play, Power, and Cultural Critique," 6; and George E. Marcus and Michael M.J. Fischer, *Anthropology as Cultural Critique: An Experimental Moment in the Human Sciences* (Chicago: University of Chicago Press, 1986), 169.

7. See James Clifford, "On Ethnographic Self-Fashioning: Conrad Laid Malinowski," in *The Predicament of Culture: Twentieth-Century Ethnography, Literature, and Art* (Cambridge: Harvard University Press, 1988), 92–113. For a discussion of the term "participant observation" see George W. Stocking, Jr., "The Ethnographer's Magic: Fieldwork in British Anthropology from Tylor to Malinowski," *History of Anthropology 1* (1983), 70–120. The term is important because it emphasizes the empirical importance newly attached by Malinowski and contemporaries like Rivers and Boas to the solitary fieldworker's act of

witnessing cultural phenomena with his own eyes. "All would be well," Malinowski stated. "once the anthropologist stepped outside the 'closed study of the theorist' and came down from 'the verandah of the missionary compound' into the open air of the anthropological field ("Myths in Primitive Psychology" (1936); cited by Stocking, 112).

8. Clifford, "Ethnographic Self-Fashioning," 93. It is widely recognized that the discourse on truth and lie in *Heart of Darkness* derives from Nietzsche's insights in "On Truth and Lie in an Extra-moral Sense," an essay Clifford observes might well have been called "On Truth and Lie in a *Cultural* Sense." For two readings crediting Malinowski with Nietzschean insight info the acculturation of the fieldworker, see Marilyn Strathern, "Out of Context: The Persuasive Fictions of Anthropology," in Manganaro (ed.), *Modernist Anthropology*. 95, and Thornton, "'Imagine yourself set down...,'" 10.

9. The "pure experience" of radical empiricism consists of "affectional facts," which are indistinguishable from material facts. The radical empiricist includes in his description no element that is not directly experienced, and aims to exclude nothing that is. See William James, *Essays in Radical Empiricism* (Cambridge, MA: Harvard University Press, 1976), 69–77 and 22. For a detailed account of the importance of James' formulation to anthropological description, see Roger D. Abrahams, "Ordinary and Extraordinary Experience," in Victor Turner and Edward Bruner (eds.), *The Anthropology of Experience* (Urbana and Chicago: University of Illinois Press, 1986), 45–72.

10. William James, *Essays in Radical Empiricism*, 81. Or as James also puts it, "To be radical, an experience must not admit into its construction any element that is not directly experienced...." (22). James' willingness to regard "experience" as "truth" is based partly on pragmatist principles—the perception that it and only it should serve as a guide to action: "immediate experience in its passing is always 'truth,' practical truth, *something to act on*, at its own movement" (13). It also reflects his rejection of transcendental points of reference: "Experience and reality come to the same thing," he says, because "we have no transphenomenal Absolute ready, to derealize the whole experienced world by, at a stroke" (30).

11. James, *Essays in Radical Empiricism*, 13, 22. My italics. "Pure experience" includes "affectional facts," which are inextricable from material facts. See the essay "The Place of Affectional Facts in a World of Pure Experience," *Essays in Radical Empiricism*, 69–77.

12. Malinowski to Mrs B.Z. Seligman, quoted by Clifford, "On Ethnographic Self-Fashioning," 96.

13. Thornton, "Imagine yourself set down ..."; Ernest Mach, "Frazer, Conrad, Malinowski and the Rule of Imagination in Ethnography," *Anthropology Today* 115 (1985): 7–14, at 9 (my italics). Thornton quotes Erwin N. Hiebert, "Introduction" to Ernst Mach, *Knowledge and Error* (Dordrecht, Holland: D. Reidel, 1976), xix.

14. See Thornton, "Imagine yourself set down ...," 9.

15. Malinowski, *Argonauts of the Western Pacific: An Account of Native Enterprise and Adventure in the Archipelagoes of Melanesian New Guinea* (London: Routledge, 1922), 518, 4.

16. Clifford, "Ethnographic Self-Fashioning," 110.

17. Bronislaw Malinowski. *A Diary in the Strict Sense of the Term* (New York: Harcourt Brace, 1967), 155, 162, 163.

18. Malinowski, *A Diary in the Strict Sense of the Term*, 69. For discussions of this and other references to *Heart of Darkness* in the diary, see Thornton, "Imagine yourself set down ..." 11–12, and Clifford, "On Ethnographic Self-Fashioning," 105.

19. For Marlow's editing of Kurtz, see Joseph Conrad, *Heart of Darkness*, ed. Robert Kimbrough, 3rd ed. (New York: Norton, 1988), 70.

20. Malinowski, *Argonauts of the Western Pacific*, 3–4, and "Method" (n.d.), Malinowski Papers, British Library of Political and Economic Science, London School of Economics; cited by Stocking, "The Ethnographer's Magic," 104–5.

21. Clifford, "On Ethnographic Self-Fashioning," 144.

22. *Heart of Darkness*, 65.

23. Orwell, "Inside the Whale," *The Collected Essays, Journalism and Letters of George Orwell*, 4 vols., ed. Sonia Orwell and Ian Angus (New York and London: Harcourt Brace Jovanovich, 1968), Vol. 1, 519. Subsequent references to this volume will use the abbreviation *CEJL*.

24. See Toynbee's comments from *Encounter* (August 1959), 81–2, rpt. in *George Orwell: the Critical Heritage* (London: Routledge & Kegan Paul, 1975), 115–18. The book has been described as a cross between "documentary" and "imaginative writing" (Williams, *George Orwell*, 41); "introspective autobiography" (Keith Alldrit, *The Making of George Orwell: An Essay in Literary History* (London: Edward Arnold, 1969) 67); and a "first-person proletarian novel" (Samuel Hynes, *The Auden Generation: Literature and Politics in England in the 1930's* (London: Bodley Head, 1976), 273. While Philip Dodd includes it in a study of texts from the 1930s concerned with what Charles Madge called "the anthropological study of our civilisation," his context is travel literature in general, not the professional discourse of ethnography. He classifies it as an "Into Unknown England" travel book. See Philip Dodd, "The Views of Travellers: Travel Writing in the 1930's," *Prose Studies* 511 (May 1982), 127–38, at 128, 131.

25. For example, James Hanley's *Grey Children* (1937), J.B. Priestley's *English Journey* (1934), Edwin Muir's *Scottish Journey* (1935), Cicely Hamilton, *Modern England: As Seen By an Englishwoman* (1935), and C.E.M. Joad, *The Horrors of the Countryside* (1931).

26. Disraeli coined the term for the subtitle of his novel *Sybil: or the Two Nations*, first published in May 1845.

27. See Judith Walkowitz, *City of Dreadful Delight: Narratives of Sexual Danger in Late-Victorian London* (Chicago: University of Chicago Press, 1992), 15–39.

28. Henry Mayhew, *London Labour and the London Poor*, 4 vols. (1861; rpt. Dover, 1968), 3:233; quoted by Walkowitz, *City of Dreadful Delight*, 19; George Sims, Selections from *How the Poor Live*, rpt. in Keating, *Into Unknown England* (1866–1913); Selections from the *Social Explorers* (Glasgow: William Collins and Sons, 1976), 16; Charles Booth, quoted it) Harold Pfautz, *Charles Booth on the City: Physical Pattern and Social Structure* (Chicago: University of Chicago Press, 1967), 85.

29. The phrasing is Marsha Bryant's. See *Auden and Documentary in the 1930s* (Charlottesville: University Press of Virginia, 1997), 169.

30. John Grierson, "The Course of Realism," in *Grierson on Documentary*, ed. Forsyth Hardy (London: Faber and Faber, 1946), 199–211 at 203.

31. Bryant, *Auden and Documentary in the 1930s*, 169.

32. For a full account of Malinowski's accomplishments and influence on social anthropology in Britain during the 1920s and 1930s, see Adam Kuper, *Anthropology and Anthropologists: The Modern British School*, 3rd ed. (London: Routledge, 1973), 17–34.

33. Charles Madge, "Anthropology at Home," *New Statesman & Nation*, 2 Jan. 1937. See also Julian Huxley's remarks in the Foreword to the main founding pamphlet of the movement, Charles Madge and Tom Harrisson's *Mass-Observation* (London: Frederick Muller, 1937), 5: "Within the social sciences, social anthropology holds an essential place. Yet, with few exceptions, it has started to choose its material from among primitive and out-of-the-way peoples. Here again the trend must be from the remote to the near at hand. Not only scientifically but practically it is urgent to obtain detailed and unbiased

information as to the mode of thinking of the larger, more powerful and economically more important groups of human beings. Most urgent of all is to obtain such knowledge about our own group, the English people." In the main body of the pamphlet, Madge and Harrisson describe their "dream" of creating an "anthropology of ourselves" (10).

34. See Orwell, Letter to Geoffrey Gorer, Sat. May ? 1936, *CEJL* 1, 221–22 at 22.

35. James Hanley, *Grey Children: A Study in Humbug and Misery* (London: Methuen, 1937), 147 (my italics). Hanley wrote to Orwell on 13 February 1937; see *CEJL* 1, 263.

36. Another writer who hollowed conventions from ethnographic studies of foreign cultures to describe the poor was Walter Greenwood, in the novel *Love on the Dole* (1933); Winifred Holtby called attention to the parallel between the exploitation of colonials and Britain's industrial works in her 1933 novel *Mandoa, Mandoa!*

37. See Kuper, *Anthropology and Anthropologists* 17–34, and Stocking, "The Ethnographer's Magic," 111.

38. See Clifford Geertz, "Distinguished Lecture: Anti-Anti-relativism," *American Anthropologist*, 36 (1984), 263–78. Geertz's concept of "anti-anti-relativism" shares with Orwell's "anti-anti-modernism" (or Jamesian radical empiricism) the view that rejecting epistemological certainty need not mean abandoning all duty to pursue accurate mimesis of the "actual world."

39. For an account of other ways in which Orwell defended literary modernism in the 1930s, only to reconsider that defense in the late 1940s, see Patricia Rae, "Mr. Charrington's Junk Shop: T.S. Eliot and Modernist Poetics in *Nineteen Eighty-Four*," *Twentieth Century Literature* 43/2 (Summer 1997), 196–220.

40. The classic statement of this criticism of modernist writer is found in Georg Lukács, "The Ideology of Modernism"; see *The Meaning of Contemporary Realism* (London: Merlin, 1963), 17–46, especially 20–26. Lukács directly shaped Soviet aesthetic policy in the 1930s.

41. Christopher Caudwell (Christopher St. John Sprigg), *Illusion and Reality* (London: Macmillan, 1937), 317; Jameson, "Documents," 9–11 at 11. Caudwell is endorsing Karl Radek's scathing remarks on Joyce at the fast All-Union Congress of Soviet Writers in 1934. See Radek, "Contemporary World Literature and the Tasks of Proletarian Art," in A. Zhdanov et al., *Problems of Soviet Literature: Reports and Speeches at the First Soviet Writers' Congress* (London: Martin Lawrence Ltd., 1970), 153. For other examples of writers on the Left objecting to Modernist "interiority," see Ralph Fox, *The Novel and the People* (New York International. 1945), 24–5, 36–7, 90–91, and Winifred Holtby, *Virginia Woolf: A Critical Memoir* (Chicago: Cassandra Editions, 1978). Holtby suggests that Woolf's retreat into the minds of her protagonists corresponds to a failure to engage adequately with "the material circumstances of life" (200–201).

42. *Grey Children*, 147.

43. Jameson. "Documents." 11. Daphne Patai offers the same complaint; see *The Orwell Mystique: A Study in Male Ideology*, 81.

44. See Theodor Adorno, "Reconciliation under Duress," in Fredric Jameson (ed.), *Aesthetics and Politics* (London: Verso, 1980), 151–76, especially 160.

45. Montague Slater, "The Fog Beneath the Skin," *Left Review* 1/10 (July 1935), 425–30 at 429.

46. See Fox, *The Novel and the People*, 43, 100–104. Fox called fiction that preserved this dialectic "new realism."

47. See Jameson, *Civil Journey* (London: Cassell, 1939), 64; note also 234. Theorists of socialist realism like Ralph Fox articulated the same view. See *The Novel and the People*, 43, 100–104.

48. See, for example, Ford Madox Ford, *The Good Soldier* (New York: Vintage, 1983), 7, and Conrad, *Heart of Darkness*, 30.

49. Hanley, *Grey Children*, 77.

50. See Buzard, "Mass-Observation, Modernism, and Auto-ethnography," *Modernism/Modernity* 4/3 (Sept. 1997), 98, 102, 111, 113–14. See also Samuel Hynes, *The Auden Generation* (Princeton: Princeton University Press, 1972), 285.

51. For examples of Mass-Observation's investigations into motives: see Charles Madge and Tom Harrisson (eds.), *Mass-Observation: First Year's Work 1937–38*, With an Essay on A Nation-wide Intelligence Service by Bronislaw Malinowski (London: Lindsay Drummond, 1938), 15–22, 37–40, 42–5, 67. As Malinowski himself summarized the quest for self-transcendence in the Observer, in his semi-sympathetic report on the movement's first year's work, the Observer was to transcend his biases in order to attain true "sympathy" with those under observation—in order better "to interpret psychologically the acts, ritual and personal, of [the] natives." See "A Nation-Wide Intelligence Service," 98. For details about the largely middle-class character of the Observers, and the working-class character of their subjects, see Penny Summerfield, "Mass Observation: Social Research or Social Movement?" *Journal of Contemporary History* 20 (July 1985), 439–52, at 442.

52. Madge and Harrisson, *Mass-Observation*, 35. Summerfield confirms this interpretation of the Observer's quest for self-transcendence. The Observers, she says, unlike the diarists, "were not supposed to involve their own reactions." See "Mass-Observation: Social Research or Social Movement?" 441.

53. Madge and Harrisson, *Mass-Observation*, 33.

54. For further evidence that the purpose of the "report on Self" was to cleanse the observer's reports of potentially distorting prejudices, see the instruction that it was to serve as a check on all further observations." Report no. FR A8: 5, in Mass-Observation Archive. University of Sussex; cited by Mercer, *Mass-Observation 1937–40: The Range of Research Methods*, 19. The final documents produced by Mass-Observation were to guarantee objectivity by distilling "facts" from hundreds of reports (32).

55. Madge and Harrisson, *Mass-Observation*, 15 (my italics).

56. Madge and Harrisson, *Mass-Observation*, 43.

57. For the "paradox" theory of Orwell, see note l.

58. Orwell, "Inside the Whale," *CEJL* 1, 495.

59. For a compendium of domestic anthropologists who used disguise in this way, see Cunningham, *British Writers of the Thirties*, 251–56.

60. Orwell, *Down and Out in Paris and London* (Harmondsworth: Penguin, 1989), 215 (first italics mine).

61. See Orwell's 1935 review of Hilton's *Caliban Shrieks*, *CEJL* 1, 149.

62. Orwell, "A Hanging," *CEJL* 1, 45 (my italics).

63. See, for example, "The Spike" and "Hop-Picking," *CEJL*, 42 and 61.

64. See Orwell, letter to Brenda Salkeld, early September 1934, *CEJL* 1, 139. The following comment by Radek illustrates the precise phenomenon in Joyce to which Radek objects—the kind of interiority I have been identifying as the target of "anti-modernism": "What is the basic feature in Joyce? His basic feature is the conviction that there is nothing big in life—no big events, no big people, no big ideas; and the writer can give a picture of life by just taking 'any given hero on any given day,' and reproducing [his consciousness] with exactitude. A heap of dung, crawling with worms, photographed by a cinema apparatus *through* a microscope—such is Joyce's work." See Karl Radek, "Contemporary World Literature and the Tasks of Proletarian Art," in A. Zhdanov *et al.*, *Problems of*

Soviet Literature: Reports and Speeches at the First Soviet Writers' Congress (London: Martin Lawrence Ltd., 1970), 153.

65. *CEJL* 1, 155, and August 1936 letter to Miller: *CEJL* 1, 228.

66. *CEJL* 1, 495.

67. Orwell, "Inside the Whale," *CEJL* 1. 523.

68. Patrick Reilly is the only other critic, to my knowledge, who has perceived a parallel between the journey to Wigan and Marlow's journey down the Congo: "Orwell enters the filthy lodging house" in Wigan, he writes, "as Marlow approaches Kurtz: here, at least, is reality." See *George Orwell: The Age's Adversary* (London: Macmillan, 1986), 150.

69. In a 23 July 1936 review of *Almayer's Folly*, he derides those members of the "modern intelligentsia" to whom Conrad was suspect because he was a "gentleman" (*CEJL* 1, 227). In a 17 October review of Johann Wöller's *Zest for Life*, he says Wöller is "not in the same class as Conrad," who is the master of portraying "the peculiar double homesickness which is the punishment for deserting your native land" (*CEJL* 1, 234). For an example of a complaint about Conrad from the left, see Christopher Caudwell, *Romance and Realism: A Study in English Bourgeois Literature*, ed. Samuel Hynes (Princeton: Princeton University Press, 1970), 102–3. Conrad, says Caudwell, "de-materializes" the world by using it primarily as a "spectacle" for the responses of his narrators.

70. Many of his readers in 1937, he says, were likely "as a matter of course, to be anti-imperialist" (147); for them, he says, "Foreign oppression is a much more obvious, understandable evil than economic oppression" (135).

71. See his comment "Class stigmata are comparable to a race-difference" (213). He makes a comparable effort to dramatize ignominious imperialist attitudes in "Shooting an Elephant": see *CEJL* 1: 236.

72. Gorer wrote to Orwell in 1935 praising *Burmese Days* and wondering whether he noted a parallel between "the Burmese sahib-log" who are "living a lie the whole time" and the upper-middle class in Britain. See letter to Orwell, 16 July 1935, cited by Bernard Crick, *George Orwell: A Life* (Harmondsworth: Penguin, 1982), 265. For Orwell's version of the point, see *The Road to Wigan Pier*, 139.

73. See Williams, *George Orwell*, 50. Lynette Hunter gives an admirably detailed analysis of the rhetorical strategies of this dramatic speaker in *George Orwell: The Search for a Voice* (Milton Keynes: Open University Press, 1984), 50–68. For a statement of the more common view that the narrative voice in *The Road to Wigan Pier* is non-dramatic, see Peter Stansky and William Abrahams, *Orwell: The Transformation*, in *The Unknown Orwell & Orwell: The Transformation* (Stanford: Stanford University Press, 1994), 221–2.

74. Among members of the Left Book Club. It has generally been assumed that Orwell pursued the project after it was commissioned by Victor Gollancz for the Club. In fact, as Peter Davison has recently pointed out, the Left Book Club could not have commissioned the book because it had not been formed when Orwell left for Wigan on 31 January 1936. Nonetheless, Orwell was aware of the club's existence while writing up the book (the first advertisement for the organization appeared in *The New Statesman and Nation* for 29 February 1936) and had some hope that it would become a club selection when he submitted it to his agent, Leonard Moore, on 15 December 1936. See Peter Davison, *George Orwell: A Literary Life* (London: Macmillan, 1996), 67–68. For the point that many Mass-Observers became Left Book Club members, see Summerfield, "Mass-Observation: Social Research or Social Movement?" 442.

75. Conrad's characterization of Marlow in *Heart of Darkness*, 15.

76. *Heart of Darkness*, 17 (my italics).

77. *Heart of Darkness*, 11 (my italics).

78. *Heart of Darkness*, 37, also 41 and 44.

79. See also *The Road to Wigan Pier*, 16.

80. Douglas. *Purity and Danger: An Analysis of Concepts of Pollution and Taboo* (Harmondsworth: Penguin 1966), 48, 53.

81. *Perils and Danger*, 146.

82. Orwell, *Burmese Days* (Harmondsworth: Penguin, 1989), 20. Cf. Orwell's own fear of pollution from colonial bodies, expressed in a letter to Gorer, 20 Jan. 1939, *CEJL* 1, 382.

83. See *The Road to Wigan Pier*, 149.

84. Also as the "sickly, ageing people" they grow into, "creeping round and round" labyrinthine slums and dark kitchens (14). Compare Marlow's observation that the Congolese look "like ants" (*Heart of Darkness*, 18).

85. See Orwell's description of the mine on a workday (18) and compare Marlow's visions, *Heart of Darkness*, 20, 66.

86. *Heart of Darkness*, 96.

87. Compare Marlow's comments on an ailing Congolese worker, *Heart of Darkness*, 20.

88. Arnold Krupat identifies catachresis as one of the four main categories of modernist irony in modernist anthropology. See "Irony in Anthropology: The Work of Franz Boas," *Modernist Anthropology*, 136–7.

89. *Heart of Darkness*, 31.

90. Gollancz's decision to republish Part One of the book alone reflected a sense that the two parts were not importantly interrelated. For a similar views, see David L. Kubal, *Outside the Whale: George Orwell's Art and Politics* (Notre Dame, IN: University of Notre Dame Press, 1972), 104, and Robert Pearce, "Revisiting Orwell's *Wigan Pier*," *History* 82 (1997), 410–28.

91. I propose the parodic nature of Orwell's autobiographical section despite the fact that the point cannot be definitively be proven. In doing so, I defer to Mark Jones' contention that parody is always, by nature, something about which we are unsure it is parodic. See "Parody and Its Containments: The Case of Wordsworth." *Representations* 54 (Spring 1996), 57–79.

92. Orwell also discusses the "I'm-not-a-snob" syndrome in "Charles Dickens," *CEJL* 1, 437.

93. *Heart of Darkness*, 9 (my italics).

94. See the 1939 essay "Marrakech," *CEJL* 1, 390, 392.

95. See Georg Lukács, "The Ideology of Modernism," *The Meaning of Contemporary Realism* (London: Merlin, 1963), 27.

96. See the Eliotic description of "a frightful patch of waste ground" in Sheffield, "trampled bare of grass and littered with newspapers and old saucepans" (98).

97. It is the "snobbishness" that will "stick" to him until his grave (128). Note also the reference to the dirt to be cleaned from "Orwell"'s eyelids (33). For a comparable inversion of the location of the "darkness" in Conrad, see *Heart of Darkness*, 9.

98. Note Marlow's comments about the epistemological effect of the rising sun ("A blinding sunlight drowned all this at times in a sudden recrudescence of glare" (19); "When the sun rose there was a white fog, very warm and clammy and more blinding than the night" (41)) and also his description of meeting Kurtz's "Intended," back in Brussels: "*I know that sunlight can be made to lie too*, yet one felt that no manipulation of light and

pose could have conveyed the delicate shade of truthfulness upon those features" (71, my italics).

99. *Purity and Danger*, 48, 53, and 15.

100. James, *Essays in Radical Empiricism*, 76.

101. Orwell appears to have had an ally for his project of foregrounding the ethnographic observer in Auden. Bryant discusses in detail how Auden's 1937 documentary project *Letters from Iceland* departs from other 1930s documentaries in "allowing us a look at the observers" (78), and points out how Auden's and Isherwood's 1939 *Journey to a War* foregrounds the unequal degrees of power held by the observer and the Chinese war victims under observation (164).

102. For a full discussion of Orwell's argument about the importance of appreciating the problems posed by cultural difference between classes, see Gerald Graff, "George Orwell and the Class Racket," *Salmagundi*, 70–71 (Spring–Summer 1986), 108–20.

103. See *The Road to Wigan Pier*, 201.

104. Note, for example, Gloversmith's criticism of Orwell for the fact that the final text leaves out references to working-class activists ("Changing Things," 117); Averil Gardner's observation that "where in the 'Diary' Orwell speaks of having gone down the Wigan coal mine with seven particular people, in *The Road to Wigan Pier* he mentions only one," the effect of which is to "appropriate experience for Orwell" (*George Orwell* [Boston: Twayne, 1987], 66); and Rai's observation that the book, unlike the diary, suggests that "no genuine working man grasps the deeper implications of Socialism" (*Orwell and the Politics of Despair*, 76). Peter Davison and Philip Dodd both note that Orwell revises his description of the woman kneeling in the mud by putting a train window—hence further distance—between them. See Davison, *George Orwell: A Literary Life*, 74, and Dodd, "The Views of Travellers," 133–5.

105. Robert Thornton. "Narrative Ethnography in Africa, 1840–1929: The Creation and Capture of an Appropriate Domain for Anthropology," *Man* 18 (1983), 502–20, at 517.

106. For admirable investigations into this strain of left-wing aesthetics in the 1930s, see Harvey Teres, *Renewing the Left: Politics, Imagination, and the New York Intellectuals* (Oxford: Oxford University Press, 1996), and Alan Filreis, *Modernism from Right to Left: Wallace Stevens, The Thirties, & Literary Radicalism* (Cambridge: Cambridge University Press, 1994). Orwell's argument for the compatibility of Modernist aesthetics and Socialist politics explains why he was willing to sign Trotsky's *Manifesto: Towards a Free Revolutionary Art* in 1938. As Teres explains, Trotsky defended the Socialist writer's freedom to choose his form, and especially to focus on "individual experience" (85). A defense of the role of "experience" in socially progressive art was also developed by William Phillips and Philip Rahv and other contributors to *Partisan Review*, the journal to which Orwell contributed "Inside the Whale," among many other essays. See especially Rahv's discussion in "The Cult of Experience in American Writing," *Partisan Review* 7/6 (1940). 412–24.

ANTONY SHUTTLEWORTH

The Real George Orwell:
Dis-simulation in Homage to Catalonia
and Coming Up for Air

If one could choose only one figure from the thirties to show what there is to be gained from critical reevaluation of the decade, one could do much worse than George Orwell. A controversial figure, not to say a controversialist, during the period itself, Orwell became in the postwar period perhaps the most problematic writer for those seeking to make sense of the possibilities, dangers and achievements of the period. In a series of uncommonly insightful texts Orwell brought a substantial literary intelligence to bear on the obsessions of the decade—poverty, social injustice, imperialism, fascism—while at the same time seeking to develop an inclusive attention to the details which characterized his era: "So long as I remain alive and well I shall continue to ... love the surface of the earth, and to take a pleasure in solid objects and scraps of useless information" (quoted in Cunningham 1988, 228). With the close of the thirties, however, Orwell became best known as commentator on the dangers of radical social movements. In articulating these dangers he seemed to provide an authoritative mythology for those seeking to argue that the remediation of social ills begins, and ends, in assumptions and practices more destructive than the privations and corruption it may ameliorate. Paradoxically, the political mythology that saw totalitarianism, doublethink and newspeak as the inevitable destiny of all mass politics became more powerful the more its conservative adherents were challenged by the remarkable achievements of

From *And in Our Time: Vision, Revision, and British Writing of the 1930s*: pp. 204–220. © 2003 by Rosemont Publishing and Printing Corp.

postwar social democratic government. Perhaps more problematic than this bromide for the "naivete" of the left were the ideological assumptions that appeared to underpin it, for which Orwell became, on the right as on the left, the cultural icon. This is the plain-speaking "honest George" who espoused a straightforward political and cultural empiricism, mediated through a "window pane" prose, and whose assumptions about "language, politics and ideology" became representative of a cultural order which, for many, stood in the way of any reasoned and progressive theoretical examination of social and political orders.[1] This is the Orwell who annoys several critics in *Inside the Myth, Orwell: Views from the Left* (Norris, 1984), whose own accomplishments in the exposure of the failures and oversights of classic liberal humanism have perhaps been tempered by the difficulties faced in attempts to offer comprehensive and workable alternatives to this liberal orthodoxy. It is the Orwell whom Raymond Williams declared "unreadable" as a result of his "successful impersonation of the plain man who bumps into experience in an unmediated way and is simply telling the truth about it," despite the careful and thought-provoking attention Williams gives to the causes, conditions, and effects of the figure of "Orwell" in his seminal study of the writer (quoted in Norris 1984, 242; Williams 1971). More recent accounts suggest that, if some of the innovative power of ideology-critique represented by the *Inside the Myth* critics has waned, the icon of the simpleminded "Orwell," if not the frustration surrounding him, has considerable staying power. Examining Orwell's essay "Inside the Whale," Janet Montefiore, for instance, finds it "a pleasure to read: clear, vigorous and well written" yet implies strongly that a corollary of these classically Orwellian virtues is that the text is "aggressive, misleading and full of holes" (1996, 14).

Despite the prevalence of the Orwell myth, however, there has emerged an extraordinarily suggestive reading of the post-1945 Orwell which ascribes an intelligence and circumspection to his work that his detractors and supporters barely hint at. In an essay exploring Orwell's obsession with cruelty in *Nineteen Eighty-Four* Richard Rorty has argued that, far from remaining settled in the humanist truisms usually associated with his work, Orwell offers in this novel a compelling reflection on the historical and political contingency of grounding myths such as "the human spirit" or "human nature," together with the potential dangers that proceed from this contingency (1989, 169–88). On Rorty's view, the novel presents in the figure of the Inner Party member O'Brien the terrifying prospect of an intellectual who has come to know, in an unselfconscious way, the mental enjoyment that can be had with the abandonment of moral scruple, for whom the making and unmaking of selves through the infliction of pain is the chief, the supreme, intellectual pleasure. Clearly this reading presents a radically different view of Orwell, the dangers he is seeking to describe, the assumptions his work entertains. Rorty's view that the postwar Orwell was "neither transparent nor simple" should prompt us to reexamine not only the Orwell myth but also crucial features of Orwell's prewar writing that this myth has obscured. Instead of a writer with uninspected ideas on the relation between truth, language and reality, what one discovers in the texts of the thirties is a writer unusually aware both of new ways in which social and political realities were being constructed within the interwar period, and the consequences that these new forms of construction held for the very views on "transparent" texts and "authentic" experience Orwell is commonly assumed to have held. This early attention is significant not only because of the insights it can generate into the new roles of artifice in the thirties, but also because it allows us to reconsider ideas about the "empiricist" strain in Orwell's work. And this is a strain that Rorty's discussion lets stand when, for instance, he argues that Orwell's best work challenges ideas, rooted in earlier work, such as the following:

> The crucial opposition in Orwell's thought is the standard metaphysical one between contrived appearance and naked reality. The latter is obscured by bad, unnecessarily sophisticated theory. Once the dirt is rubbed off the windowpane, the truth about any moral or political situation will be clear. Only those who have allowed their own personality ... to cloud their vision will fail to grasp the plain moral facts. (173)

In what follows I shall argue that, by contrast, these texts of the thirties suggest that Orwell values the "window pane" text not because he is a prisoner of an uninspected empiricism, much less because he believes that some unmediated idea of truth is "out there" to be bumped into, but rather because of the *absence* of any such unmediated truth. Equally, inspection of these texts reveals crucial alternatives to the sense of political impotence that haunts *Nineteen Eighty-Four*, alternatives which can be understood as one of the most valuable of the legacies of Orwell's work in the period, and indeed of the period itself.

Unreading Orwell: Artifice and Truth in HOMAGE TO CATALONIA

Orwell's reflective account of his experience during the Spanish Civil War, *Homage to Catalonia* (1938), is a key text for those seeking to understand how the representation of events had, in the thirties, become intensely problematic for even the most careful of observers. In this text the shifting barrier between mythic and reliable representations of conflict is a casualty of war which Orwell hopes to diagnose and to heal. The narrator offers himself as a lonely truth-teller, dispelling myths about the conflict wherever possible, arguing for a proper understanding of the nature of "real" war, with its countless privations, its brutality and its carnage. Orwell's task is all the more urgent because of his awareness that the Spanish war is an ideological battle, subject to the obfuscations and interpretations, not to say the deception, of ideological positions, which he hopes to untangle and question.

Yet as numerous critics have pointed out (Norris 1984, 243), a conscious effort to "speak the truth" is not, in itself, a guarantee that the truth can be told.[2] Indeed, this very effort at honesty may unwittingly disguise the fact that there is more to telling the truth than the conscious wish to avoid deceit. A notorious example concerns Orwell's role as participant, rather than spectator, in violent exchanges, where, as Valentine Cunningham has noted, he "carefully minimizes the killing he is himself actually engaged in by playing up the farcicality of his ... unit. He presents himself and his comrades as badly armed, mere children, people who can't shoot straight ... They're a harmless joke," where the war becomes a "comic opera with an occasional death," a "bloody pantomime" (1988, 424). In this description Orwell finds his ethical status as truth-telling observer in conflict with that of combatant, and plainly it is the observer whose neutrality is compromised in the narrator's attempt to limit the ethical consequences of his potentially lethal actions. Although one might reasonably claim that Orwell is fulfilling an ethical obligation in writing against myths of revolutionary heroism, it is also true that in viewing the Spanish war as a "comedy," and as a "false" war, Orwell further undermines his neutral stance by invoking uninspected assumptions about what a "real" war might be like. Furthermore, his sense of the war as comic, rather than heroic, implies an opposition that is deeply mediated by Orwell's own cultural background. Certainly this may not be a war of heroes, if any war is; it does not follow, though, that the war must be a comedy continually teetering on the brink of farce, or of meaninglessness.

It is plain, therefore, that Orwell does not meet his own standards of neutrality in his description of the Spanish conflict. What is interesting about his narrative, however, is how Orwell himself begins to recognize this failure, and briefly entertains the possibility that the criterion of neutrality is not simply a difficult one to live up to for even as strenuously an objective reporter as himself, but is in fact from the beginning an impossible goal. Urging his readers to distrust even his own account Orwell notes that: "I believe that on such an issue as this no one is or can be completely truthful. It is difficult to be certain about anything except what you have seen with your own eyes, and consciously or unconsciously everyone writes as a partisan" (230–31).

The expressed caution in these lines can be read as a kind of ideological ruse, where the narrator's disquiet about the possibilities of untruthfulness actually serve to increase the reader's confidence in his narration. Here, one might think, is an observer so scrupulous about the need for honesty that he urges caution even about his own story; here is an observer who can, therefore, be trusted. More interesting about this declaration, though, is what Orwell is prepared, and unprepared, to recognize about the conditions of truth that obtain in his narrative. He allows that everyone can be "unconsciously" influenced by one's partisanship in describing a particular state of affairs, yet also insists that one can be certain that some things are beyond distortion by this partisanship. One can be certain about "what you have seen with your own eyes." Obviously this statement is in a certain sense deceptive. It implies that one can witness events without selection or interpretation, and indeed that the very act of witnessing is not an act of selection to begin with, and that the act of selection is not itself an act of interpretation. Statements such as this underpin the icon of Orwell as simpleminded empiricist. Yet it is this kind of certainty, I would argue, that Orwell came to doubt, and that he sought to question in his writing that followed *Homage to Catalonia*. This doubt led not to a repudiation of any notion of certainty, but rather to an account of the ways in which one may and may not be certain of what one sees. This is not an account of how there can be no certainty, but rather an account of how by understanding the ways in which the kind of certainty expressed in the above statement is mistaken, and is actually linked to numerous other false certainties that characterize modernity, a more properly reasoned notion of certainty can be attained. Orwell's project becomes, then, not that of considering what one can be certain of, but of exploring what it is to be certain.

The Incomplete Angler: Ersatz and Artifice in COMING UP FOR AIR

As Valentine Cunningham has noted (1988, 256), the world George Bowling inhabits in *Coming Up for Air* (1939), from "new false teeth" that open the novel to the pseudo-natural suburb of Pixie Glen that closes it, is dominated by the ersatz. This falseness seemingly militates against the possibility of adequate judgment that might form grounds for certainty. Like Conrad's Marlow, Bowling distinguishes himself from his fellows by his ability to discern and despise the fake, although his insights do not initially extend to ways of effectively resisting or of escaping from a modernity dominated by the counterfeit. His work in insurance, he states quite baldly, is an "open swindle," the suburban environment consists, despite appearances, of "a prison with the cells all in a row" (13), with a "line of semi-detached torture-chambers where the poor little five-to-ten-pound-a-weekers quake and shiver, every one of them with the boss twisting his tail and the wife riding him like the nightmare and the kids sucking his blood like leeches" (12). As "the cleverest racket of modern times" building societies extort money but also, more importantly, loyalty from their patrons:

> The really subtle swindle, the one that makes me feel old Crum deserved his baronetcy, is the mental one. Merely because of the illusion that we own our houses and have what's called "a stake in the country," we poor saps in the Hesperides, and in all such places, are turned into Crum's devoted slaves for ever. We're all respectable householders—that's to say Tories, yes-men and bumsuckers ... And the fact that actually we aren't house-holders, that we're all in the middle of paying for our houses and eaten up with the ghastly fear that something might happen before we've made the last payment, merely increases the effect. (15)

Although one may be tempted to see Bowling's modernity as an undifferentiated mass of falsehood, his environment in fact contains different kinds of artifice, different forms of deceit. Bowling's comments above, for instance, suggest fabrication of the old within the new. His householders are not modernist-rationalist dwellers of a radiant city, but rather stout yeomen, householders whose homes are castles, where the appearance of privileges and power that have long been obsolete conceal new forms of subordination and servitude.

By contrast, an explicitly "modern" environment is characterized by a different kind of artifice, a new kind of deception, where the suggestion of opportunity and futurity is constantly emphasized in design, only to be mocked in practice. Perhaps the most telling example of this false modernity is Bowling's "fish dog" meal at a newly opened milk-bar:

> There's a kind of atmosphere about these places that gets me down. Everything slick and shiny and streamlined; mirrors; enamel and chromium plate whichever direction you look in. Everything spent on the decorations and nothing on the food ...
>
> The frankfurter had a rubber skin, of course, and my temporary teeth weren't much of a fit ... But the taste! For a moment I just couldn't believe it. Then I rolled my tongue around it again and had another try. It was *fish!* A sausage, a thing calling itself a frankfurter, filled with fish. I got up and walked straight out

without touching my coffee. God knows what that might have tasted of. (25, 27)

Bowling's encounter indicates that food has become a kind of "propaganda" for a specific interpretation of modernity, where "nothing matters except slickness and shininess and streamlining":

> I read in the paper somewhere about these food-factories in Germany where everything's made out of something else. Ersatz, they call it. I remembered reading that *they* were making sausages out of fish, and fish, no doubt, out of something different. It gave me a feeling that I'd bitten into the modern world and discovered what it was really made of. That's the way we're going nowadays. Everything slick and streamlined, everything made out of something else. Celluloid, rubber, chromium-steel everywhere, arc-lamps blazing all night, glass roofs over your head, radios all playing the same tune, no vegetation left, everything cemented over, mock-turtles grazing under the neutral fruit-trees. But when you get down to brass tacks and get your teeth into something solid, a sausage for instance, that's what you get. Rotten fish in a rubber skin. Bombs of filth bursting in your mouth. (27–28)

Accompanying a false "old," then, is a new environment in which objects are false: imitations, saturated with the suggestion of qualities that they actually lack. Yet despite the functional redundance of streamlining in buildings, there is nothing obviously false about objects that are "slick and streamlined." These are not copies of something that is genuinely slick and streamlined. They are deceptive, however, in the way they falsely suggest that the new is in reality accompanied by development, by productive energy. This is not merely a new world that is dominated by the primacy of replication and signification, then, where a specious old sits alongside the specious objects that make up the new. Just as importantly, this is a false "new" because its suggestion of rapid and astonishing change, exhilaration, liberty from the constraints of the old, is only a parody of what such circumstances might actually be like. Bowling rails against the reign of a newness that replaces authenticity with counterfeits, but at the same time he points to the absence of a genuine modernity, a state of affairs that is genuinely new, genuinely progressive. When Bowling rails against the present he is lamenting the loss of the past, then, but also making it possible to long for a new and different future.

It is this new future that can inform our reading of the state of the new in Bowling's world, as can his desire to revisit the past, to "come up for air" in an alternative world that stands outside the reign of the fake. Concomitant with the desire to reexperience a lost authenticity, Bowling seeks to free himself from the anxiety that is caused and supposedly ameliorated by the present: "Fear! We swim in it. It's our element. Everyone that isn't scared stiff of losing his job is scared stiff of war, or Fascism, or Communism, or something. Jews sweating when they think of Hitler" (18). By contrast, the rural Binfield of Bowling's youth, though marked by physical hardship and poverty—"It isn't that life was softer then than now. Actually it was harsher" (124)—was also marked by a stolid sense of the reality of things, the undeceptiveness of observation: "What was it that people had in those days? ... It was a feeling of security, even when they weren't secure. More exactly it was a feeling of continuity ... All of them knew they'd got to die ... but what they didn't know was that the order of things could change" (125). In certain ways, as I shall show, this sense of continuity is itself deceptive, yet for Bowling it is this notion of continuing values, where history has long established what will remain and what will pass away, what is genuine and can be trusted, that most distinguishes the society of the past from that of the present:

> It's easy enough to die if the things you care about are going to survive ... Individually they were finished, but their way of life would continue. Their good and evil would remain good and evil. They didn't feel the ground they stood on shifting under their feet ...
>
> They were a bit shaken, and sometimes a little dispirited. But at least they never lived to know that everything they'd believed in was just so much junk. They lived at the end of an epoch, when everything was dissolving into a sort of ghastly flux, and they didn't know it. They thought it was eternity. You couldn't blame them. That was what it felt like. (126–7)

What is interesting here is the concern with how the inhabitants of the past "know" what is permanent, and the extent to which, in "knowing" a permanence that is shortly to be disrupted, they may be subject to an illusion. One must consider the degree to which the society that Orwell describes is not a permanent one so much as it is a stagnating one, unable to create opportunities for the young to fully develop within it, and unable to adapt to a changing world in a way that can preserve what is important to it, to ensure that its own values and practices will endure. These doubts about the self-representation of the Binfield of the past complicate the sense of a society in contact with the real. They are, however, subordinated in Bowling's description to the sense that the world of the past offers important insights into how the present fails to offer this sense of solidity. Moreover, they are subordinated within a questioning of the "reality" of Binfield that is, in the course of the novel, more thoroughgoing than the suggestion that traditional Binfielders are failing to keep up with the times. Paradoxically, it is only when the full insubstantiality of the new is established in the novel, how much the "ground shifts under one's feet," that the illusions of the old world, and of Bowling's description of it, are revealed.

Central to this examination is the image, and practice, that for Bowling typifies life in old Binfield: that of fishing. Fishing for Bowling is "the opposite of war" (97), and it is war that is said to bring about the insubstantiality of the modern. In phrases that prefigure *Nineteen Eighty-Four* ("War Is Peace") war is not simply something that changes the existing order, but is itself a metaphor for the conditions that obtain during the modern: "It was like an enormous machine that had got hold of you. You'd no sense of acting of your own free will, and at the same time no notion of trying to resist" (131). Fishing can stand as the opposite of war not only because it is a time-honored tradition through which a sense of continuity is felt, but because it marks time between youth and age, and because it allows a sense of the substance of things, the qualities that the artificialities of modernity destroys: "I knew that I wasn't a kid any longer, I was a boy at last. And it's a wonderful thing to be a boy, to go roaming where grown-ups can't catch you, and to chase rats and kill birds and shy stones and cheek carters and shout dirty words. It's a kind of strong, rank feeling, a feeling of knowing everything and fearing nothing, and it's all bound up with breaking rules and killing things" (75). What fishing does is concentrate the sense of power that comes through "killing things" and locates it within a mental state that is all but absent from modernity:

> As soon as you think of fishing you think of things that don't belong to the modern world. The very idea of sitting all day under a willow tree beside a quiet pool—and being able to find a quiet pool to sit beside—belongs to the time before the war, before the radio, before aeroplanes, before Hitler. There's a kind of peacefulness even in the names of English coarse fish. Roach, rudd, dace, bleak, barbel, bream, gudgeon, pike, chub, carp, tench. They're solid kind of names. The people who made them up hadn't heard of machine-guns, and they didn't live in terror of the sack or spend their time eating aspirins, going to the pictures and wondering how to keep out of concentration camps. (87)

If fishing gives a sense of continuity within the external world, it also allows this external world to grant a solidity to the self. On discovering a secret pond, unfished for years, Orwell offers an image of how this solidity is experienced, as well as what it means:

> It was several hundred yards behind the house and completely hidden in the beach woods, but it was a good-sized pool ... It was astonishing, and even at that age it astonished me, that there, a hundred miles from Reading and not fifty from London, you could have so much solitude. You felt as much alone as if you'd been on the banks of the Amazon. The pool was ringed completely round by the enormous beach trees, which in one place came down to the edge and were reflected in the water. On the other side there was a patch of grass where there was a hollow with beds of wild peppermint, and up at one end of the pool an old wooden boathouse was rotting among the bulrushes. (89)

Set next to this rich landscape is a pool that, supposedly, only the young Bowling knows about; it is ignored and teeming with life:

> It was a small pool not more than twenty yards wide, and rather dark because of the boughs that overhung it. But it was very clear water and immensely deep. I could see ten or fifteen feet down into it. I hung about for a bit, enjoying the dampness and the rotten boggy smell, the way a boy does. (91)

The pool is an image of rich solitude, depth, interiority, the very things that modernity, and by extension fascism, seeks to occupy, exploit, or prohibit. Fascism's prohibition of these interior spaces is concomitant with the exclusion of their private meanings, as Orwell indicates in his description of the politics of self-righteous hatred that seems to preclude any form of genuine politics:

> Just like a gramophone. Turn the handle, press the button and it starts. Democracy, Fascism, Fascism, Democracy ... Every slogan's gospel truth to him. If you cut him open all you'd find inside would be Democracy-Fascism-Democracy. Interesting to know a chap like that in private life. But does he have a private life? Or does he only go round from platform to platform, working up hatred? Perhaps even his dreams are slogans. (172)

Alongside this "automatic" consciousness which cannot accommodate a sense of the private, reflective self, is the whipped-up fantasy of violence, the identity-breaking image of "face-smashing" into which politics degenerates. At a political meeting Bowling observes:

> What he's saying is merely that Hitler's after us and we must all get together and have a good hate ... But what he's *seeing* is something quite different. It's a picture of himself smashing people's faces in with a spanner. Fascist faces, of course. I *know* that's what he was seeing. It was what I saw myself for the second or two that I was inside him. (175)

This sense of contemporary politics gaining power by the occupation of private, internal space was not Orwell's alone.[3] Yet Orwell is perhaps more explicit than other writers in the nature of this occupation, the images it works with, and indeed with the way in which these images, by their very nature, prohibit other forms of interiority, while erecting a spurious subjectivity that emerges out of fear—"Every thinking person nowadays is stiff with fright" (175)—and exists merely through the imaginary destruction of others. Politics devolves into the destruction of enemies. The self is what emerges through this destruction. And this kind of false subjectivity is, for Bowling, characteristic of the form of the future that will come as the intensification of modernity, rather than its disruption:

> The world we're going into, the kind of hate-world, the slogan world. The coloured shirts, the barbed wire ... the crowds of a million people all cheering for the Leader till they deafen themselves into thinking that they really worship him, and all the time, underneath, they hate him so that they want to puke. It's all going to happen. Or isn't it? Some days I know it's impossible, other days I know it's inevitable. (176)

Bowling's uncertainty captures nicely a sense that the world he inhabits is both bizarrely unpredictable and brutally straightforward. The world has only power, and the exercising of power, at its roots. At the same time, the coming of this world seems one minute absurdly far-fetched, the next only too chillingly plausible, not least because only the few seem to understand what fate lies in wait for the many.

Modernity, however, does not merely prohibit, but also replicates previous forms of subjectivity. Revisiting the earthy, reliable town of his youth Bowling confronts its supplanting by a new town of concrete and light industry, and, perhaps most troublingly, with its replication in the kitsch pseudo-world of "Upper Binfield Estate." The deep, clear, swarming pool of his youth has been turned into a rubbish dump, a copse renamed for its pretentious newcomers:

> "Ah, that! That is sacrosanct. We have decided never to build in it. It is sacred to the young people. Nature, you know ... we call it the Pixy Glen."
>   The Pixy Glen. I got rid of him, went back to the car and drove to Lower Binfield. The Pixy Glen.... doesn't it make you puke sometimes to see what they're doing to England, with their bird-baths and their plaster gnomes, and their pixies and tin cans, where the beechwoods used to be? (257)

Bowling's specific reference to "beechwoods" bespeaks the discerning, solid eye of a man of the country, schooled in particular knowledge of solid words and robust worlds, that indicates the absurdity of the simulated environment together with its attractions for the unwary, who can pleasure their desire for "nature" by indulging in its pastiche, replicate the experiences of "natural" awareness through their synthetic and kitschy substitutes.

If fishing is the opposite of war, then it is so because it is the opposite of fraud, self-deception, ersatz and kitsch. The uncertainty of the conditions of reality generated by the regime of the false add urgency and moral seriousness to Bowling's "sentimental" reminiscences of the experience of his youth. If the loss of this experience, that is to say, is to be regretted, its exploitation by the "word of hate" is terrifying and atrocious. The loss of authenticity is concomitant with its exploitation and replication. Bowling's unlikely role is to distinguish between the real and the fake versions of the authentic. Clearly this role is not an unusual one in Orwell's canon. Indeed, the single figure in possession of the truth is the very image of "honest George" that so many of his later twentieth-century readers found hard to countenance. One thing that *Coming Up for Air* might teach, though, is that the implied ontological heroism of this position is thoroughly mitigated by a sense of impotency that is close to despair, and that the novel is careful in indicating how this despair can be plausibly felt: tools of resistance, slight at best, can be replicated and co-opted so that they become tools for the consolidation of emerging totalitarian power. Powerlessness intensifies in direct proportion to one's "authenticity" as one's authentic experience is duplicated by the mass media; the false is the real, the real the false; the living are the dead, the dead the living:

Here was all this new life swarming to and from, and here was I, a poor old fatty with false teeth, watching them from a window and mumbling stuff that nobody wanted to listen to about things that happened thirty and forty years ago. Christ! I thought, I was wrong to think that I was seeing ghosts. I'm the ghost myself. I'm dead and they're alive. (233)

Critics who attack Orwell with an uninspected faith in his own certitude and truth have failed to allow for the insight he shows into how these virtual environments are created, what purposes they serve, and how they are attractive. But more importantly, one can underestimate the emphasis Orwell grants to the failure of authenticity in his work, to the sense that, whatever claims to certitude he might have, these claims are indicative of impotence rather than authority, an impotence that militates against the received image of Orwell as "furious papa," descending upon his aberrant charges with bracing doses of truth. Still, what does seem to remain here is the figure of Bowling as a "last man" doomed by his integrity to wander a universe where truth has become meaningless. Bowling may be "dead," but he still knows the truth.

In the novel as a whole, however, Orwell challenges this sense of impotence, and does so by suggesting that the kind of certitude Bowling relies on, along with the experience of depth and unmediated interiority that grounds his certitude, is in a particular sense illusory. For the end result of this novel is not to demarcate a sense of truth that modernity defiles, but to indicate how any such sense of unmediated truth can be seen as illusory, yet also, and crucially, that a sense of truth can have value *because* there is no absolute truth "out there," as Rorty might put it, against which one might measure its claims. The novel dramatizes an awareness of truth that is thought to be imperiled, but which is then shown to be vertiginously illusory, yet which is validated not because truth is independently available to those who would seek it, but because of the consequences of its unavailability, and because a real purchase on the gears of resistance can be gained only by the recognition that it is not available.

How can an illusion have value? How can the recognition of the illusoriness of independent truth countermand the sense of impotence from which Bowling suffers? Orwell's clue as to how these questions might be resolved occurs in his use of the figure of the fish in water as metaphor for what is most fake, but also most real, in Bowling's world. Bowling is drowning in fear, and in the irreality which both causes and seeks to ameliorate this fear. Against this is the image of the Binfield fish, swimming in the clear, deep waters of a solid, authentic rural environment. However, in just the same way that the falseness of a simulation does not necessarily make an original "authentic" (it too may be a simulation), the fakery and paucity of urban experience does not make the rural experience it replaces "pure." In other words, Bowling's experience of a pure interiority, unmediated by language, culture, history, a solitary space in which the solid reality of things is brought about by the pure action of consciousness, and of a "solid" language that accompanies this consciousness, is an empiricist's fantasy, just as the "solid" sounding names of fish are a false guide to the "reality" supposed to exist within past societies. Names are no more valid than one another as designators because some of them might sound more "solid" than others. No words get "closer" than others to reality, if by "closer" one means that they escape the condition of designating or of describing the world, and that they can be identical with that world. The reader might seem, then, to be in the position of having to choose only between different kinds of deception and mystification, between the simulated universe of the world that has replaced Binfield, and equally mystified awareness of "pure" depth and interiority, supposed to be outside the language and culture that preceded this universe. This concern leaves aside questions of whether Binfield misunderstands itself—whether it is a "continuous" society or a stagnating one, unable to make any steps to ameliorate its poverty, under-education and limited opportunities while still maintaining its character. It leaves aside the question of how individually reliable Bowling may be as an observer and social critic. Instead it raises questions about the reliability of any kind of observation that claims to function in a pure and unmediated way. Bowling's idea of a transparent world of observation where things are simply what they are, and of a pure interior space that corresponds to this world, is vulnerable to the vertiginous sense that a "fake" world is set against an "original" which itself turns out to be an error, one which is perhaps all the more troubling in that its construction is hidden from one who is otherwise capable at distinguishing between the artificial and the real.

Yet it is here, I would argue, that Orwell's identity of "honest George" and his concern with a "transparent," a "window pane" text comes most fully and most usefully into play as a vehicle for inspecting the construction of reality in the thirties. One way of reading Bowling's vertiginous position is to suggest that because there can be no access to an unmediated truth "out there" one must suspect claims to have found it more than one attacks those who abandon the search for it. But Bowling's vision of an unmediated, pure interiority and its corresponding language has more to tell us than that such a search is futile. Bowling's description of Binfield, of course, challenges and subverts the humiliating redescription of this experience that he encounters in modernity. And unwittingly, Bowling's mistaken notion of a "real" Binfield which modernity simulates adds a further level of critique to the appearances generated by this modernity. Rather than simply being a fake, the new Binfield is the counterfeit of an error, consisting of a faked version of an "authentic" Binfield—or a Binfield of "authenticity"—that, as Bowling shows, cannot have actually existed. Yet Bowling's erroneous view of Binfield does not need to be corrected by the reader by recourse to an idea of yet another Binfield that is somehow more real, more true, than the one he describes. Although one might certainly point to errors in Bowling's description of Binfield, what is more important is what we can understand by the idea of correcting the view of Binfield as a place in which unmediated observation is possible. One corrects this error with a notion of representation, within and of Binfield, that is more aware of its own status as mediation, as "true" only within the conditions generated by a particular language. This notion, crucially, need not exclude an idea of "transparency," but rather seeks to redescribe what transparency is. In this sense, "transparency" is not "in correspondence with how things are," where this correspondence assumes the achievement of what Rorty calls "The One Right Description" (40). Rather, transparency can be understood as a coherent claim to truth, one which is unclouded by error, illusion, and deception, including the error of assuming that the language game one employs, in being coherent, matches up with the way things are and thus forms the One Right Description. Indeed, since truth is a property of language, and not of the world, a particular mediation of the word can have validity only if it admits the possibility of other mediations, other truths, that obtain within other descriptions and redescriptions, other language games, other vocabularies. A "window pane," therefore, is precisely that—one windowpane among others.

Thus we can distinguish between the *way* Bowling thinks he has experienced Binfield and the actual content of his experience, consisting of the real, if mediated, experience of a particular town in a particular place at a particular time. But in asserting that this content has validity, one must also assert that it cannot be the *only* content that can have validity, nor can it be the only description or windowpane that might claim truth value. The point might seem trivial enough, and even imply a happy plurality of perspectives, each transparent to themselves, free of error and deception. Yet a deeply unsettling consequence is that this plurality cannot logically exclude a windowpane that is coherent and "true," but which exists to advance the truth-claims of power in, for instance, describing Binfield as a convenient and efficient location for a Big Brother Internment Camp. The point is that although such a description would surely be, from any recognizable moral perspective, evil, it *need* not be erroneous, incoherent, or untransparent within the terms of its vocabulary, although of course the chances are that it would be just that.

This possibility, which once recognized simply cannot be closed down, would lend support to the suggestion that in seeking a "transparent" text Orwell was not only, seeking to identify and expose error, delusion and deception in his historical moment. Still less was he seeking to do so from a position that claimed unmediated access to a discovered truth that lay outside of language and human construction. Rather he was seeking to establish a valid sense of truth that could withstand the efforts of competing truths to undermine or overpower it, and to establish this sense by *making* a truth that would remain true even if it were not the One Right Description, even if it were only one description among others. From this perspective, Orwell did not oppose power only because it was untrue, or because it was *only* untrue; instead he made it possible to argue for conditions of valid truth because he opposed power. Just as one's vocabulary may be challenged by another, that vocabulary must be resisted with one's own. The difficulty comes, of course, in distinguishing between a different vocabulary and the unsuccessful (erroneous) application of an existing vocabulary, and in recognizing circumstances where opposition to a hateful vocabulary effectively closes down the possibility of generating new vocabularies. Hence, the importance of recognizing both the opportunities and dangers of competing vocabularies, as well as the need to insist on the validity of one's own vocabulary *precisely because* it must stand against others, rather than because it offers the perspective that is uniquely and exclusively true. Thus, Orwell can show the validity of attempts to combat illusion and error embedded in power, but more importantly his situation suggests that the strenuous resistance to power involves recognition of the perils and freedoms that obtain in the absence of One Right Description of the world, together with the labor necessary to create a language adequate to this discomforting vision.

Notes

1. "One can write nothing readable unless one constantly struggles to efface one's personality. Good prose is like a window pane" (Orwell 1970, 29–30). Christopher Norris (1984) has summarized as "empiricist" the view that "reality exists independently of the mind which perceives or interprets it. The unmediated *facts* of real-life experience are appealed to as a bedrock guarantee that we can, after all, speak the truth of that experience by sticking to straightforward accurate description and not letting words or ideologies get in the way" (243). Writing, however, of a historical and cultural moment with striking parallels to that explored by texts of the thirties examined in the present essay, Norris (1992) has modified his emphasis, arguing against thinkers like Rorty, in what one could call a "Neo-Orwellian" vein, that "*getting things right* as regards the historical record is the only adequate means of counteracting the various myths, pseudo-histories, propaganda ploys or strong revisionist narratives that can otherwise be invented pretty much to order by those with the power to intervene in the production of socially-acceptable truth" (129–30). In what follows I will suggest that, although one hopes that the necessary

goal of "getting things right" is not obscured as a result of Rorty's work, Orwell's texts suggest that exposing error is not all that is involved in "getting things right," and that the significant problems in "socially accepted truth" surface when there is more than one way of describing what can properly count as truth.

2. See also Keith Williams's comments in Williams and Matthews (1997, 163–81) and Williams (1996, 1–4), and Lynette Hunter's discussion in Williams and Matthews (1997, 202–16).

3. See, for instance, the passage in Isherwood's *Lions and Shadows* concerning the secret attractiveness of authoritarian models of "The Test," where the narrator fantasizes about being "an austere young prefect" and, against the odds, whips into proper order a "bad" public school house and thereby emerges "a Man." The narrator comments: "It is so very easy ... to sneer at all this homosexual romanticism. But the rulers of Fascist states do not sneer—they profoundly understand and make use of just these phantasies and longings" (1985, 48).

Works Cited

Cunningham, Valentine. 1988. *British Writers of the Thirties*. Oxford; Oxford University Press.

Hunter, Lynette. 1997. Blood and Marmalade: Negotiations between the Domestic and the State in George Orwell's Early Novels. In *Rewriting the Thirties: Modernism and After*, edited by Keith Williams and Steve Matthews, 202–16. New York: Longman.

Isherwood, Christopher. [1938] 1985. *Lions and Shadows: An Education in the Twenties*. London: Methuen.

Montefiore, Janet. 1996. *Men and Women Writers of the 1930s: The Dangerous Flood of History*. London: Routledge.

Norris, Christopher, ed. 1984. *Inside the Myth, Orwell: Views from the Left*. London: Lawrence and Wishart.

———. 1992. *Uncritical Theory: Postmodernism, Intellectuals and the Gulf War*. Amherst, MA: University of Massachusetts Press.

Orwell, George. 1938. *Homage to Catalonia*. New York: Harcourt.

———. 1939. *Coming Up for Air*. New York: Harcourt.

———. 1970. *The Collected Essays, Journalism and Letters of George Orwell. Vol. 1. An Age Like This 1920–1940*, edited by Sonia Orwell and Ian Angus. Harmondsworth: Penguin.

Rorty, Richard. 1989. *Contingency, Irony and Solidarity*. Cambridge: Cambridge University Press.

Williams, Keith. 1996. *British Writers and the Media 1930–1945*. New York: St. Martin's Press.

Williams, Keith, and Steven Matthews, eds. 1997. *Rewriting the Thirties: Modernism and After*. New York: Longman.

Williams, Raymond. 1971. *Orwell*. London: Fontana.

WILLIAM E. CAIN

Orwell's Perversity:
An Approach to the Collected Essays

The question I want to raise and explore is: What gives Orwell's literary and political criticism its abiding interest and vitality? And in brief I think the answer is that it is perverse. In part the perversity exists in the bracing unexpectedness of Orwell's analyses and judgments but, even more, it is the result of his form of expression—the slant of his phrases, the shape of his sentences.

I am drawn to and curious about the operations of Orwell's language, and the dimension of it in particular that strikes me as perverse—the persistently oppositional and contradictory turns of his thinking, patterned in the style. Orwell's perversity makes his work as a literary and cultural critic extraordinarily good, yet it sometimes makes him predictable (a strange thing to say about such an independent mind) and hard to lay hold of.

Getting underway on this essay, I began reading volume 4 of *The Collected Essays, Journalism, and Letters*. The first essay in that volume, from November 1945, is "Revenge Is Sour," where Orwell describes acts of revenge taken by Jews against SS officers after Nazi control of the death camps had ended. Former prisoners could hardly be blamed for their behavior, he concedes, but he adds that his observations "brought home to me that the whole idea of revenge and punishment is a childish daydream": "Properly speaking, there is no such thing as revenge. Revenge is an act which you want to commit

From *George Orwell into the Twenty-first Century*: pp. 215–228. © 2004 by Paradigm Publishers.

when you are powerless and because you are powerless: as soon as the sense of impotence is removed, the desire evaporates also."[1]

My first response was, Orwell is wrong: Countless people and nations have craved the power that would enable them to exact revenge, often through legal channels, but often too, as in Eastern Europe and Africa in the 1990s, through monstrously violent actions. Orwell's remote tone seemed wrong as well, oddly detached from the reality of Nazi victimization of Jews, which was itself a genocidal form of revenge—he gives this just a single sentence. But it then occurred to me that the more accurate term for Orwell's claim is *perverse*, and that, furthermore, perversity is his signature.

Perverse, like *perverted*, has through its Latin root a range of meanings— *turn*, but also *crooked, slanted, askew*, even *turned upside down or over*. *Perverse* implies obstinate persistence and stubbornness, a deep disposition toward being oppositional and contradictory, and unpleasantly so. Orwell employs the word in this sense, for example, in *Burmese Days* (1934): "It was the first time they [Flory and Elizabeth] had definitely quarrelled. He was too miserable even to ask himself how it was that he offended her. He did not realize that this constant striving to interest her in Oriental things struck her only as *perverse*, ungentlemanly, a deliberate seeking after the squalid and the 'beastly.'"[2] Later, Elizabeth lingers over Flory's upsetting behavior: "For there had always been something dubious about Flory; his age, his birthmark, his queer, *perverse* way of talking—that 'highbrow' talk that was at once unintelligible and disquieting."[3]

In *Nineteen Eighty-Four*, Orwell gives *perverse* a political charge: "Goldstein was delivering his usual venomous attack upon the doctrines of the Party—an attack so exaggerated and *perverse* that a child should have been able to see through it, and yet just plausible enough to fill one with an alarmed feeling that other people, less level-headed than oneself, might be taken in by it."[4]

Perverse and affiliated words also appear in a number of Orwell's essays, in, for instance, these two passages: "English is peculiarly subject to jargons. Doctors, scientists, businessmen, officials, sportsmen, economists, and political theorists all have their characteristic *perversion* of the language";[5] and "I am now reading a new life of Dickens by Hesketh Pearson, which I have to review. It isn't awfully good. There doesn't seem to be a perfect life of Dickens *perverse* & unfair though it is, I really think Kingsmill's book is the best."[6]

In Orwell's era and our own, *perverse* and *perverted* have been deployed as demeaning words for homosexuals, and these words continue to be invoked as designation and code for disturbed sexual imaginings and practices, as in Orwell's essay on Salvador Dali: "But from his Surrealist paintings and photographs the two things that stand out are sexual *perversity* and necrophilia.... He professes an especial affection for the year 1900, and claims that every ornamental object of 1900 is full of mystery, poetry, eroticism, madness, *perversity*, etc."[7] This suggests a path into sexual themes in Orwell's work—his uneasy comments about homosexuals, his account of Winston Smith's sadistic sexual fantasies, and related topics pertaining to gender roles that Daphne Patai examines with a prosecutor's zeal in *The Orwell Mystique* (1984). But I'm after something more general, closer to a defining perversity of temperament and to the nature of Orwell's "peculiar and impressive personality" (Stuart Hampshire's phrase)—his sense of himself and the impact he made on other people and the effects he renders in his prose.

Commonly it is said that in Orwell's case the style is the man. But, in truth, critics do not agree on the relationship of the life to the writing, the man to the work. Lionel Trilling describes Orwell as one of those men "who live their visions as well as write them, who *are* what they write, whom we think of as standing for something as men because of what they have written in their books."[8] The political scientist Ian Slater says, decisively, the opposite: "he was *not* what he wrote."[9] The self presented in the books, Slater contends, calculatedly differs from the biographical self: the Orwell created on the page lives at a remove from the composite Eric Blair/George Orwell whose actual experiences, opinions, friendships, and sexual activities his biographers have traced.

I lean toward Trilling rather than Slater on this issue. But that is because I see elements of perversity in both the writing and the life, complicatedly bonding them together, and I doubt that Trilling would go along with that. Yet there is, among the recollections and anecdotes, a good deal of evidence for the term I propose. Many who knew Orwell have highlighted contradictions and tensions in his attitudes and behaviors that reached such a high degree they seemed perverse, or were saved from perversity only because his rare virtue and wholeness engagingly atoned for them.

"Orwell was original in himself," recalled Malcolm Muggeridge: "If not witty, he was intrinsically funny. For instance, in the extraordinary prejudices he entertained and the naïve confidence with which he propounded them. Thus, he would come out with the proposition: 'All tobacconists are Fascists!', as though this was something so obvious that no one could possibly question his statement."[10] Richard Rees describes Orwell as "strenuous and self-martyrizing" yet "diffusing" all the while an "atmosphere of cosiness."[11] Bernard Crick says: "Orwell saw himself as a violent unmasker of published pretentiousness, hypocrisy, and self-deceit, telling people what they did not want to hear; but in private he was a gentle and tolerant man."[12] Reviewing *Nineteen Eighty-Four*, Diana Trilling found herself "thrown off" by "something in the book's temper, a fierceness of intention, which seems to violate the very principles Mr. Orwell would wish to preserve in the world."[13] "A penchant for the painful, the demeaning and the repulsive," notes Dwight Macdonald more ominously, "runs throughout Orwell's work."[14] Orwell "turned his life into an experiment in classlessness," the critic Louis Menand states, "and the intensity of his commitment to that experiment was the main reason that his friends and colleagues found him a perverse and sometimes exasperating man."[15] In a similar vein, Timothy Garton Ash offers this brief biography: "The bare biographical facts are curious enough: a talented scholar at Eton perversely goes off to become an imperial policeman in Burma, a dishwasher in Paris, and a tramp in London; runs a village shop, fights in the Spanish Civil War, abandons left-wing literary London for a farm on a remote Scottish island and dies of tuberculosis at the moment of literary triumph, aged forty-six."[16]

The accent on Orwell's perversity is there, too, in Steven Marcus's reference to "Orwell's irresistible inclination throughout his life toward situations in which he would live in hardship, deprivation, and suffering."[17] One notices it in a comment by V.S. Pritchett, who, during the bombing of Britain, visited Orwell's flat on the top of a building in St. John's Wood: "He seemed to want to live as near to a bomb as possible."[18] "I think it's clear beyond all doubt that he didn't like himself much," remarks Christopher Hitchens.[19] This sounds accurate yet incongruous about a figure whom many, past and present, have admired, celebrated, wished they could become.[20]

Orwell, notoriously, angers and exasperates readers on the left, who find him extremely perverse, false, and dangerous, and their denunciations hit repeatedly at the perversity of his behaviors and views. The extreme personal distaste extends back and forth from Orwell to the positions he took. The foreign correspondent Alaric Jacob, for instance, says, "After coasting gently through Eton, earning no laurels but making no enemies, Orwell went tamely to Burma at the age of nineteen for lack of anything better to do. I could not understand how anyone of even moderate intelligence could have taken so retrograde a step."[21] Christopher Norris, commenting on Orwell's relation to "the broad tradition of British socialist politics," concludes, "He turned against that tradition while persistently claiming to speak for it; took over its most rooted assumptions in the service of antagonistic aims; and produced, in short, a point-for-point travesty of socialist argument."[22] Finally, Raymond Williams writes, "The recruitment of very private feelings against socialism becomes intolerable by 1984. It is profoundly offensive to state as a general truth, as Orwell does, that people will always betray each other. If human beings are like that, what could be the meaning of a democratic socialism?"[23]

Critics like Williams find Orwell exasperating not only for the essays and books he wrote but also for the claims he made about his intentions in them. Referring to *Nineteen Eighty-Four*, Orwell observes: "My recent novel is NOT intended as an attack on Socialism or on the British Labour Party (of which I am a supporter) but as a show-up of the *perversions* to which a centralised economy is liable and which have already been partly realised in Communism and Fascism."[24] This, to those on the left, is perverse: they see Orwell in *Nineteen Eighty-Four* engaged in exactly the discrediting of socialism and the British Labour Party that he here denies.

Other readers—Left, Right, and Center—Orwell simply annoys. They do not warm to his quickness to take the other side, an inherent recalcitrance of mood that, they claim, verges on or edges into perversity. John Morris, a BBC colleague, found a "strange expression" in Orwell's eyes, "a combination of benevolence and fanaticism."[25] "Whatever was 'in' affected him with a kind of violent claustrophobia," says Mary McCarthy: "he wanted out."[26] Stephen Spender says: "Just as D. H. Lawrence disapproved of everyone else's sex, so Orwell disapproved of everyone else's socialism!"[27] This, from John Bayley: "Like T. E. Lawrence in *Seven Pillars of Wisdom*, Orwell unconsciously strove both to be a man of action and destiny and to reveal what a fraud he was in that role." Pritchett, both impressed and suspicious, contends that Orwell's relentless regard for the truth was "perverse."[28]

As a writer Orwell is highly perverse, and I am interested in when that's a good thing and when it's not. It's nearly always a good thing when the perversity is in the detailed quality of observation—the direct seeing-and-saying capped with a flourish or given a keen edge that distinguishes Orwell's settings and scenes, as in this passage early in *The Road to Wigan Pier* where he depicts his lodgings at Mrs. Brooker's:

> Downstairs there was the usual kitchen living-room with its huge open range burning night and day. It was lighted only by a skylight, for on one side of it was the shop and on the other the larder, which opened into some dark subterranean place where the tripe was stored. Partly blocking the door of the larder there was a shapeless sofa upon which Mrs. Brooker, our landlady, lay permanently ill, festooned in grimy blankets. She had a big, pale yellow, anxious face. No one knew for certain what was the matter with her; I suspect that her only real trouble was overeating. In front of the fire there was almost always a line of damp washing, and in the middle of the room was the big kitchen table at which the family and all the lodgers ate. I never saw this table completely uncovered, but I saw its various wrappings at

different times. At the bottom there was a layer of old newspapers stained by Worcester Sauce; above that a sheet of sticky white oilcloth; above that a green serge cloth; above that a coarse linen cloth, never changed and seldom taken off. Generally the crumbs from breakfast were still on the table at supper. I used to get to know individual crumbs by sight and watch their progress up and down the table from day to day.[29]

The brilliant perversity is in the Dickensian fantasia of the personified crumbs, as Orwell enlivens a dreary setting so that its pathos and degradation seem a bit sprightly. Frequently Orwell gives the bleakest place some lightly redemptive touch or comical exaggeration. He has the eye of a skillful cartoonist, as the sketch of Mrs. Brooker shows, in "grimy blankets" but "festooned" with them, as if adorned with a garland of flowers. He takes pleasure in the properties of the English language, savoring the details of vocabulary and phrase that define the English literary tradition of Shakespeare and the King James Bible, and of Orwell's favorites, Jonathan Swift and Charles Dickens.

Another, more direct, harder element of Orwell's perversity, however, is linked to the judgments he makes and our response to them. How, after all, do we tell the difference between good and bad perversity in his, or in any critic's or intellectual's, judgments? When is a writer not boldly incisive or enlightening but perverse (that is, "merely" perverse)? When, on the other hand, is a writer brave and honorable precisely because he or she is perverse, cutting against the grain of received wisdom or confronting power like Milton's Abdiel, "faithful found; / Among the faithless, faithful only he"?

Perversity can function as a heroic force in a writer's style of judgment making. One concurs with Irving Howe's assessment: "In his readiness to stand alone and take on all comers, [Orwell] was a model for every writer of our age."[30] But then again, perversity can be unthinking and lead to formulaic writing. When this happens, we grow accustomed to the perversity: the writer's sentences take their turns but exert no pressure on the reader. You know what to expect—perversity, an always contrarian angle whatever the subject. Oscar Wilde, George Bernard Shaw, H. L. Mencken: each can come to feel mannered, his thought grooved, predictable in a fondness for unpredictability, paradox, and mockery of traditional views and values.

A complication arises: we say that a writer is perverse, but is perversity really a position that someone can occupy? It isn't self-sufficient: you are perverse only in relation to something that you turn against or away from. Alfred Kazin touches on this point when he remarks of Orwell that he "conceives the beginning but cannot bear the end.... He knew best what he was against."[31] The risk of perverse writing and thinking is a dead end: a critic is against this, but, perversely, is against *that* too. No system, state, or institution will do, and this implies a perpetual dissatisfaction that has the ring of relativism. What is Orwell for if everything he says he is *for* is flawed? Perversity: Isn't *this* what he is for?

Capitalism, Orwell believed, is a system that no decent person wants; he declared in 1947 that it "has manifestly no future."[32] Socialism is the better way—one recalls the memorable pages on socialism in chapter 8 of *Homage to Catalonia*. But the problem for Orwell is that socialists have perversely equated their cause with the defense of Stalin's Russia and hence dwell in an echo chamber of unrealities. Who could accept the betrayal of conscience required to stand with them? Where, then, is Orwell standing?

My concern about relativism may be mistaken. Surely perversity can be classified and distinguished, this kind from that—we believe we can make distinctions about Orwell and other authors. Perversity of a bad kind means that someone is really wrong—history has confirmed it. Perversity of a good kind means that someone was or is really right, as when we say: Perverse to many in his own era because of his critique of the Left, Orwell now represents the truth that others at that time failed to see and give voice to; now, as Christopher Hitchens has argued, he is the touchstone that retrospectively exposes the perversity of others who embraced Soviet dogma uncritically.[33]

Comparisons might help my inquiry. To whom might we compare Orwell, as exemplars of bad and good perversity? When the African American intellectual W. E. B. Du Bois exalted Stalin and supported the Soviet crackdown on the Hungarians in 1956, he was being perverse in a bad way. He wrote, for example, "Joseph Stalin was a great man: few other men of the 20th century approach his stature. He was simple, calm and courageous. He seldom lost his poise; pondered his problems slowly, made his decisions clearly and firmly; never yielded to ostentation nor coyly refrained from holding his rightful place with dignity."[34] Another instance is the ill-tempered introduction that Edmund Wilson wrote in November 1961 for *Patriotic Gore* (1962), his magisterial study of Civil War literature. Aligning the Civil War with the cold war, Wilson tenders the cranky claim that virtues, values, and ideologies are irrelevant, totally delusional: ultimately, there is "at bottom the irrational instinct of an active power organism in the presence of another such organism, of a sea slug of vigorous voracity in the presence of another such sea slug."[35] Such a formidable, intellectually curious writer is Wilson, and yet this Darwinian moral equivalence is hectoring and reductive, perverse.

Examples come to mind of writers who started with good perversity and ended in bad perversity. The British literary critic F. R. Leavis preached powerfully in the 1940s and 1950s for D. H. Lawrence's achievements as a novelist and critic, but he grew so wedded to his conception of Lawrence's "supreme intelligence"[36] that other writers eventually loomed for him as defective and unhealthy. An equally notable case is the art critic Clement Greenberg, who almost alone spoke and wrote as an advocate of the abstract expressionists (above all, Jackson Pollock) in the 1940s.[37] He praised their work before anyone else and developed from it an influential understanding of modernism and color field painting. Yet Greenberg became dogmatic, ever more narrowing in his interests and sympathies. Enslaved to a formula, Greenberg later in his career was left with only three or four artists to care much about.

These points of comparison, however, dramatize for me the special interest and richness of Orwell's perversity: he is more successfully and consistently perverse than are other writers. Orwell's perversity is everywhere in his style, in his approach to an issue, in the way he attacks it and compels attention to it. His perversity is central to his poised wit, to his irony. Here is the first sentence of "Bookshop Memories" (November 1936): "When I worked in a second-hand bookshop—so easily pictured, if you don't work in one, as a kind of paradise where charming old gentlemen browse eternally among calf-bound folios—the thing that chiefly struck me was the rarity of really bookish people."[38] And this, from the first page of "The Lion and the Unicorn" (February 1941):

> Also, one must admit that the divisions between nation and nation are founded on real differences of outlook. Till recently it was thought proper to pretend that all human beings are very much alike, but in fact anyone able to use his eyes knows that the average of human behaviour differs enormously from country to country. Things that could happen in one country could not happen in another. Hitler's June purge, for instance, could not have happened in England.[39]

For me the most potent examples of Orwell's perversity occur during the period from 1945 to 1950, with the cold war shadowing and then dominating political discussion and debate, argument and analysis.[40] "Considering how likely we all are to be blown to pieces by it within the next five years," Orwell says, "the atomic bomb has not roused so much discussion as might have been expected."[41] And then in "Catastrophic Gradualism" (November 1945): "In his much-discussed essay, [Arthur] Koestler is generally assumed to have come down heavily on the side of the Yogi. Actually, if one assumes the Yogi and the Commissar to be at opposite points of the scale, Koestler is somewhat nearer to the Commissar's end."[42]

Orwell typically seizes on a topic or theme that seems settled, where a consensus of opinion resides, a feeling shared by nearly all, and then he briskly tacks the other way. He relishes this moment. "Whatever the subject," says Michael Shelden, "Orwell was always tempted to look at it from both sides. And when he considered another point of view, he did not usually do it halfheartedly. He became immersed in it and used all the powers of his imagination to identify with it."[43]

More Orwellian perversity, an eagerness to destabilize and unnerve the reader, appears in this first sentence from a book review: "If one were obliged to write a history of the world, would it be better to record the true facts, so far as one could discover them, or would it be better simply to make the whole thing up? The answer is not so self-evident as it appears."[44] We are familiar with this question and (so we tell ourselves) know the answer, which is exactly the answer that Orwell challenges in the second sentence, his hook. He is an exceptionally honest writer, but he is indeed a writer, agile and crafty; he is attuned from start to finish to the expectations and responses of readers to his sentences, and he is working with *that* every step of the way.

Perversity is also a central feature of Orwell's literary criticism, as in "Good Bad Books" (November 2, 1945), where he states that the "supreme example" is *Uncle Tom's Cabin*: "It is an unintentionally ludicrous book, full of preposterous melodramatic incidents; it is also deeply moving and essentially true; it is hard to say which quality outweighs the other."[45] And in his introduction to Jack London's *Love of Life and Other Stories* (November 1945): "On several points London was right where nearly all other prophets were wrong.... His best stories have the curious quality of being well told and yet not well written."[46] Then, this review of *The Prussian Officer and Other Stories* (November 16, 1945), where he observes of D. H. Lawrence: "Yet he does often seem to have an extraordinary power of knowing imaginatively something that he could not have known by observation."[47]

Perverse he may be, yet Orwell possesses a strangely adhesive literary personality—a lively, probing intelligence, stimulating and credible even when the reader is prompted to disagree with the judgments presented. Perversity in Orwell is frequently first confessional ("this is how I felt") and then a lot or a little coercive ("this is how you feel, or should"), but one is struck by how little one minds this. Some do mind it, but the fervor of their criticisms shows that Orwell has seized them: he will not let them go; they cannot let go of him.

"In a political and moral sense I am against him, so far as I understand him," states Orwell about Jonathan Swift: "Yet curiously enough he is one of the writers I admire with least reserve, and *Gulliver's Travels*, in particular, is a book which it seems impossible for me to grow tired of."[48] There's this firm pair of sentences from "Lear, Tolstoy, and the Fool" (March 1947): "One's first feeling is that in describing Shakespeare as a bad writer [Tolstoy] is saying something demonstrably untrue. But that is not the case."[49] Orwell *pushes* from the point taken for granted, turning away and turning aside.

Orwell says what he thinks, even if what he says makes him seem bizarre or outrageous or inconsistent, and because hardly anyone does that, he affects readers as perverse. He famously launches "Reflections on Gandhi" (January 1949): "Saints should always be judged guilty until they are proved innocent...." There's the shock to received opinion. Yet the sentence is not done: "... but the tests that have to be applied to them are not, of course, the same in all cases."[50] He invokes a sense of obligation that likely was not there in us ("have to be applied"), with the phrase "of course" enforcing the enigmatic obligation and aligning itself with the equally insistent "always." The reader has been made captive.

Orwell's style "can be deceptive," Richard Rees proposes: "It is so swift and simple and unpretentious that his best arguments sometimes appear much easier and more obvious than they really are."[51] But there is another aspect to the perverse style, to which the literary critic Hugh Kenner alludes when he avers that the "plain style" practiced by Orwell is "the most disorienting form of discourse yet invented by man."[52] Few readers ever become lost amid Orwell's sentences, but they are disorienting, unbalancing, even as they give pleasure in their plainness. Few dare to write and sound like that. Though we tend to think of the plain style as the basic or foundational style, and other styles as its perversions, the reality (so Kenner, I think, implies) is the reverse: it's the plain style, pitched against other styles, that's the oddity, that's perverse.

The illusions, delusions, and folly of the attitudes that people cling to—these are among the favorite topics that Orwell rubs against the grain of his prose:

> I am always amazed when I hear people saying that sport creates goodwill between the nations, and that if only the common peoples of the world could meet one another at football or cricket, they would have no inclination to meet on the battlefield.... International sporting contests lead to orgies of hatred.[53]

> Every generation imagines itself to be more intelligent than the one that went before it, and wiser than the one that comes after it. This is an illusion, and one should recognise it as such, but one ought also to stick to one's own world-view, even at the price of seeming old-fashioned: for that world-view springs out

of experiences that the younger generation has not had, and to abandon it is to kill one's intellectual roots.[54]

We are all capable of believing things which we know to be untrue, and then, when we are finally proved wrong, impudently twisting the facts so as to show that we were right.... To see what is in front of one's nose needs a constant struggle.[55]

Orwell insists that much thinking is perverse. Not said, but of course intimated, is that a writer must be rare, quite perverse, to gain mastery over common and embedded perversity. It is terribly difficult to cease looking sideways and, redirected, see what is right in front of us. Someone thrust against the face makes us uncomfortable, intruding on space that does not belong to them. Would you prefer someone to stand smack in front of your nose, or to be off a ways? When we look to the side or away, there's more room to feel at ease, to invent, embellish, pretend, lie.

Orwell's political writing features the perversity I have been describing—paradoxically, the perverse look is the straight-on look—and there it is still more pronounced and morally stiffening.

The organized lying practiced by totalitarian states is not, as is sometimes claimed, a temporary expedient of the same nature as military deception. It is something integral to totalitarianism, something that would continue even if concentration camps and secret police forces had ceased to be necessary.[56]

Politico-literary intellectuals are not usually frightened of mass opinion. What they are frightened of is the prevailing opinion within their own group. At any given moment there is always an orthodoxy, a parrot-cry which must be repeated, and in the more active section of the Left the orthodoxy of the moment is anti-Americanism.[57]

Perversity, for Orwell himself, is a resistance to orthodoxy, and that mandates a rigorous clarity in the uses of language as he takes aim at the perversity he identifies in others. As he maintains in "The Prevention of Literature" (January 1946): "To write in plain, vigorous language one has to think fearlessly, and if one thinks fearlessly one cannot be politically orthodox."[58] Orwell locates himself in relation to orthodoxy, and once he has it defined, his style is energized: he has *that* to turn against:

It is queer to look back and think that only a dozen years ago the abolition of the death penalty was one of those things that every enlightened person advocated as a matter of course, like divorce reform or the independence of India. Now, on the other hand, it is a mark of enlightenment not merely to approve of executions but to raise an outcry because there are not more of them.[59]

Nearly the whole of the English Left has been driven to accept the Russian regime as "Socialist," while silently recognizing that its spirit and practice are quite alien to anything that is meant by "Socialism" in this country. Hence there has arisen a sort of schizophrenic manner of thinking, in which words like "democracy" can bear two irreconcilable meanings, and such things as concentration camps and mass deportations can be right and wrong simultaneously.[60]

Yet I must acknowledge that Orwell's perversity is sometimes too perverse, as in the conclusion he draws in the following passage about literary censorship in the USSR:

The thing that politicians are seemingly unable to understand is that you cannot produce a vigorous literature by terrorizing everyone into conformity. A writer's inventive faculties will not work unless he is allowed to say approximately what he feels. You can destroy spontaneity and produce a literature which is orthodox but feeble, or you can let people say what they choose and take the risk that some of them will utter heresies. There is no way out of that dilemma so long as books have to be written by individuals. That is why, in a way, I feel sorrier for the persecutors than for the victims.[61]

Orwell is wrong: the persecutors do not deserve sympathy more than their victims. But, perversely, Orwell feels the need to add that twist, knowing that readers will respond to it as I have done. Irritatingly, Orwell is sharper than you or me: he bothers and jostles, making readers inhabit untried attitudes and experience uncomfortable points of view about subjects upon which it has been agreed that the truth is already known. What Orwell says in this example is surprising, but I am not surprised he says it. If I do not hurry to criticize him, his manner of thinking may do me some good.

Sometimes, as Morris Dickstein pointed out to me, Orwell seems to be constructing an orthodoxy that he can then, perversely, take issue with. True, I think, yet Orwell often implicates himself in the orthodoxies and anti-orthodoxies he challenges, as in this passages from "Politics and the English Language" (November 1946): "Look back through this essay, and for certain you will find that I have again and again committed the very faults I am protesting against."[62] Orwell's point is that such faults are inevitable, but his tone implies his own willfulness—"again and again committed," as though he knew where the "faults" were and chose to leave them in.

There is also a theatrical quality to some of Orwell's perverse passages, where he leaves the reader wondering: Does he really mean this, or is it a potent ploy, a strategic joke, he means for me to see through? Consider this, from "Such, Such Were the Joys":

> You were supposed to love God, and I did not question this. Till the age of about fourteen I believed in God, and believed that the accounts given of him were true. But I was well aware that I did not love him. On the contrary, I hated him, just as I hated Jesus and the Hebrew patriarchs. If I had sympathetic feelings towards any character in the Old Testament, it was towards such people as Cain, Jezebel, Haman, Agag, Sisera; in the New Testament, my friends, if any, were Ananias, Caiaphas, Judas, and Pontius Pilate.[63]

Few writers sought truth telling and integrity as intently as did Orwell, yet here he names as his boyhood compatriots the Bible's best-known murderers, hypocrites, liars, and traitors. "What is truth?" Pilate asked (John 18:38), a question that Francis Bacon, William Cowper, William Blake, Gerard Manly Hopkins, and Aldous Huxley, among others in the English literary tradition, responded to. The sheer asking of the question, in Pilate's case, exposes his own failure of vision, for Jesus, the figure of truth, is standing before his eyes ("... that I should bear witness to the truth. Every one that is of the truth heareth my voice" [John 18:37]). It is hard to imagine a more spectacular case of moral blindness, with the possible exception of the panoramic blindness to Soviet crime that Orwell himself called attention to and denounced. Orwell thus ends his sentence, with delicious perversity, with the name that stands in most glaring contrast to the kind of writer he became.

I asserted at the outset that Orwell is hard to get hold of, and that's where I must move now, as the final consequence of his perversity. An honest man, a plain writer: as we read and think about him, Orwell embodies these simple phrases with depth and power. Yet his irony, paradox, perversity: Can you say you know him, this resistant writer and critic? "If you state your principles clearly and stick to them," Orwell professed, "it is wonderful how people come round to you in the end."[64] What I want to know is this: Is perversity, the motivating principle that I see in Orwell, a principle that others can adopt? Is the lesson he teaches: be perverse?

Orwell's perversity was always there, in the reversal and anticonsensus thrust of his style and operations of mind. Yet it is more starkly present and disquieting in his work of the mid- to late 1940s. He makes more statements like these, which declare the perversity, as he envisioned it, of his enterprise as a writer:

> When one considers how things have gone since 1930 or thereabouts, it is not easy to believe in the survival of civilization.... I think one must continue the political struggle, just as a doctor must try to save the life of a patient who is probably going to die.... Exactly at the moment when there is, or could be, plenty of everything for everybody, nearly our whole energies have to be taken up in trying to grab territories, markets and raw materials from one another. Exactly at the moment when wealth might be so generally diffused that no government need fear serious opposition, political liberty is declared to be impossible and half the world is ruled by secret police forces. Exactly at the moment when superstition crumbles and a rational attitude towards the universe becomes feasible, the right to think one's own thoughts is denied as never before. The fact is that human beings only started fighting one another in earnest when there was no longer anything to fight about.[65]

Postwar history tends in the wrong direction, taken astray by humanity's friends and foes alike. But Orwell's deeper implication is that human beings are intrinsically perverse: *that* is what he is in contact with, and *that* is why he perceives an inner perversity in history's bad design.

"Part of our minds—in any normal person it is the dominant part— believes that man is a noble animal and life is worth living," Orwell reflects. He completes the sentence: "but there is also a sort of inner self which at least intermittently stands aghast at the horror of existence."[66] Normality is believing—in order to get through the day—in something that may not be true: the impact of this sentence is apparent if one switches its parts, with the horror first, and the doughty accommodation to it second, as the sentence's place of rest.

Here is one of Orwell's assertions: "The civilization of nineteenth-century America was capitalist civilization at its best." He continues: "Soon after the Civil War, the inevitable deterioration started."[67] Conspicuous by its absence is any mention of slavery, which Orwell either neglects or fails to see. But more noteworthy is his "inevitable," with its accent of mordant certainty that a high point never endures. What's striking is less Orwell's historical blind spot than the rhythm of his thinking in these sentences, the cadence of decline and decay.

This perverse passage has an odd but revealing relationship to another, in "Such, Such Were the Joys": "How difficult it is for a child to have any real independence of attitude could be seen in our behavior towards Flip. I think it would be true to say that every boy in the school hated and feared her. Yet we all fawned on her in the most abject way, and the top layer of our feelings towards her was a sort of guilt-stricken loyalty."[68]

"Independence of attitude": this is Orwell's distinction. Yet he emphasizes that such an attitude in a child is dreadfully hard to secure. Hate and fear are the true feelings, but the behavior in response to them, perversely, is abject fawning. In Orwell's tone is the same chord of inevitability—this, always, is how persons tend to behave. The conduct of the boys prophesies the submissiveness to authority they will display as adults.

The ultimate perversity, for Orwell, is the absurdity of the human predicament, its unchanging core. History pursues its course, and we are who we are: "From time to time a human being may dye his hair or become converted to Roman Catholicism, but he cannot change himself fundamentally."[69] The sane thing in a way would be to stop working. Why write at all? This is a question that Orwell wondered about, and for which he provides a complex, illuminating, and egregious answer:

> I give all this background information because I do not think one can assess a writer's motives without knowing something of his early development. His subject matter will be determined by the age he lives in—at least this is true in tumultuous, revolutionary ages like our own—but before he ever begins to write he will have acquired an emotional attitude from which he will never completely escape. It is his job, no doubt, to discipline his temperament and avoid getting stuck at some immature stage, or in some *perverse* mood: but if he escapes from his early influences altogether, he will have killed his impulse to write.[70]

> In a reasonable world a writer who had said his say would simply take up some other profession. In a competitive society he feels, just as a politician does, that retirement is death. So he continues long after his impulse is spent, and, as a rule, the less conscious he is of imitating himself, the more grossly he does it.[71]

There is, Orwell believes, no stopping work, even if the work is grossly imitative, because stopping would mean death. But in Orwell's case, as his biographers have recorded, he drove himself with near-suicidal intensity to complete *Nineteen Eighty-Four* amid wracking illness. His execution of this book ensured his death. Why do that? It's pointless, yet for Orwell utterly necessary.

Orwell was a writer: he kept working: he had to work. And his impact has been astounding. In the turn of his sentences and judgments, he remains brilliantly and memorably perverse.

Notes

1. George Orwell, *The Collected Essays, Journalism and Letters*, ed. Sonia Orwell and Ian Angus (New York: Harcourt Brace Jovanovich, 1968), 4:5. (Henceforth referred to as *CEJL*.)

2. George Orwell, *Burmese Days* (New York: Harcourt Brace Jovanovich, 1962), 133.

3. Orwell, *Burmese Days*, 176.

4. George Orwell, *Nineteen Eighty-Four* (New York: Harcourt Brace Jovanovich, 1982), 10.

5. Orwell, "The English People," *CEJL*, 3:26.

6. Orwell, *CEJL*, 4:479.

7. Orwell, *CEJL*, 3:158, 3:163.

8. Lionel Trilling, "George Orwell and the Politics of Truth," in *The Opposing Self: Nine Essays in Criticism* (New York: Viking, 1955), 155.

9. Ian Slater, *Orwell: The Road to Airstrip One* (New York: W.W. Norton, 1985), 183.

10. Malcolm Muggeridge, "A Knight of the Woeful Countenance," in *Nineteen Eighty-Four to 1984: A Companion to the Classic Novel of Our Time*, ed. C. J. Kuppig (New York: Carroll and Graf, 1984), 276–77.

11. Richard Rees, *George Orwell: Fugitive from the Camp of Victory* (Carbondale: Southern Illinois University Press, 1962), 147.

12. Bernard Crick, *George Orwell: A Life* (New York: Penguin, 1982), 362.

13. Diana Trilling, "Fiction in Review," *The Nation*, June 25, 1949, 717.

14. Dwight Macdonald, "Trotsky, Orwell, and Socialism," *The New Yorker*, March 28, 1959, reprinted in *Discriminations: Essays and Afterthoughts* (New York: Da Capo, 1985), 341.

15. Louis Menand, "Honest, Decent, Wrong: The Invention of George Orwell," *The New Yorker*, January 27, 2003, 87.

16. Timothy Garton Ash, "Orwell in 1998," *The New York Review of Books*, October 22, 1998.

17. Steven Marcus, "George Orwell: Biography as Literature," *Partisan Review* (Winter 1993): 46.

18. V. S. Pritchett, "Orwell in Life," *The New York Review of Books*, December 15, 1966.

19. Christopher Hitchens, "The Power of Facing" (interview), *Atlantic Unbound* (http://www.theatlantic.com/unbound/unb_index.htm), October 23, 2002.

20. A brief digression: In his survey of biographical accounts of Orwell's "prep school" experiences, Robert Pearce concludes: "These writers, aware that Orwell did not always tell the whole truth, nevertheless insist that he did not lie: he produced an account which, to use one of his own favorite phrases, was 'essentially true.'" (Robert Pearce, "Truth and Falsehood: George Orwell's Prep School Woes," *The Review of English Studies*, new series, 43, no. 171 [August 1992]: 367–86.) This is convincing but curious, more than a little perverse if not dangerous: When does the shading of truth reach a point when the essential truth becomes discredited? Or is the idea that if you know that something is essentially true, you can take liberties that the reader may never detect?

21. Alaric Jacob, "Sharing Orwell's 'Joys'—But Not His Fears," in *Inside the Myth: Orwell: Views from the Left* (London: Lawrence and Wishart, 1984), 73.

22. Christopher Norris, "Language, Truth, and Ideology: Orwell and the Post-War Left," in *Inside the Myth*, 249–50.

23. Raymond Williams, *Politics and Letters: Interviews with the New Left Review* (London: Verso, 1979), 390.

24. Orwell, *CEJL*, 4:502.

25. Audrey Coppard and Bernard Crick, eds., *Orwell Remembered* (New York: Facts on File, 1984), 171.

26. Mary McCarthy, "The Writing on the Wall," *The New York Review of Books*, January 30, 1969.

27. Stephen Spender, "The Truth about Orwell," *The New York Review of Books*, November 16, 1972.

28. Quoted in Miriam Gross, ed., *The World of George Orwell* (New York: Simon & Schuster, 1971), 80.

29. Orwell, *The Road to Wigan Pier* (New York: Harcourt, Brace, Jovanovich, 1958), 20–21.

30. Irving Howe, "George Orwell: 'As the Bones Know,'" in *Decline of the New* (New York: Horizon, 1970), 270.

31. Alfred Kazin, "'Not One of Us,'" *The New York Review of Books*, June 14, 1984.

32. Orwell, *CEJL*, 4:375.

33. Christopher Hitchens, *Why Orwell Matters* (New York: Basic Books, 2002).

34. W. E. B. Du Bois, "On Stalin," *National Guardian*, March 16, 1953, reprinted in *Newspaper Columns*, vol. 2, 1945–1961, ed. Herbert Aptheker (White Plains, N.Y: Kraus-Thomson, 1986), 910.

35. Edmund Wilson, *Patriotic Gore: Studies in the Literature of the American Civil War* (New York: Oxford University Press, 1962), xxxii.

36. F. R. Leavis, *D. H. Lawrence: Novelist* (New York: Simon and Schuster, 1969), 14.

37. Clement Greenberg, *The Collected Essays and Criticism*, vols. 1 and 2, ed. John O'Brian (Chicago: University of Chicago Press, 1986).

38. Orwell, *CEJL*, 1:242.

39. Orwell, *CEJL*, 2:56.

40. Volume 4 of the *Collected Essays, Journalism and Letters* reprints many of Orwell's best-known and most-admired pieces from 1945 to 1950, including "The Prevention of Literature," "Politics and the English Language," "James Burnham and the Managerial Revolution" (as well as a later piece on Burnham), "Politics vs. Literature: An Examination of *Gulliver's Travels*," "How the Poor Die," "Lear, Tolstoy, and the Fool," "Writers and Leviathan," "George Gissing," and "Reflections on Gandhi."

41. Orwell, *CEJL*, 4:6.

42. Orwell, *CEJL*, 4:17.

43. Michael Shelden, *Orwell: The Authorized Biography* (New York: HarperCollins, 1991).

44. Orwell, *CEJL*, 4:116.

45. Orwell, *CEJL*, 4:22.

46. Orwell, *CEJL*, 4:24, 4:29.

47. Orwell, *CEJL*, 4:32.

48. Orwell, *CEJL*, 4:220

49. Orwell, *CEJL*, 4:290.

50. Orwell, *CEJL*, 4:463.

51. Rees, *George Orwell*, 111.

52. Hugh Kenner, "The Politics of the Plain Style" (1984), in *Mazes: Essays* (San Francisco: North Point Press, 1989), 261–69.

53. Orwell, *CEJL*, 4:41.

54. Orwell, *CEJL*, 4:51.

55. Orwell, *CEJL*, 4:124, 4:125.

56. Orwell, *CEJL*, 4:63; see also 4:158.

57. Orwell, *CEJL*, 4:398; see also 4:409.

58. Orwell, *CEJL*, 4:66; see also 4:135.

59. Orwell, *CEJL*, 4:240.

60. Orwell, *CEJL*, 4:410.

61. Orwell, *CEJL*, 4:267.

62. Orwell, *CEJL*, 4:137.

63. Orwell, *CEJL*, 4:360.

64. Orwell, *CEJL*, 4:399–400.

65. Orwell, *CEJL*, 4:248–49.

66. Orwell, *CEJL*, 4:222.

67. Orwell, *CEJL*, 4:247.

68. Orwell, *CEJL*, 4:350.

69. Orwell, *CEJL*, 4:276.

70. Orwell, *CEJL*, 1:3.

71. Orwell, *CEJL*, 4:253.

JAMES M. DECKER

George Orwell's 1984 and Political Ideology

From its release in 1949, George Orwell's *1984* has been considered a stinging indictment of totalitarian ideology. Unlike many other texts, Orwell's novel seems overtly to suggest its ideological underpinnings and place aesthetic considerations squarely in the background.[1] For critics such as Richard Lowenthal (1983, 209) and Tosco R. Fyvel (1984, 33), Orwell provides a transparent—but nevertheless powerful—condemnation of Stalinism and a prescient warning against the proliferation of totalitarian methods. In this light, Orwell, working from a 'common sense' socialist position that eschews dogmatic rhetoric, exposes the dehumanizing qualities of systemic terror. Both sympathetic and hostile critics usually ground their discussions of *1984* in the assumption that Orwell offers 'substantially little more than an extension into the near future or the present structure and policy of Stalinism' (Rahv 1987, 14). For the inhabitants of Oceania, ideology—irrational and sadistic—crushes not only the feeble resistance of 'rebels' like Winston Smith and Julia, but also disintegrates the human spirit and transmogrifies it into a repository of platitudes. Aided by what Rob Kroes deems a 'dislocation of human understanding by linguistic sabotage,' the Inner Party employs ideology to eliminate the very possibility of thought (Kroes 1985, 85). According to such interpretations, Orwell sets his dystopia

From *Ideology*: pp. 146–158. © 2004 by James M. Decker.

in England as a check against factions within British socialism that he feels are open to influence from Stalinism.

Alternately, however, Erich Fromm, in a tantalizingly brief section in his discussion of the novel, points readers of *1984* not only toward the Soviet Union but toward the United States and the West as well. For Fromm, Orwell excoriates the capitalist West for many of the same tendencies evident in totalitarian states, claiming that 'managerial industrialism, in which man [sic] builds machines which act like men and develops men who act like machines, is conducive to an era of dehumanization and complete alienation, in which men are transformed into things and become appendices to the process of production and consumption' (Fromm 1983, 267). Fromm's assessment of Orwell's dual purpose seems apt, for while Big Brother and Emmanuel Goldstein certainly resemble Stalin and Trotsky in both physiognomy and philosophy, using the geographic 'logic' of the novel, the setting is awry, for a disguised Soviet Union would appear to suggest Eurasia rather than Oceania. Airstrip One owes its allegiance, moreover, to a more distantly western entity, which certainly suggests the United States.[2] In a three-superpower world (Eastasia/China represents the third power), totalitarianism has spread far beyond its Stalinist roots. Antony Easthope validates such a perspective, observing that 'liberal democracy is complicit with the totalitarianism it would condemn in that it supports the undemocratic structures of corporate capitalism and state paternalism' (Easthope 1984, 267). Although Lowenthal rejects postulations such as those offered by Fromm and Easthope, arguing that 'Orwell did *not* believe ... that the social conformity of advanced capitalist democracies ... was essentially similar to totalitarian party dictatorship,' he offers little in the way of evidence to support his purported knowledge of Eric Blair's thoughts (Lowenthall 1983, 209). Indeed, one cannot simply dismiss Fromm's intriguing comments out of hand, for they at least offer a potential explanation for the demise of free market capitalism and its leading exponent, the United States, an account that asserts that the 'danger [of totalitarianism is] ... relatively independent of ideology' (Fromm 1983, 267). One might, in fact, posit that Orwell's use of totalitarianism predicates itself on the end of ideology.

In his best-selling *The End of History and the Last Man* (1992), Francis Fukuyama examines the demise of totalitarianism in Eastern Europe and suggests that the victory of liberal democracy, which represents an 'ideology of potential universality,' portends the end of history—and, thus, ideology (42). In its attempt to dominate, the totalitarian state swims meekly against the relentless current of human progress. For Fukuyama, the whole point of empirical methodology is to bolster human security and conquer nature in order to fulfill material wants (76). Because totalitarian governments emphasize collective security rather than individual desire, they fail to mesh with what Fukuyama regards as the inevitable course of human history. While occasional ruptures or discontinuities have appeared, the fundamental historical pattern indicates a consistent prejudice for liberal democracy. Totalitarianism ignores this controlling principle and, thus, with its 'bankruptcy of serious ideas,' cannot sustain its internal logic indefinitely (39). Simply stated, there is 'now no ideology with pretensions to universality that is in a position to challenge liberal democracy' (45). China's ideological threat 'is finished' (36) and Islam 'has virtually no appeal outside those areas that were culturally Islamic to begin with' (46). With astonishing surety, Fukuyama posits that liberal democracy (usually of the capitalist variety) echoes the innermost desires of humanity and, in its purest form, will mark the end of history. Although 'a host of problems like unemployment, pollution, drugs, crime, and the like' will still exist, the absence of any 'deeper sources of discontentment' will preclude a return to history and its ideological posturing (288).

Opposing Orwell's vision of totalitarianism, Fukuyama holds that 'the most fundamental failure of totalitarianism was its failure to control thought' (1992, 29). While doublethink and thoughtcrime might serve for interesting fiction, Fukuyama is clearly skeptical of their practical applications. Despite concerted attempts to exercise state authority within the confines of the human mind, the innate need for *thymos* (self-recognition) undercuts efforts to control individual imagination (162). Confidently employing an essentialist view of 'human nature,' Fukuyama suggests that psychological terror of the son practiced by O'Brien can never completely efface the quasi-instinctive drive to improve material conditions and seek recognition. Discontent might become liminal, but it will ultimately explode (if the regime's own decaying infrastructure does not collapse beforehand). Totalitarianism, based on a *megalothymian* principle of state superiority, must fail in the face of isothymia, 'the desire to be recognized as the equal of other people' (190). Because 'recognition based on groups is ultimately irrational,' the neo-Hegelian Fukuyama inverts Marx's premise and argues that totalitarian communism holds its contradiction within itself (242). Control based on abstractions—even ostensibly positive ones—pales in comparison to control based on collective practice. In denying the agency of its citizens, totalitarianism grounds itself in limited self-interest (consequently, Fukuyama would not accept O'Brien's notion of self-perpetuating power). Because its discipline derives from innate tendencies, liberal democracy stands a much stronger chance of outlasting history. Based on the 'scientific' fulfillment of the human desire for comfort (the economic imperative) and the 'natural' drive for rational autonomy, the final incarnation of capitalist democracy—according to Fukuyama—would result in a 'completely satisfying' state (206).

Fukuyama characterizes his world-without-history as a peaceful place where wars are irrelevant (ideological jealousy being obsolete) and humans are content (1992, 311). Interestingly, he also holds with Alexandre Kojève that art and philosophy will disappear for want of subject matter: the possibility of change would not exist (311). As with well-fed dogs dozing in the sun, humans would have no need to look beyond their own noses (311). If they were inclined, artists could repeat themes and approaches, but they could not innovate. Fukuyama does not lament such a loss, however, for the absence of ontological and epistemological friction would create conditions so blissful that no one would desire to pursue visions of a better life. Creativity would be channeled through other means, such as economic and scientific activity (315). While survival would not depend on entrepreneurs or increased efficiency, the natural desire for *thymos* would find an outlet in such activities.[3] Plenty of opportunity, then, would exist for those who felt some inner compulsion to do more than simply scratch their full bellies or enjoy the latest gadget. The 'homogeneous' world, therefore, would not constitute the ontological equivalent of a coma, but rather would represent the culmination of all human desires and instincts. Unlike Ursula LeGuin's Omelas, however, such a utopia would not be founded—according to Fukuyama—upon an essential injustice but upon ideology-free, 'natural' principles that all humans hold in common. Any inequality that remains at the end of history would not be traced to systemic imbalances but rather to the 'natural inequality of talents' (291). For Orwell, however, the end of history is far from the sunny paradise that Fukuyama envisions.

In *1984*, Orwell depicts not only Stalinist brutality pursued to its vicious extreme. The narrative also presents a horrifying vision of the consequences of absorbing an ideology so completely, so unquestioningly, as to eliminate ideology altogether. In this way, *1984* represents not an *example* of ideology but a world *without* ideology. As Winston's position in the Ministry of Truth reveals, history has ended in Oceania, replaced by a ubiquitous present less convinced of its oven righteousness than unaware of any alternate ontological possibilities. Unlike Fukuyama, Orwell conceptualizes the end of history as a grim, vacuous realm where struggle has ceased and canine-like contentment is omnipresent. Paradoxically, Orwell's Oceania, free of political strife and economic dissatisfaction, represents not a utopia but a dystopia. Curiously, Orwell depicts ideology—utterly vanquished and annihilated beyond possibility—in a romantic, even nostalgic, way in *1984*, for its absence leads to a dispassionate, soulless existence that must manufacture a faux ideological opponent to avoid the risk of mass psychological implosion. For Orwell, the prospect of erasing ideological difference elicits not celebration but fear, for a society without debate—even among a tiny elite—is a society that breeds terror. As Winston's tormentor O'Brien points out, Oceania's ideology-free system substitutes self-perpetuating 'collective' power for inefficient individual power, which is based on the possibility of resistance and dies with its owner (Orwell 1983, 218). Oceania contains no endings, no beginnings, no history. It is.

Although the system that Oceania represents is definitely suggestive of totalitarianism, it would be better characterized as post-totalitarian. Irving Howe calls for such an interpretation, remarking that 'the world of *1984* is *not* totalitarianism as we know it, but totalitarianism after its world triumph' (Howe 1982, 332). One finds more support for Howe's observation in Hannah Arendt's magisterial work on totalitarianism. For Arendt, totalitarianism represents an attempt to destroy the creed for *consensus iuris*, the process whereby society agrees to a set of laws, and 'make mankind itself the embodiment of law' (Arendt 1968, 462). In this way, 'totalitarian policy claims to transform the human species into an active carrier of a law to which human beings would otherwise only passively and reluctantly be subjected' (462). Arendt's formulation of totalitarianism, furthermore, states that 'ideologies are never interested in the miracle of being,' preferring the realms of 'becoming' and 'perishing' to the victory itself (469). Arendt focuses on process, on the heinous but dynamic act of bending a people to the 'will' of in idea. Totalitarianism gains its momentum from both the rhetoric and act of terror, inscribing the latter within the former terror is the method by which the idea will be absorbed by—not imposed on—an unwilling and foolish public (for its own good). Much as suspects, under extreme duress, honestly confess to crimes that they did not commit, the inhabitants of a totalitarian society eventually come to believe in the very government that injures them. The pain stops when acceptance is absolute. Arendt, however, clearly suggests that totalitarianism without an enemy or a backslider portends the end of ideology: 'it would mean the end of history itself if rudimentary classes did not form so that they in turn could "wither away" under the hands of totalitarian rulers' (464). Such is the state of affairs in Oceania.

The 'becoming' and 'perishing' of which Arendt speaks do not exist in Oceania, a realm of the infinite present. Orwell indicates that the process of becoming ended years ago for the leaders of Oceania and its enemies: 'the purpose of all of them was to arrest progress and freeze history at a chosen moment' (1983, 167). Isaac Deutscher views such comments as evidence that 'Orwell saw totalitarianism as bringing history to a standstill' (Deutscher 1982, 342). While the state continues to 'fight' its enemies, Goldstein's *The Theory and Practice of Oligarchical Collectivism* (a parody of Trotsky's *The Revolution Betrayed* [1937]) reveals that a geographic and technologic equilibrium prevents the three superpowers from expanding their territories in any but the most tentative way.[4] In effect, the regimes engage in the simulacrum of war in order to prop up an obsolete class structure. While Ruth Ann Lief argues that 'Party unity is assured by adherence to a common ideology,' her proposition assumes a conscious sense of direction lacking (even according to O'Brien) in Oceania, where hollow ritual has replaced burning idealism (Lief 1969, 93). The phenomenon that Fukuyama labels the 'crisis of authoritarianism,' the inability for *megalothymian* self-interest to subsume human desire, fails to materialize in Oceania, and the system continues to lumber on long after its original practitioners are dead (Fukuyama 1992, 13). Although totalitarian measures still exist, they are no longer required to transform the overwhelming majority into zealots for the party. As Fyvel points out, 'there is not even any political ideology left to oppose, so that resistance becomes nonsensical' (Fyvel 1984, 77). So effectively has the system reprogrammed the citizens of London—and by extension all of Oceania—that rebellion has to be either fabricated, as in the case of the innocuous Parsons, or else cultivated, as with Winston. While the former represents the discovery of 'repressed' anti-Big Brother sentiment by children, the latter signifies a more curious situation in which Winston's halting gestures against conformity had been observed and tolerated for at least eleven years (Orwell 1983, 212). A totalitarian state, no doubt, would have crushed such behavior at its first signs, but a post-totalitarian government, in search of any 'enemy' that could regenerate the 'becoming'/'perishing' binary, might attempt to 'grow' Winston's discontent like a hothouse flower, cutting it down only after it had reached full bloom. While Winston assumes that 'purges and vaporizations were a necessary part of government,' such instances seem to stem more from habit than from necessity (41). The citizens have internalized doublethink and need little in the way of real monitoring: even the telescreens, representing a high-tech panopticon, frequently have no guardian on the other side, for everyone lived 'from habit that became instinct' as though 'every sound [they] made was overheard' (6–7).[5]

Oceania thus exists as a paradox, for while it craves enemies, with their concomitant positionality (spatio-temporal starting/ending points), it nonetheless cannot subvert its own ultimate victory as represented in its atemporality. The defamiliarization of time, most famously represented in the novel by the clock striking thirteen, is the culmination of Oceania's decades-long project of obliterating; the past and making the future irrelevant (5). O'Brien sums up this tendency as he catechizes Winston during his 'reintegration': 'who controls the past controls the future; who controls the present controls the past' (204). Consequently, the Party places complete stress on the immediate moment, blurring any chance of temporal comparison. Winston, for example, can only crudely determine the year ('it was never possible nowadays to pin down any date within a year or two'), for the continuum itself represents the unthinkable: time before Oceania (10). The speaker at a Hate Week rally, furthermore, finds no problem in informing the crowd mid-sentence in condemnation of Eurasia that their enemy is, and always was, Eastasia (149). Julia has little conception of how many sexual partners she has had, and the old prole whom Winston queries seems not to project any knowledge of life before the Party. Five-year plans never seem to end, and Big Brother (or Goldstein, for that matter) never ages. Winston's own memories seem impossible, and the antique shop he frequents is fraudulent (perhaps everything it contains has been created by members of the Party) and superfluous: there is no call for antiquities in a society of ubiquitous presence. The Party has, in effect, ruptured the very fabric of time and rendered it meaningless outside of the present. Unlike Fukuyama and his contention that the end of history will be characterized by the 'smallness of its actual remaining inequalities,' Orwell views such omnipresence with fear and loathing (Fukuyama 1992, 295). For Orwell, the bureaucratization of society that Fukuyama anticipates in a post-historical society yields not only efficiency but an enervating lack of motivation. Because the past does not exist, no one exhibits a sense of progress (apart from the pseudo-progress depicted in counterfeit reports of 'record' output of consumption goods and the like), and, as the future is an alien concept, no one can set long-term goals and is doomed to a static death-in-life. By implication, Orwell suggests that as long as ideology exists, struggle prevails and hope continues. In Oceania, the Party has vanquished hope forever, the Brotherhood not withstanding.

Oceania's post-ideological status manifests itself most clearly in Winston's job at the Ministry of Truth. Charged with expunging errors from printed material, Winston's department adjusts all texts to conform with the requirements of the present. Since the Party cannot make mistakes, any discrepancies between the printed word and official policy must be eliminated: 'all history was a palimpsest, scraped clean and reinscribed exactly as often as was necessary' (Orwell 1983, 36). Such a step, however, is superfluous, for the Party's doctrine is so pervasive as to constitute reality rather than ideology. Even should references to Party miscalculations escape detection, it is doubtful that anyone would notice because the sheer weight of the present would overwhelm the past. Old newspapers, like Winston's 'ancient' paperweight/talisman, would hold no appeal for the Party faithful, who would subscribe to whatever the current speaker imparted. Just as doublethink could explain away anti-Eurasia war posters as the work of Goldstein-influenced saboteurs, it could ascribe images of non-persons or narrative inconsistencies to the handiwork of Big Brother's enemies. The parameters of thought are such that—except in the increasingly sporadic cases of 'pure' subversion evident in the (literally) dying breed of Winston's generation—Party inaccuracy is utterly impossible. Even had Winston retained the surreptitious photograph of Jones, Aaronson, and Rutherford, he would hardly have been in a position to convince anyone of its origin, despite his belief that 'it was enough to blow the Party to atoms' (67). O'Brien, for example, easily dismisses it as pure 'invention,' even though Winston has seen the picture, prompting Winston to question his own sanity (211). While smuggled copies of Solzhenitsyn or Pasternak may have resonated with furtive Soviet dissidents, their Oceanic counterparts would have been viewed as the products of Oceania's 'enemies' and, thus, discounted accordingly. Counter-ideology is invisible, particularly among children and young adults who, of course, were born after the Party's hegemony was complete. As O'Brien tells Winston, the Party 'cut the links between child and parent' (220). Even the hazy memory of ideology is recast as fantastic. Winston's rebellion, therefore, amuses, rather than infuriates, the Inner Party, and exemplifies the futility of resistance. No one hears him.

Apparently, most people in Oceania unquestioningly accept their system as signifying the terminus of human development. No viable alternative to the Oceanic worldview exists, for Orwell suggests that Eastasia and Eurasia are quite similar in outlook: they 'are not divided by any genuine ideological difference' (153). More important, however, is the absence of even the *sub rosa* desire for such an option. Orwell's largely undifferentiated characters— caricatures, really—truly seem to bask in their existence, reveling in their hate for Goldstein and applauding Big Brother in 'electric thrill' (244). Of those characters that Orwell does delineate in more detail, only Winston and Julia rebel overtly, and for Winston, Julia's resistance is 'from the waist downwards,' a phenomenon indicating instinctive physical hunger, rather than ontological questioning (129).[6] The *thymos* that Fukuyama requires for ontological viability seems for all but a few citizens—such as Winston—to manifest itself in unwavering dedication either to bureaucratic functions or to various social superstructures such as group hikes or the Spies. Art and philosophy are produced—quite efficiently—by machine, and political dissent is rare to the point of suggesting mental aberration. People throw themselves eagerly into state-sponsored activities such as the Junior Anti-Sex League and the two-minutes hate. Apart from Winston, fear, which Philip Rahv claims results in a 'psychology of capitulation,' seems eerily absent from Oceania (Rahv 1987, 16). Contentment, a prerequisite for Fukuyama's post-ideological world, is rampant.

The bounty that Fukuyama anticipates for such a society, however, materializes only in tepid gin, razor blade shortages, and chocolate of dubious quality. The efficiency that Fukuyama claims will outpace traditional social groups and portend the fulfillment of desire, furthermore, aids only disembodied power (Fukuyama 1992, 77). Inequality is institutionalized and revered: 'freedom is slavery' (Orwell 1983, 17). While the average citizens of Oceania have little to do with war per se, they nonetheless endorse it, despite Fukuyama's assertion that post-historical contentment will yield the cessation of war (Fukuyama 1992, 311). In effect, Orwell seems not only to have envisioned the end of history long before Fukuyama, but he turns that vision on its head. For Orwell, Winston may represent the 'last man,' but he certainly does not present a very compelling case for the end of history.[7] As an ideological warrior, Winston appears woefully inadequate. Lacking any sense of ideology apart from a vague and instinctive emptiness, Winston gropes along without purpose. Despite numerous outward signs that would preclude collaboration, Winston attempts to enlist Julia and O'Brien in his 'cause,' a foolish decision given that Winston has little idea as to their goals. Physically and mentally mediocre, Winston represents hope in a world devoid of struggle. His ultimate impotence (underscored by his initial inability to achieve an erection with Julia) manifests itself both in his wildly imprudent actions— particularly his establishing a love nest and failing to destroy Goldstein's book upon detection—and his ultimate 'reintegration' and love for Big Brother. O'Brien, assured that no ideological alternative exists, extirpates Winston's heterodoxy with ease: Winston's 'mind shriveled' (Orwell 1983, 214). Orwell clearly has little faith in the potential for revolution in a post-totalitarian state.

Even Goldstein's book offers little in the way of ideological opposition to the Party, a fact stemming, no doubt, from its being a product of O'Brien's authorship. Winston learns the answer to his question 'why?' but he certainly fails to discover any ontological alternative. Although Orwell's imitation of Trotsky's prose style presents a lucid history of Oceania's post-totalitarian methods—including the use of war to destroy surplus goods (155) and the principles of doublethink (176)—it does not appear to spur Winston on to consider ideological alternatives. Julia, moreover, falls asleep when Winston reads her *The Theory and Practice of Oligarchical Collectivism* not only because of her general contentment but because Goldstein's book fails to generate any revolutionary ideas. Orwell suggests that were Big Brother himself to read the text over the telescreen the impact would not be enough to overcome the desensitization to ideological conflict inherent in a post-totalitarian society. Rob Kroes considers such a phenomenon the result of 'an effort aimed at the total surrender of intellectual and moral sense' (Kroes 1935, 36). Oceania's residents, including Winston ('what most oppressed him was the consciousness of his own intellectual inferiority'), have ceded their ability to think to the system itself (Orwell 1983, 211). The country's political machinery is exposed to Winston, but without a viable counter-ideology he lacks the critical vocabulary to articulate alternatives and work toward its realization. Oceania's citizens are so stripped of independent thought that they cannot reinterpret society and imagine a distinctly different entity. Access to sexual partners, the refinement of Newspeak, the possession of a glass object—these acts hardly qualify as full-scale ideological rebellion. Winston exists at the margins of the party, but he never leaves the circle itself, for his creative abilities are simply too atrophied to reenvision society. Once he is imprisoned, for example, Winston hardly proves a worthy adversary to O'Brien, who, convinced that history has culminated in the concept of pure, self-perpetuating power, glibly swats away the criminal's confused objections. In Orwell's formulation, once the threshold of totalitarianism has been passed, a return to ideological struggle is impossible. While Fukuyama argues that totalitarianism is a historical aberration that represents a 'pathological condition' that will inevitably be corrected, Orwell's dystopia presents a stark counterpoint that explicitly maintains the 'condition' could become permanent if other ideologies are rendered unthinkable (Fukuyama 1992, 123).

Orwell's fear, therefore, lies less in the propositions of a particular ideology than in the absence of ideology. Nearly all ideologies advance a mythic future wherein its enemies have been vanquished. Concurring with Fukuyama, such self-mythologies present claims to historical finality, postulating that the past merely represents a prelude to the wondrous realm wherein every human desire will be fulfilled. In presenting Oceania as a society divested of possibility, Orwell critiques the principle of ideological inevitability and presents not a heavenly dream but a hellish nightmare. Valorizing the liberal subject, Orwell depicts Oceania as a subhuman society filled with witless citizens who cannot recognize their own subjugation. Even the elite class has been stripped of mental responsibility, for power itself is in control. The compartmentalization of human behavior and emotion has resulted in a bureaucratized, soulless state that cannot even remember its own original idealism. Once intent on destroying its ideological rivals, Oceania now drifts through an endless gray day of empty slogans and pointless tasks. As with unthinking beasts, the denizens of Oceania represent interchangeable parts of a collective unconcerned with individuation; the collective lurches instinctively forward, protecting its power for no other reason than to survive, like so many gnats forgoing sustenance in order to produce the next generation. According to Orwell's conception, all of the human attributes that Fukuyama links lo historical struggle—Art, Philosophy, Beauty, Truth, Justice, Love—vanish when a society loses its contrasts, but unlike Fukuyama's paradigm, Orwell's model inscribes total contentment as a pejorative. Such a notion is unquestionably intertwined with what Marx would deem bourgeois liberalism, but it also functions in a rather conservative way, a trait noted by Philip Goldstein (2000, 44) and Carl Freedman, who points out Orwell's ambivalence toward the socialist project (1988, 167).

Written in a post-war era when Britain's status as imperial power had diminished considerably and permanently, *1984* mightily resists the changes promised by either American capitalism or Soviet communism. The novel elides the process whereby the superpowers entrenched their positions, but it emphasizes how their respective ideologies would produce draining, homogenizing effects if extended to their logical conclusions. Orwell, then, clearly rejects the utopian vision for which Fukuyama yearns. Far from yielding self-actualization, a conflict-free society irreparably damages the very essence of humanity and transforms life into a perfunctory trudge toward undifferentiated existence. The dingy milieu of Oceania betokens political stasis, ideological uniformity—which is to say it has no ideology at all. Any political system—be it communist, capitalist, or otherwise—that totally expunges dissent risks a devolution into utter imbecility. While O'Brien prizes Oceania's methods as being superior to the crude tactics of Hitler and Stalin and recognizes in his society's system the apotheosis of power itself, he fails to acknowledge that complete efficiency robs that power of significance. None of the powerless even discern that they lack power, and Inner Party members—being utterly interchangeable—lack true understanding beyond their function. All sense of irony has been banished, and O'Brien, like Symes before him, is too good at his job and will inevitably be reprogrammed himself. As many critics, such as Lowenthal (1983, 210) and Gordon Beauchamp (1984, 75), have pointed out, Orwell offers not a prophecy in *1984* but a warning. He rails against all ideologies with pretensions toward comprehensive explanation, against any system so hubris-filled as to intimate that human civilization could not transcend its 'truths.' Orwell strongly suggests that the importance of Life lies, far beyond issues of economics and political creeds, within the process of resistance. Even Winston's meek overtures of rebellion constitute a grand Life when contrasted with the jingoist bravura of an Inner Party member, who, like Fukuyama's dog, merely exists. Ultimately, Orwell reveals a vision wherein Fukuyama's complacent, post-historical dog should be euthanized in order to clear the way for the return of ideological chaos and its attendant humanity.

Notes

1. Numerous critics, including Anthony Burgess and Jeffrey Meyers, have chided Orwell for his rather cumbersome style in *1984*.

2. Orwell writes that Airstrip One is a 'province' of Oceania, which subverts any notion that English Socialism has led to totalitarianism (1983, 7). Clearly, totalitarianism was imported to London from a futuristic America.

3. In this context, any 'art' would be more akin to that described in Donald Trump's *The Art of the Deal* than to the discussions in Walter Pater's *The Renaissance: Studies in Art and Poetry*.

4. Of course, the war has very real consequences for the subaltern populations existing at the margins of the central powers. The constant upheaval reifies these peoples into a slave class and obstructs the avenues of assimilation or subversion possible in a time of peace. Their status as chattel represents a far more dangerous and dehumanizing prospect than the bleak but 'secure' existence experienced by the inhabitants of Oceania. Even criminals such as Winston eventually find their suffering abated—albeit via reeducation and death—but the subalterns must face eternal bondage without even a bottle of Victory Gin to dim their consciousness.

5. Vita Fortunati perceptively remarks that 'Oceania represents the panoptic *society par excellence*' (1987, 145). Michel Foucault, of course, famously describes the theory and practice of the panopticon in *Discipline and Punish: The Birth of the Prison* (1995, 195–228).

6. If one accepts the veracity of Winston's clandestine photograph, then one might count the three disgraced Party leaders as providing dissent above the waist. Given the Thought Police's methods, however, one must be wary about the authenticity of the document. 'Charrington,' Goldstein's book, O'Brien's 'look'—all of these represent counterfeit sedition designed to entrap Winston.

7. Christopher Norris reminds his readers that the working title of *1984* was *The Last Man in Europe* (1984, 256). Such a title clearly indicates Orwell's disgust for end-of-history complacency.

PAUL KIRSCHNER

The Dual Purpose of Animal Farm

After nearly sixty years debate continues over the ultimate political meaning of *Animal Farm*, owing partly to its use as propaganda, but also to Orwell's original purpose, which was artistic as well as political. This article concentrates on the former purpose. It shows how fictional rhetorical strategies inevitably led to a pessimistic conclusion contradicting Orwell's own political actions and opinions during the period 1936–46, and attributes that contradiction to the effect of Orwell's chosen literary genre, combining elements of the fable and the fairy tale. The subtitle, 'A Fairy Story', indicates a neglected aspect of *Animal Farm*—literary parody of the 'proletarian' fairy tale that thrived in the 1920s and 1930s in Germany, the United States, and, tepidly, in England. A rare example of such a tale from the 1930s is quoted in full as an archetype of the politicized children's stories Orwell may have been parodying: it displays striking rhetorical and structural parallels with *Animal Farm*. The appealing form of such stories, adopted by Orwell, interfered with the full and accurate expression of his political thought. *Animal Farm* owes both its power and its ambiguity to the force and autonomy of literature itself, today menaced more than ever by the 'gramophone mind' Orwell detested.

From *The Review of English Studies* 55, no. 222 (2004): pp. 759–786. © 2004 by Oxford University Press.

> Whoever feels the value of literature, whoever sees the central part it plays in the development of human history, must also see the life and death necessity of resisting totalitarianism, whether it is imposed on us from without or from within.

> There is some hope ... that the liberal habit of mind, which thinks of truth as something outside yourself, something to be discovered, and not something that you can make up as you go along, will survive.

> (The Collected Essays,
> Journalism and Letters of George Orwell)

When, a couple of years ago, *Animal Farm* was put on stage in China, the long uncertainty about its ultimate meaning should have been dispelled. It dated back to 1945, when William Empson warned Orwell that, since allegory 'inherently means more than the author means', his book might mean 'very different things to different readers'.[1] Sure enough, English communists attacked *Animal Farm* as anti-Soviet, while a conservative chided Orwell for forgetting that private property is a prerequisite of personal freedom.[2] Western propagandists hijacked the book after Orwell's death, but twenty years later George Woodcock found it showed the identity of governing-class interests everywhere, and by 1980 Bernard Crick had to caution against reading it as a case *for* revolution.[3] In 1998 critics were still debating whether *Animal Farm* implied 'that revolution always ends badly for the underdog, hence to hell with it and hail the status quo'.[4] The confusion, as Empson saw, came not only from readers' prejudices but also from the story itself.

To show why, I shall explore Orwell's claim to have tried deliberately in *Animal Farm* 'to fuse political purpose and artistic purpose into one whole' (i. 29).[5] My purpose will be equally dual: first, to infer Orwell's purpose from his political views; secondly, to explain the built-in artistic contradictions that made *Animal Farm* fine meat for propagandists, and suggest how they may be, if not resolved, at least transcended. In fusing my own purposes, I shall not hesitate to evoke a social and intellectual ethos that today may seem quaintly archaic.

I

Defining his 'political' purpose in *Animal Farm* to the American critic Dwight Macdonald, Orwell showed he was no crusading anti-communist:

> I think that if the USSR were conquered by some foreign country the working classes everywhere would lose heart ... I wouldn't want to see the USSR destroyed and think it ought to be defended if necessary. But I want people to become disillusioned about it and to realize that they must build their own Socialist movement ... and I want the existence of democratic Socialism in the West to exert a regenerative influence upon Russia.[6]

Orwell's artistic aim was to remedy what England lacked: 'a literature of disillusionment about the Soviet Union' (iii. 272). If we apply Tolstoy's definition of art (which includes Orwellian hallmarks of simplicity, clarity, and accessibility) as the evocation of a feeling once experienced so as to make others feel it, Orwell had to evoke his disillusion over the Russian failure to achieve what to English Conservatives was anathema: social equality.

The disillusion is conveyed by continuous negation of what is being said, through wit, dramatized irony and intertextuality. The punning presentment of old Major as a 'prize Middle White boar' (p. 1)[7] makes a poor introduction to any speaker. His boast, 'I have had much time for thought as I lay alone in my stall, and I think I may say that I understand the nature of life on this earth as well as any animal now living' (p. 3), not only betrays woolly-minded, pigsty philosophizing; it impugns animal wisdom in general. Similarly, his personal resume, 'I am twelve years old and have had over four hundred children. Such is the natural life of a pig' (p. 5), makes it doubtful that social revolution can improve animal nature, and his optimistic prophecy that English fields 'Shall be trod by beasts alone' (p. 7) is unsettling. Major's axiom that 'All animals are comrades' is quickly exploded as the dogs chase the rats and then vote against accepting them as comrades, while the cat, who hasn't even listened, hedges her bets by voting on both sides. And with a blast from his shotgun, after which the whole farm is 'asleep in a moment' (p. 8), Jones completely deflates Major's oratory.

Intertextually, Major unwittingly parodies Saint-Simon and Marx in calling Man 'the only creature that consumes without producing' (p. 4), since Man does produce, as the animals find when they have to trade with him. More ominously, Major's reference to animal life as 'miserable, laborious and short' (p. 3) echoes the famous verdict on human life as 'solitary, poor, nasty, brutish, and short' by Hobbes,[8] whom Orwell saw as forecasting totalitarianism,[9] and the name of Animal Farm's leader recalls a Dostoyevskian view that everywhere there is always

> 'a first person and a second person. The first acts and the second takes.... In France there was a revolution and every one

was executed. Napoleon came along and took everything. The revolution is the first person, and Napoleon the second person. But it turned out that the revolution became the second person and Napoleon became the first person.'[10]

The Battle of the Cowshed likewise evokes not only the failed Western interventions against the Soviets in 1918–20, but also the defeat of Europe by the French republic in 1792–5. The Battle of the Windmill rings a special bell: the repulse of the duke of Brunswick in 1792, following the Prussian bombardment that made the windmill of Valmy famous. More significantly, in 1802 Napoleon restored slavery, abolished by the Convention in 1794. The Rebellion and its fate exemplify a historical paradigm.[11]

More obviously, the switch from Major's anthem 'Beasts of England' to the patriotic 'Animal Farm' parodies that from Lenin's internationalism to Stalin's 'Socialism in One Country'. The Rebellion, however, copies the February, not the October, Revolution. In a pamphlet[12] Orwell marked 'very rare' and cited (iv. 85), Maxim Litvinov, the first Soviet ambassador to England, told how spontaneous protests by women in food queues led to riots in which Cossacks, then Guards, joined the people, so that 'before anyone was properly aware, the capital was in the hands of the workers and soldiers'.[13] The Rebellion, sparked by Jones's failure to feed the animals, is similarly unplanned: they win the day 'almost before they knew what was happening' (p. 12). With history as his guide, Orwell divides the feelings that start a revolt from the ideology used afterwards to pervert it. Similarly, the spontaneous courage displayed in the Battle of the Cowshed is embalmed in the titles 'Animal Hero—First and Second Class': the first official nod to class distinction.

Naturalistic description is at first whimsical (Clover, cradling ducklings maternally with her foreleg, 'had never quite got her figure back after her fourth foal', p. 2), but as the Commandments are chipped away and the pig-managers increasingly resemble farmers, the allegory requires balancing. Physical details, previously anthropomorphic, now remind us that Napoleon is a pig, since morally he begins to seem all too human. Snowball draws plans for the windmill ('with a piece of chalk gripped between the knuckles of his trotter, he would move rapidly to and fro ... uttering little whimpers of excitement' (p. 33)), and Napoleon urinates over them. He signals his *coup d'état* by 'a high-pitched whimper of a kind no one had ever heard him utter before' (p. 35). Animality is preserved by wordplay when Napoleon hires a human solicitor named Whymper—the sound, we now recognize, made by a pig.

Disillusion is best transmitted by narration from the animals' point of view. When Muriel spells out the altered commandment 'No animal shall kill any other animal *without cause*' (p. 61), we find that the animals have forgotten the last two words of the original commandment. But are our memories better? Ransacking them, we feel the animals' fading hopes. And having been kept, like them, ignorant of their leader's manoeuvres, we share their shock at learning that Napoleon has sold the timber to Frederick and been cheated with forged banknotes. The aim isn't just to mimic the diplomatic minuet of West and East, each hoping Hitler would attack the other first; it is to make us share the animals' gradual conversion to Benjamin's view that their lot *cannot* improve—only worsen. Yet the very devices vindicating Benjamin's pessimism bolster sympathy with the rank-and-file animals. When, after their initial victory, we are told: 'Some hams hanging in the kitchen were taken out for burial' (p. 14), the humorous conceit is endearing; but deeper sympathy is gained by an inside view. After a new 'rebellion' is crushed (the word 'revolution', implying lasting change, is avoided) and the commandment against murder is broken, a view of the farm on a clear spring evening dissolves into the mind of Clover, lying on the knoll where she once feted victory:

> If she herself had had any picture of the future, it had been of a society of animals set free from hunger and the whip, all equal, each working according to his capacity, the strong protecting the weak, as she had protected the lost brood of ducklings with her foreleg on the night of Major's speech. Instead—she did not know why—they had come to a time when no one dared speak his mind, when fierce, growling dogs roamed, everywhere, and when you had to watch your comrades torn to pieces after confessing to shocking crimes. There was no thought of rebellion or disobedience in her mind. She knew that even as things were they were far better off than they had been in the days of Jones, and that before all else it was needful to prevent the return of the human beings. Whatever happened, she would remain faithful, work hard, carry out the orders that were given to her, and accept the leadership of Napoleon. But still, it was not for this that she and all the other animals had hoped and toiled.... Such were her thoughts, though she lacked the words to express them. (pp. 58–9)

The inarticulate, duped by the articulate, have been evicted not from paradise, but from a dream of one: now the very idea of rebellion is dead. Disenchantment is complete before the end of the book, as Squealer proclaims victory over Frederick, and the loyal Boxer asks, 'What victory?'

(p. 71), widening his chink of doubt over Snowball's 'crimes'. Yet to the last, the 'lower animals', now unable to remember better days, continue to hope. (Memory for them is the enemy of hope.) Literary form—their quality as animals—adds the deeper sadness of losers in the battle of evolution.

II

So pessimistic an outlook is belied by Orwell's own life and opinions during the years 1936–45. Benjamin's gloomy scepticism is sometimes attributed to Orwell's disillusionment with socialism after Stalinist treachery in Spain, covered up by the 'capitalist anti-Fascist press' (i. 318). The truth, is just the opposite. Orwell had seen through the USSR long before Spain. In 1940 he wrote: 'All people who are morally sound have known since about 1931 [the peak of forced collectivization] that the Russian regime stinks' (i. 583). In 1947 he spoke of regarding it 'with plain horror' for 'quite 15 years' (iv. 355). Yet, two weeks before leaving Spain, after the Barcelona fighting and being wounded at the front, he declared: 'I ... at last really believe in Socialism, which I never did before' (1. 301). In *The Lion and the Unicorn* (1941) Orwell advocated nationalization of land, mines, railways, banks, and big industries; income ceilings; classless education; and Dominion status for India. In 1946 he recalled: 'The Spanish war and other events in 1936–7 turned the scale and thereafter I knew where I stood. Every line of serious work that I have written since 1936 has been written, directly or indirectly, *against* totalitarianism and for democratic Socialism, as I understand it' (i. 28). 'Socialism' meant equality; not, as its enemies claimed, loss of liberty. On the contrary, 'the only regime which, in the long run, will dare to permit freedom of speech is a Socialist regime' (i. 373). 'Liberty' began with fairer income distribution: 'The glaring inequality of wealth that existed in England before the war must not be allowed to recur' (iii. 51). While rejecting 'the inherently mechanistic Marxist notion that if you make the necessary technical advance the moral advance will follow of itself' (i. 583), he defended Marx on novel grounds claiming that:

> the most important part of Marx's theory is contained in the saying: 'Where your treasure is, there will your heart be also.' [Luke 12: 34] But before Marx developed it, what force had that saying had? Who had paid any attention to it? Who had inferred from it—what it certainly implies—that laws, religions and moral codes are all a superstructure built over existing property relations? It was Christ, according to the Gospel, who uttered the text, but it was Marx who brought it to life. And ever since

he did so the motives of politicians, priests, judges, moralists and millionaires have been under the deepest suspicion—which, of course, is why they hate him so much. (iii. 121–2)[14]

Although by 'Communism' Orwell usually meant the Russian regime or its advocacy ('the "Communism" of the English intellectual is ... the patriotism of the deracinated' (i. 565)), he also used the word in an ideal sense:

> In mid-nineteenth-century America men felt themselves free and equal, *were* free and equal, so far as that is possible outside a society of pure Communism. (i. 547)

> One can accept, and most enlightened people would accept, the Communist thesis that pure freedom will only exist in a classless society, and that one is most nearly free when one is working to bring such a society about. (iv. 84)

What he did *not* accept was 'the quite unfounded claim that the Communist Party is itself aiming at the establishment of the classless society and that in the U.S.S.R. this aim is actually on the way to being realized' (iv. 84).

But while recognizing similarities in practice between Nazi and Soviet regimes, Orwell never equated fascism or Nazism with either socialism or communism. In 1936 he observed that, in reading Marxist literary criticism, 'even a quite intelligent outsider can be taken in by the vulgar lie, now so popular, that "Communism and Fascism are the same thing"' (i. 291). He saw German fascism as 'a form of capitalism that borrows from Socialism just such features as will make it efficient for war purposes' (ii. 101), and drew a basic distinction:

> the idea underlying Fascism is irreconcilably different from that which underlies Socialism. Socialism aims, ultimately, at a world-state of free and equal human beings. It takes the equality of human beings for granted. Nazism assumes just the opposite. The driving force behind the Nazi movement is the belief in human *inequality*, the superiority of Germans to all other races, the right of Germany to rule the world. (ii. 102)

For Orwell, Stalinism was the betrayal of an ideal, Nazism the fulfilment of one. In 1937 he warned: 'Fascism after all is only a development of capitalism, and the mildest democracy, so-called, is liable to turn into Fascism when the pinch comes' (i. 318). The next year he joined the Independent Labour Party and gave his reasons: 'It is not possible for any thinking person to live in such a society as our own without wanting to change it.... One has got to be actively a Socialist, not merely sympathetic to Socialism' (i. 374).

The tendency to equate the sceptical Benjamin with Orwell therefore looks odd, until one notices that it is Benjamin who untypically comes galloping, braying at the top of his lungs, 'Come at once! They're taking Boxer away!' and that, as the animals stupidly wave goodbye to Boxer in the van, it is Benjamin who shouts: 'Fools! Do you not see what is written on the side of that van? ... Do you not understand what that means? They are taking Boxer to the knacker's!' (pp. 81–2). The scene echoes the GPU's abduction of Trotsky, related by his wife: 'I shouted to the men who were carrying Lev D[avidovitch] down the stairs and demanded that they let out my sons, the elder of whom was to accompany us into exile.... On the way down the stairs, Lvova rang all the door-bells, shouting: "They're carrying Comrade Trotsky away!"'[15] Internally, however, what matters is that Benjamin tells the animals what they cannot 'read' for themselves, *as the author/narrator has been doing for us*. By usurping authorial function, Benjamin suddenly *becomes* the author—not by prudently keeping silent, but by placing sympathy before safety. He becomes 'Orwell' when, through him, the 'author' suddenly seems to drop his mask and show where his heart lies.

In portraying Stalinist betrayal, in fact, Orwell implicitly arraigns capitalism as well. Timothy Cook first remarked in print that Boxer's motto 'I will work harder' echoes that of the immigrant 'workhorse' Jurgis in Upton Sinclair's exposure of the Chicago meat-packing industry in *The Jungle* (1906).[16] The echo is probably deliberate—Orwell once praised Sinclair's factual accuracy (i. 262)—but it is too simple to say, as Cook does, that *Animal Farm* is an 'answer to the hopeful message'[17] of Sinclair's book, to which Jurgis listens only after the work accident that—analogously to Boxer's physical decline—puts him on the capitalist scrap-heap. Cook skips Sinclair's most sensational revelation: the processing for sale as lard of workers who fell into the rendering vats—a cannibalistic touch paralleled in *Animal Farm* when the pigs buy a case of whisky with the money they get for Boxer, who fulfils Major's prediction that *Jones* will one day sell him to the knacker's. Boxer's fate, in other words, isn't specific to the USSR. Far from refuting socialism, *Animal Farm* shows that totalitarianism in socialist clothing ends in the very evils of capitalism that led Orwell in 1941 to consider socialism inevitable: 'The inefficiency of private capitalism has been proved all over Europe. Its injustice has been proved in the East End of London' (ii. 117). *After* writing *Animal Farm* he called capitalism 'doomed' and 'not worth saving anyway' (iii. 266).

What Orwell discredited was not socialism but its sham: genuine progress, he believed, 'can only happen through increasing enlightenment, which means the continuous destruction of myths' (iv. 56). This has been the writer's task since Aristophanes, and in the 1940s it was not confined to exposing Russian communism. When, in 1949, Arthur Miller's naive free-enterprise idealist Willy Loman, sacked after thirty-four years by his former boss's son, belatedly discovered an unmarketable value—'You can't eat an orange and throw the peel away—a man is not a piece of fruit!'—Miller effectively demythologized his own country's economic system. Decades later he recalled how Columbia Pictures first weakened the movie *Death of a Salesman*, then asked him to issue an anti-communist publicity statement and preface the film by interviews praising selling as a profession.[18] On the other side of the ideological divide British publishers, kowtowing to left-wing readers and a wartime ally, similarly rejected *Animal Farm*. Orwell's proposed preface was prescient:

> For all I know, by the time this book is published my view of the Soviet regime may be the generally-accepted one. But what use would that be in itself? To exchange one orthodoxy for another is not necessarily an advance. The enemy is the gramophone mind, whether or not one agrees with the record that is being played at the moment. (p. 106)

At the closing banquet Soviet tyranny mirrors its capitalist counterpart. Orwell claimed, however, that he meant to end not with a 'complete reconciliation of the pigs and the humans', but on 'a loud note of discord', 'for I wrote it immediately after the Teheran Conference which everybody thought had established the best possible relations between the USSR and the West. I personally did not believe that such good relations would last long; and, as events have shown, I wasn't far wrong' (p. 113). But if the banquet parodies Teheran, the shot that goes home is Pilkington's solidarity with Animal Farm's proprietors in extracting more work for less food than any other farmer in the country: 'If you have your lower animals to contend with ... we have our lower classes!' (p. 92). Whom 'we' stood for, Orwell made clear in 1942:

> The war has brought the class nature of their society very sharply home to English people, in two ways. First of all there is the unmistakable fact that all real power depends on class privilege. You can only get certain jobs if you have been to one of the right schools, and if you fail and have to be sacked, then somebody

else from one of the right schools takes over, and so it continues. This may go unnoticed when things are prospering, but becomes obvious in moments of disaster. (ii. 241)

Asked if he had intended a statement about revolution in general, Orwell said that he had meant that

> *that kind* of revolution (violent conspiratorial revolution, led by unconsciously power-hungry people) can only lead to a change of masters. I meant the moral to be that revolutions only effect a radical improvement when the masses are alert and know how to chuck out their leaders as soon as the latter have done their job. The turning-point of the story was supposed to be when the pigs kept the milk and apples for themselves (Kronstadt). If the other animals had had the sense to put their foot down then, it would have been all right.... In the case of the Trotskyists ... they feel responsible for the events in the USSR up to about 1926 and have to assume that a sudden degeneration took place about that date, whereas I think the whole process was foreseeable—and was foreseen by a few people, e.g. Bertrand Russell—from the very nature of the Bolshevik party. What I was trying to say was, 'You can't have a revolution unless you make it for yourself; there is no such thing as a benevolent dictatorship.'[19]

So much for Eliot's dismissal of the 'positive point of view' in *Animal Farm* as 'generally Trotskyite'.[20] Yet Orwell's own exegesis is uneasy, since the initial revolt, despite indoctrination by the pigs, is not conspiratorial but spontaneous. It also begs vital questions. How *can* revolution be achieved? How should the 'masses' 'chuck out' leaders who have seized power? Lenin hoped—reckoning without Stalin—that education and mass participation would naturally follow a violent conspiratorial revolution—for him the only kind feasible. Similarly, Orwell assumed in 1940 that revolution would come automatically through winning the war, but later saw he had 'underrated the enormous strength of the forces of reaction' (iii. 339). He continued to back Russia 'because I think the U.S.S.R. cannot altogether escape its past and retains enough of the original ideas of the Revolution to make it a more hopeful phenomenon than Nazi Germany' (iii. 178), but he nailed the root cause of revolutionary failure:

> Throughout history, one revolution after another ... has simply led to a change of masters, because no serious effort has been

made to eliminate the power instinct.... In the minds of active revolutionaries, at any rate the ones who 'got there', the longing for a just society has always been fatally mixed up with the intention to secure power for themselves. (iv. 36)

In this light, Eliot's cavil, 'after all, your pigs are far more intelligent than the other animals, and therefore the best qualified to run the farm ... so that what was needed (someone might argue) was not more communism but more public-spirited pigs',[21] looks cagily facetious. What was needed (someone might reply) was, precisely, real implementation of the ideal perverted by the self-serving pigs—something Eliot, with his personal investment in religious conservatism, would hardly have approved. Even Empson's objection that the Revolution appeared foredoomed is redundant: Orwell knew that 'all the seeds of evil were there from the start' (iv. 35). The depth of his disillusion is nevertheless a measure of his sympathy with the hopes betrayed. Fearing a sell-out of socialism by those waving its flag at home, he chose the Independent Labour Party because it alone provided 'the certainty that I would never be led up the garden path in the name of capitalist democracy' (i. 375). When Attlee took over in 1945 Orwell was on his guard: 'A Labour government may be said to mean business if it (a) nationalizes land, coal mines, railways, public utilities and banks, (b) offers India immediate Dominion Status (this is a minimum), and (c) purges the bureaucracy, the army, the diplomatic service, etc., so thoroughly as to forestall sabotage from the Right' (iii. 448). He faced the dilemma: 'Capitalism leads to dole queues, the scramble for markets, and war. Collectivism leads to concentration camps, leader worship, and war. There is no way out of this unless a planned economy can be somehow combined with the freedom of the intellect, which can only happen if the concept of right and wrong is restored to politics' (iii. 144). Yet he scorned the flattering unction of 'neo-pessimists': 'Men cannot be made better by act of Parliament; therefore I may as well go on drawing my dividends' (iii. 82). His answer was to 'dissociate Socialism from Utopianism' (iii. 83) and seek progress through failure itself: 'Perhaps some degree of suffering is ineradicable from human life, perhaps the choice before man is always a choice of evils, perhaps even the aim of Socialism is not to make the world perfect but to make it better. All revolutions are failures, but they are not all the same failure' (iii. 282).

III

None of this philosophy comes across in *Animal Farm*. In fact, Eliot's red herring highlights a troubling correlation. 'Class' in *Animal Farm*—unlike in England—is determined by *native* intelligence. It is 'the more intelligent animals' (p. 9) whose outlook is transformed by Major's speech. The pigs rule by brainpower ('The other animals understood how to vote, but could never think of any resolutions of their own' (p. 19)). Except for the author's alter ego Benjamin, the pigs alone learn to read perfectly. On the other hand, the noble, selfless Boxer, who has 'no wish to take life, not even human life' (p. 28), is of 'stupid appearance' and 'not of first-rate intelligence' (p. 2). It is hard not to suspect that it is *because* he is stupid—that he is good; that power-hunger *must* accompany intelligence—unless checked by an instinct of self-preservation (Benjamin, who can read as well as any pig, wisely abstains from doing so). Intelligence—aiming at power, safety, or animal comforts—itself becomes a satirical target. The Rebellion is at first beneficial (a detail professional anti-communists naturally ignored). The fault lies not in the theory but in the theorists. In the passage Orwell deemed crucial, the clever pigs, including both Napoleon and Snowball, privatize the milk and apples instead of sharing them out equally, arguing that they are brain workers and that Science has proved milk and apples necessary for their well-being, without which Jones will come again. A new class system is born based on *biological* inequality, its commandments issued not by the sugar-candy religion of the preaching raven Moses, but by the intellectual religion of Science (Lenin's 'scientific socialism'). As their pilfered privileges coalesce, the pigs learn to walk on their hind legs, and accordingly teach the sheep to chant, 'Four legs good—two legs better', thereby hypostatizing managerial function into ruling-class status. The last altered commandment on the barn wall—that new English proverb 'All animals are equal, but some are more equal than others'—may come from *Paradise Lost*, when Eve decides that hiding her ill-gotten knowledge from Adam will render her 'more equal, and perhaps / A thing not undesirable, sometime Superior' (a professed aim of *removing* inequality masks a desire to *reverse* it). Crick cites Orwell's claim to have discovered 'the joy of mere words'[22] reading *Paradise Lost* at Eton, and the attribution is apposite both to lost paradises and to intellectual power-seeking: it is the clever animals who become 'more equal'.

This exaltation of brainwork follows allegorical logic rather than Soviet dogma. 'Even the most stubborn among the "intellectuals"', Litvinov predicted in 1918, 'will soon learn that, after all, the people is a much better master than the capitalist, and that a Socialist regime is likely to render them more happy than a bourgeois regime.'[23] *Animal Farm*, however, inverts Hobbes's apology for absolutism: it is not equality of faculties that fosters dangerous 'equality of hope'[24] but equality of hope that founders on unequal faculties. Empson saw the paradox:

> the effect of the farmyard, with its unescapable racial differences, is to suggest that the Russian scene had unescapable social differences too—so the metaphor suggests that the Russian revolution was always a pathetically impossible attempt.... the pigs can turn into men, but the story is far from making one feel that any of the other animals could have turned into men ...[25]

The implication is probably the last thing Orwell intended: he, if anyone, knew that nothing suits a ruling class better than a genetic alibi. Rather, he meant that animalkind's dream of equality founders because the very brains needed to achieve it demand superior status: the power of reason becomes the reason of power.

Stressing the pigs' cleverness may have been a swipe at British intellectuals, who alone accepted the 'ruthless ideologies of the Continent' and formed an 'island of bigotry amid the general vagueness' (iii. 31). In 1940 Orwell noted, 'The thing that frightens me about the modern intelligentsia is their inability to see that human society must be based on common decency, whatever the political and economic forms may be.' His 'chief hope' was the ordinary person's moral code: 'I have never had the slightest fear of a dictatorship of the proletariat.... But I admit to having a perfect horror of a dictatorship of theorists' (i. 582–3). After writing *Animal Farm* he called British intellectuals 'more totalitarian-minded than the common people' (iii. 143) and observed: 'In our country ... it is the liberals who fear liberty and the intellectuals who want to do dirt on the intellect' (p. 107).

The pigs' intellect, however, may also reflect a historical scruple. Orwell admitted that his knowledge of Russia consisted 'only of what can be learned by reading books and newspapers' (p. 111). One book he mentions respectfully, John Reed's *Ten Days That Shook the World* (p. 170), mirrors the paradox of *Animal Farm*. Reed, also anti-intellectual but on other grounds, insists that the revolution was made by the masses; that the Bolsheviks were 'not rich in trained and educated men'.[26] He identifies 'intellectuals' with the provisional government, citing a young woman's sneer at soldiers and workmen arriving at the Congress of Soviets: 'See how rough and ignorant they look!'[27] When an anarchist calls the Bolsheviks 'common, rude, ignorant persons, without aesthetic sensibilities', Reed snorts: 'He was a real specimen of the Russian *intelligentsia*'. Yet, paradoxically, he hails 'great Lenin' as 'a leader purely by virtue of intellect; colourless, humourless, uncompromising and detached, without picturesque idiosyncrasies—but with the power of explaining profound ideas in simple terms, of analysing a concrete situation. And combined with shrewdness, the greatest intellectual audacity.'[28]

This kind of thing baffled British journalists. E. H. Wilson complained that Lenin frequently introduced 'political and economic conceptions which can hardly be intelligible to untrained minds'. Philips Price recalled him unflatteringly as 'a short man with a round head, small pig-like eyes, and close-cropped hair.... One sat spellbound at his command of language and the passion of his denunciation. But when it was all over one felt inclined to scratch one's head and wonder what it was all about.'[29] Robert Bruce Lockhart, in *Memoirs of a British Agent*, learned to respect Lenin's 'intellectual capacity', but at first was more impressed by 'his tremendous will-power, his relentless determination, and his lack of emotion. He furnished a complete antithesis to Trotsky.... Trotsky was a great organiser and a man of immense physical courage. But, morally, he was as incapable of standing against Lenin as a flea would be against an elephant.'[30]

Orwell's view of Lenin was hypothetical. In 1944 he generalized that 'all efforts to regenerate society by *violent means* lead to the cellars of the O.G.P.U. Lenin leads to Stalin, and would have come to resemble Stalin if he had happened to survive' (iii. 278). In 1946 he coupled Lenin with Cromwell as 'one of those politicians who win an undeserved reputation by dying prematurely. Had he lived, it is probable that he would either have been thrown out, like Trotsky,[31] or would have kept himself in power by methods as barbarous, or nearly as barbarous, as those of Stalin' (iv. 200–1). This does not, nevertheless, make Napoleon a composite. Although Lockhart's simile fits Snowball and Napoleon, the latter prevails not by intellectual and moral ascendancy—no pig matches Lenin there—but by self-seeking cunning. Orwell specified his target by altering his text to Napoleon's advantage when the windmill is blown up, to be 'fair to J[oseph] S[talin], as he did stay in Moscow during the German advance' (iii. 407). If he bent over backwards to be fair to a 'disgusting murderer' (ii. 461), he might have felt a qualm in parodying the Revolution minus its mastermind. The clever pigs would make amends: if 'the symmetry of the story' (p. 113) meant leaving Lenin out, his distinguishing mark, at least, could be left in.

IV

In any case, Orwell was bound by the form he used, one responsible both for the contradictions of *Animal Farm* and for its permanent appeal. Initially, he described it as 'a kind of parable'.[32] A parable makes a point, not fine distinctions, and a fable is also limited.[33] It may be because Orwell felt constricted by the parable form that he redefined his book as 'a little fairy story ... with a political meaning'[34] and finally subtitled it 'A Fairy Story'.

The misnomer merits attention. *Animal Farm* has none of the fairies, princes, witches, spells, magic transformations, or happy endings associated with the 'fairy story'.[35] Once the metaphor is established, the rest is history. In fact, *Animal Farm* has been called a 'fable', defined as a 'brief, single episode' in which speaking animals, plants, objects, and humans metaphorically illustrate and satirize human conduct, although 'in practice it is occasionally rendered in terms of other generic forms: for instance as märchen [folk tales] (e.g. "Little Red Riding Hood")'.[36] Chesterton more acutely compared persons in a fable to algebraic abstractions or chess pieces, whereas the fairy tale

> absolutely revolves on the pivot of human personality. If no hero were there to fight the dragons, we should not even know that they were dragons.... If there is no personal prince to find the Sleeping Beauty, she will simply sleep. Fables repose on quite the opposite idea; that everything is itself, and will in any case speak for itself. The wolf will always be wolfish; the fox will always be foxy.[37]

Animal Farm spans both genres: the sheep remain sheep; the dogs, dogs; the cat, a cat; but the pigs, horses, and donkey all display elements of 'human personality', although Benjamin's world-pessimism goes back to Æsop's fable 'The Oxen and the Butchers', in which an old ox stops his brothers from rising against the butchers, arguing that they at least cause no needless pain, but that, if they are killed, inexperienced slaughterers will replace them and inflict greater suffering: 'For you may be sure that, even though all the Butchers perish, mankind will never go without their beef.'[38] 'Fairy tale' of course may simply signify fantasy, but this hardly fits *Animal Farm*, which derives its authority precisely from historical events that are in turn illuminated by it. The subtitle points, therefore, to a parodic impulse, like that which the Teheran conference inspired. But why parody a 'fairy story' for 'political' purposes?

The answer may again lie in the springs of Orwell's inspiration. In his preface to the Ukrainian edition he mentions having seen a carthorse whipped and thinking that 'men exploit animals in much the same way as the rich exploit the proletariat' (p. 112), but this skirts the issue.[39] Other suggested 'sources' are equally unconvincing.[40] The parodic mode is more fertile. Parodies of magic tales go back to their inception, and fables have also been parodied,[41] but Charles Dickens provided the precedent of fairy-tale parody at one remove. When George Cruikshank 'altered the text of a fairy Story' to propagate 'doctrines of Total Abstinence, Prohibition of the sale of spirituous liquors, Free Trade, and Popular Education',[42] Dickens vowed:

Half playfully & half seriously I mean to protest most strongly against alteration)—for any purpose—of the beautiful little stories which are so tenderly & humanly useful to us in these times when the world is too much with us, early & late; and then to re-write Cinderella according to Total-abstinence, Peace Society, and Bloomer principles, and especially for their propagation.[43]

Dickens kept his word. In 'Frauds on the Fairies' he denounced 'the intrusion of a Whole Hog of unwieldy dimensions into the fairy flower garden',[44] adding a moralistic parody of 'Cinderella'. The same year he used fairy-tale imagery in *Hard Times* to attack education aimed solely at grooming the poor to serve the rich.[45]

Orwell may well have known 'Frauds on the Fairies'. During a five-month sanatorium cure in 1938 he kept Dickens's collected works in his room.[46] In 1947 he himself contemplated a BBC version of 'Cinderella', calling it 'the tops so far as fairy tales go but ... too visual to be suitable for the air'. He imagined Cinderella as a wonderful singer unable to sing in tune (not a bad self-parody), and a godmother who cures her: 'One could make it quite comic with the wicked sisters singing in screeching voices' (iv. 318–19). Orwell's parodic idea sprang from technical necessities, but he knew that pastiche 'usually implies a real affection for the thing parodied' (iii. 193). Dickens parodied an *abuse* of the fairy tale.

During the 1920s and 1930s children's stories in the Weimar Republic, the United States, and, to a lesser extent, England were again altered by a 'proletarian' or 'left-wing' slant to counter classic fairy tales seen as a tool of bourgeois socialization.[47] Orwell at first thought of participating. In May 1940, after denouncing right-wing bias in boys' stories, he wrote to Robert Geoffrey Trease (author of a left-wing version of Robin Hood): 'this matter of intelligent fiction for kids is very important and I believe the time is approaching when it might be possible to do something about it'. Orwell, Trease recalled, had in mind

some Leftish juvenile publishing scheme, pink in shade, perhaps backed by the T.U.C. or the Liberal *News Chronicle*. Not having read *Homage to Catalonia*, and being unaware of his disenchantment with the official Communist line, I did not fully appreciate his quip that, if Laurence and Wishart [Trease's left-wing publishers] did it, they would want books like 'boys of the Ogpu' or 'The Young Liquidators.'

Later Trease realized that 'perhaps Orwell's quip had helped—that false history from the Right should not be countered with false history from the Left'.[48]

Whether Orwell feared that left-wing boys' stories would turn out like the communist tract quoted in his 'Boys' Weeklies' essay (i. 529), or whether he was chastened by Frank Richards's robust reply (i. 531–40),[49] he dropped the idea and instead pursued his interest in children's literature by adapting Andersen's 'The Emperor's New Clothes' for the BBC in November 1943, just before he set out to counter 'false history from the Left' by stripping the USSR of its emperor's clothes in *Animal Farm*.

In doing so, he may have been partly reacting in a Dickensian way to left-wing children's stories. One I recall vividly from my own childhood was the title story of a booklet by Helen Kay (pseud. Helen Colodny Goldfrank) called *Battle in the Barnyard*.[50] The preface, 'To the Children of the Working Class', read:

Dear Comrades:

Once upon a time, a long long time ago, a book appeared called, 'Fairy Tales for Workers' Children.' But this was a long time ago, and the book has since run out of print.

Now, we are starting anew. I offer this book as a challenge—a challenge to every reader to write for 'Us Kids.'

These stories were penned when I was a 'Pioneer.' As a member of the Young Pioneers of America, I felt the need of such a children's book. Later, when I came to work with younger comrades, I even more clearly saw the demand for such stories.

Today, the Pioneer movement is growing.... Farmers' children and kids of unemployed parents are rapidly joining our ranks. We must furnish them with our literature. I am glad to make this start.

Several of these stories deal with real and living children. All tell of the class struggle. An older comrade told me some. Every one was written for you. I hope you'll like them.

Comradely yours,
Helen Kay

Kay's prototype was a collection of German 'proletarian' fairy tales by Hermynia Zur Mühlen, translated and published in Chicago by the Daily Worker Press in 1925,[51] and she saw herself as marching in the ranks of revolutionary history. (Note her claim to authority: 'An older comrade told me some'.) Paraphrase would not adequately convey the spirit of her story. I therefore give it in full:

Battle in the Barnyard

Out in the country where the fields are green and the sunshine is golden, an old farm stands between two groves of tall poplar trees. On this farm there lived at one time a happy colony of healthy chickens.

Now the yard where these chickens lived was filled with very fertile soil. The rich ground contained a plentiful amount of worms upon which the chickens lived. There were long skinny worms, short stubby worms, and big fat worms. There were as many kinds of worms as there are people. Besides worms a great variety of caterpillars and bugs helped these chicks lead a healthy well-nourished life.

In a corner of the yard where the chickens scratched away their time ran a refreshing spring. This spring was used by the chickens to quench their parched throats in the hot summer days.

Many a happy day was passed by these roosters and hens. The chickens would rise with the sun, scratch for worms, drink water from the spring, cackling and crowing merrily all the while. The hens would lay eggs—and then tell the world about it in delight.

'Cut-cut-cut-ca-deh-cut!' they would cry. Just as if they were trying to say, 'I've laid an egg, the loveliest white egg!'

The little downy chicks would play tag and leapfrog between their eating times, to while away the time until they in turn would grow up and become hens and roosters.

The cocks would strut about the farm in their conceited manner, crowing and asking the world if it had not noticed their handsome plumage. 'Cock-a-doodle-do!' 'Am I not a handsome bird. Am I not. Am I not!'

Then at the setting of the sun the chicken farm would become dark and silent—closed in the embrace of slumber.

On this farm, however, there was one very sly ugly rooster, who had lost most of his fine feathers in his quarrels and fights with the other more sociable inmates of the farm. He would always take advantage of the young chicks. Being a very lazy fellow he would try to get out of doing his own scratching for worms.

For instance, when a younger cock would dig up a dainty morsel from the rich loam, such as a lively young earthworm, this ugly monster would immediately pounce upon his comrade's dinner and gobble it all up. Yes, every single bit of it. This nasty habit made him very much hated by all the others on the farm.

One day the entire colony was amazed. They were in fact so astonished at the sight before their eyes that words actually failed them. Even some of the more talkative hens who always had something to cackle about, couldn't find their tongues.

Dear little comrades, it actually was an unusual sight, for there before their eyes, they saw for the first time this nasty rooster scratching away for worms! But what surprised them even more was that this greedy creature did not eat the worms he unearthed. He put them away. As many worms as he dug up he would lay in a pile on the ground.

The inhabitants of the colony became nervous. Such a state of affairs was impossible. They were unable to understand it. Something had to be done about it.

One evening at the setting of the sun, a huge mass meeting was called. It was advertised far and wide by the young cocks, who would perch themselves on high fences and, flapping their wings, would crow the order for the meeting.

At this gathering the rooster was asked by the patriarchs and industrious hens of the colony, what the meaning of the huge pile of worms meant [sic].

The rooster promptly answered. 'Here, I have a huge pile of tasty bugs, caterpillars [sic], and worms ...' He paused cleverly to let the audience take in the sight. 'If you will give me the corner of this yard where the spring runs—and allow me to keep it all to myself—I will give you in return that huge pile of food.'

Without further thought the chicken community decided to do as the rooster bargained. His food was evenly divided among all the members of the village and in return he received that section of the yard where the cool spring ran.

The chickens gossiped among themselves—telling each other how stupid the old rooster was to desire that bit of land in return for the delicious pile of eatables. After an hour or so everyone retired for the night. The sun set and the farm was dark and silent.

The next morning the chickens arose as usual. The sun was up and shining brightly. The day became very hot and uncomfortable. The inmates of the farm grew very thirsty and as was their habit they strolled over to the spring to quench their thirst. However, as they came within reach of the precious water, the mean rooster arose and said:

> 'Cock-a-doodle-do!
> This spring does not belong to you.
> It's mine, you cannot drink here!'

The thirsty chickens exclaimed, 'What do you mean, yours! It is everyone's.'

The cock immediately answered, 'Didn't you sell it to me yesterday in return for the food that you have already eaten.'

A young rebellious cock cried out, 'But we are thirsty. You cannot keep the water from us. We wish to drink.'

The rooster replied, 'For ever drink of water that you take out of my spring, I will in return take two worms!'

Since the chickens were very thirsty they consented to this arrangement.

The pile of worms which the old miserly cock reaped from the toil of the chickens began to grow by leaps and bounds. As a matter of fact it grew so large that he alone could not care for it. So he hired ten of the strongest young roosters on the farm to be his policemen.

Their job was to take care of and to protect his hoard of worms. In return, he promised to give them enough water and food to live on, no more nor no less. No less—because he had to have strong husky well-nourished policemen to take care of and guard the surplus that he now lived upon. He would give them no more—because this wicked rooster wanted more and more for himself.

This state of affairs went on for a long time. The chicken colony lost its usual happy satisfied expression. They did not crow as joyously as they did before. The young chickens were afraid to be merry. They were underfed and undernourished. They could no longer play without fear of disturbing the selfish cock. The hens could no longer lay good eggs, because they lacked food, and entertainment. They now had to labor from sunrise to sunset so that they could have enough food to live on, and enough food to give to the cruel rooster in return for the water that they so badly needed.

The chicks who were born during this period were generally not strong enough to live. Most of them died and the tragic part was that those who did survive took the condition that now existed for granted. They thought it was impossible to live any other way.

On the other hand the rooster grew bigger and fatter. His daughter also grew bigger and fatter. Neither had to work. They merely ate and played all day. They lived off the toil and sweat of their fellow chicks.

Now, on the farm there was a duck, a very handsome graceful duck. He would waddle and quack all through the chicken farm. One day the rooster decided to marry his daughter to the duck, in order that she would become a duchess, and so be one of the nobility.

The rooster went up to the duck and said, 'If you marry my daughter, and so make her a duchess, I will give you a share of my grounds and make you a partner in my food association. You will not have to scratch for your worms, but will live off the worms that the other chickens scratch up. You will lead a life of luxury and play, if you do this.'

The duck agreed. And so they were married. They had little aristocratic duck-chicks born to lead lives of idleness.

One day one of the roosters was tired of feeding the mean cock, and going hungry himself. He ran up single handed to the old miser and started to fight him. Of course, he was immediately killed by the police. This incident added to the suffering and to the downtrodden conditions of the other chickens. But they always remembered the brave young cock.

Soon after this occurred, the ugly miser got another idea. He called over some more chickens. He told them that he would pay them more than the policeman if they would act as preachers.

'Your duty,' he said, 'is to tell the chickens to be submissive and obey me, the apostle of the lord in the heavens above. If they are submissive and do everything I and my family order them to do, when they die they will go to heaven, and there lead happy lives. But, if they rebel they will go down to the fires of hell and burn forever. The harder they work here on earth, the better time they will have in heaven.'

As time went on the chickens slaved harder and harder, and the rooster grew richer and richer. They began to believe whatever the preacher chickens told them. They thought that conditions must always be as they are. That the greater amount of chickens should be poor and that a privileged few must live off the wealth that the poor chickens scratched up.

One young and energetic cock who was deeply impressed by all the goings on, began to think. He thought and planned, and others helped him. Then they all decided that the only way to save the chickens of the farm, and themselves, from endless slavery was by driving out the selfish rooster, his daughter, the duchess, her husband, the duck, and the aristocratic duck-chicks, also their protectors, the policemen, and especially the preachers.

Secret leaflets were printed and spread over the colony for the chickens to read and to learn the truth. Huge mass meetings were called and the exploited chicks were organized into battalions to drive out their oppressors.

The chicken colony was in a state of excitement. If they won the battle they would again be free chickens. If they lost—no one wanted to think of that. They must win. And dear little comrades, they did win. They certainly were victorious. They drove the old rooster and his protectors out of their lives forever. The mean cock and his lazy good-for-nothing family were killed. The preachers and policemen fled from the farm. No one has ever heard of them since. Perhaps the wolves ate them.

Now in the summer when the fields are green and the sunshine is golden in the country you can see the hens happily laying eggs, and the other chickens scratching away for worms. They have learned their lesson, and never again will anyone be able to trick them into slavery. The little chicks play tag and leap-frog in their merry way. You can hear them go 'Peep-peep-peep!' The roosters strut around the farm and crow, 'Cock-a-doodle-do!' The hens cry, 'Cluck-cluck-cluck!' They are all contented and equal.

As far as I know, the only extant copy of Kay's booklet is in Harvard's Wiedner Library. A student of mine[52] traced it for me twenty-five years ago: other libraries, he said, had 'removed' it during Senator Joe McCarthy's inquisition. On a fall evening in 1995 I visited the Wiedner and asked to see it. A guard, happily waiving the rules, took me down to the stacks, and there it was, its soft brown and buff cover as I had last seen it well over half a century before in the guest lounge of a holiday camp patronized by skilled low-paid workers. It was then (like myself) nine or ten years old, but still circulating. Like Combray from a teacup, a bygone hopeful ethos rose before my mental vision as I leafed through Kay's stories—'Bread', 'High Hat Ants',

'Strike Secret'—and saw what had worried librarians. In one story, 'Us Alley Kids', black and white children defying Jim Crow organized the poor of both races against exploitation: a threat that nearly materialized thirty years later in the last, 'integrated' march Martin Luther King was planning at the time he was murdered. By then Workers Library Publishers was long extinct.[53] Today, the premise of *Battle in the Barnyard* is obsolete. As a *Financial Times* journalist sanguinely remarked: 'Long considered a basic right, water is now being looked at as a good investment.'[54] The word 'Comrade' (which Orwell thought put people off socialism) needn't be banned, as it finally is on Animal Farm, for there is little risk of its use between members of contending national, religious, ethnic, linguistic, or sexual interest groups. In the new Russia the Song of the Volga Businessman proclaims the blessings brought to workers and pensioners by Soviet apparatchiks, turned freebooting capitalists—giving Orwell's ending a prophetic resonance missing from Kay's.[55]

Yet, despite such progress, few 'great books' I have read since childhood have left me with as vivid a memory as Kay's, down to the cover drawing of the rout of the miserly rooster and his clan. That fact seems to me relevant to the enduring power of *Animal Farm*. The secret of Kay's impact on me as a child lay not in content but in form. Max Frisch once ascribed the peculiar force of marionettes to the fact that, unlike actors, they don't have to 'make believe', but are bodied forth as naked creations of the spirit.[56] Animals representing humans operate similarly.[57] Like 'Battle in the Barnyard', *Animal Farm* gains force from elements of the fable and the magic folk tale while corresponding strictly to neither. Orwell's story structurally mirrors Kay's. Kay's idyllic prelude closed by a peaceful night's slumber precedes the insidious rise of a selfish capitalist tyrant, ultimately provoking conspiratorial revolt and a return to the idyllic status quo ante. Orwell's parodic utopian prelude is also followed by a peaceful night's sleep, but then by conspiracy and a rebellion paving the way for the insidious rise of a collectivist, ideological tyrant and even more hopeless oppression. Kay fares less well than Orwell in fusing artistic and political purpose. Beneath the communist catchwords, her nostalgia for a happy state of nature is closer to Rousseau than to Marx or Lenin, far from the open-ended stories of Zur Mühlen, whom she claimed as a model.[58] Nevertheless, the kinship between Orwell's story and Kay's is obvious: the collective protagonist, the gradual habituation to oppression, the word 'Comrade' used seductively by Kay, ironically by Orwell, and the calculated slippage from symbolic to direct statement (having established the young roosters as the miser's policemen Kay can say that the hungry rooster was 'killed by the police'; Orwell, after having Napoleon's dogs rip out the young pigs' throats in a metaphor conveying forced confession and execution, can credit Napoleon with the cry 'Death to humanity'). Both stories use preachers and private police, Orwell's more subtly. When Napoleon's private army of dogs wag their tails to their master, they remind us that a dog is Man's best friend. And when the preaching raven Moses, initially chased off the farm, later reappears, the pigs tolerate him, even giving him a daily gill of beer, as if to say 'Stick around, you may be needed.' This has been taken to symbolize Stalin's wartime entente with the Orthodox Church; more generally it reflects the potential convenience of religion to dictators (Hitler viewed his concordat with the Catholic Church as propitious for his war on Jews).[59] Finally, if Orwell and Kay both play on words, Kay's duck-duchess and hens that 'always had something to cackle about' seem frivolous, whereas Orwell's ham-burial has dramatic point. In both stories the key word is 'equal', but Orwell's turns it upside down.

V

Despite, or because of, their differences, the family likeness between Kay's story and Orwell's makes *Animal Farm* look like *literary* parody. Was parody intended? In 1946 Orwell recognized, 'I am not able, and I do not want, completely to abandon the world-view that I acquired in childhood' (i. 28). Magic tales, although escapist, were part of that world-view. In 1947, while contemplating a parody of 'Cinderella' and hoping for a re-broadcast of 'The Emperor's New Clothes', Orwell agreed to adapt 'Little Red Riding Hood' for the BBC's *Children's Hour*. Like Dickens, he would probably have resented the abuse of fairy tales for propaganda, which he detested.[60] With his penchant for parody, he might well have regarded *Animal Farm*, once written, as a pastiche of left-wing children's literature.

Whether he intended it as such is more conjectural. There is no evidence that he knew of Kay or Zur Mühlen, whose stories were not published in England. On the other hand, for an omnivorous reader with cosmopolitan left-wing contacts[61] and a special interest in 'proletarian' literature and ephemeral writing—who had worked in 1934–5 in a Hampstead second-hand bookshop doing 'a good deal of business in children's books ... rather horrible things' (i. 274),—nothing can be quite ruled out. In any case Orwell could have seen a mild strain of left-wing children's literature in the Cooperative Union's 'Cooperative Books for Young People': 'fairy plays' and stories—envisaging factories where no worker was ever sacked owing to bad trade.[62] In 1937, the year in which Orwell said he first thought of *Animal Farm*, Gollancz's Left Book Club published both *The Road to Wigan Pier* and a left-wing children's book, *The Adventures of the Little Pig and Other Stories* by F. Le Gros and Ida Clark.[63] Gollancz may have planted a seed.[64]

Orwell's political opinions were, besides, hardly original. Some had been inscribed in literary history by that versatile *femme de lettres* and nostalgic historian of rural manners George Sand during the revolution of 1848. Privately, Sand declared herself communist

> as people were Christian in the year 50 of our era. For me it is the ideal of advancing "societies, the religion that will live a few centuries hence. Thus I cannot be tied by any of the present communist formulas, since all are rather dictatorial and think they can be set up without the aid of morals, habits and convictions. No religion is established by force.

Publicly, she denounced elections organized in May 1848 against 'chimerical communists':

> If by communism you mean a conspiracy ready to try a grab for dictatorship ... we are not communists.... But if, by communism, you mean the desire and the will that, by all means lawful and admitted by the public conscience, the revolting inequality of extreme wealth and extreme poverty should hereby vanish to make way for the start of true equality, yes, we are communists and dare to tell you so.[65]

Like Orwell, she wanted a revolution preserving 'common decency'.

Nor was Orwell alone on the left in condemning Russian communists. Whatever the seeds of *Animal Farm* they were encouraged to sprout by an anarchist pamphlet in his collection: *The Russian Myth*.[66] Although George Woodcock caught him out on the title, Orwell called it 'a terrific and very able anti-Soviet pamphlet' (ii. 210, 259). The cover read:

> To Communists and others, criticism of the Russian political and economic system is taboo. According to them, to criticise is to betray the 'Worker's State' and play into the hands of the capitalist class.
>
> But in this pamphlet we ask the question: is Russia a Socialist country? ...
>
> If we define a Socialist State or Country as one in which inequality is abolished and where economic and political freedom exist, then it can be conclusively shown that none of these pre-requisites exist in Russia today. By clinging to their illusions; by looking to the Russian regime as the goal of the British workers;

and by stubbornly refusing to face the facts, the Communist rank and file, however sincere they may be in their beliefs, are misleading the workers of this country.

The Russian Myth anticipated the premise of *Animal Farm*:

> Bolshevist tactics wherever they are applied will always lead not to the emancipation of the workers from the chains which now enslave them, nor even to the dictatorship of the proletariat. They lead inevitably to the absolute or totalitarian state. By allowing power over the instruments of production to pass out of their own hands into those of a so-called revolutionary government, the workers will achieve not liberty but a slavery as bad or worse than that they sought to escape from.[67]

It distinguished true socialism from what the Bolsheviks had established:

> The propagandists of Marxism ... urge *State* control of industry and agriculture as the aim of revolution. But Anarchists regards socialism as the *emancipation of the workers from all the forces which fetter free development....* To overthrow private capitalism only to enthrone State capitalism in its place will only appear progress to the blindest devotees of utopian gradualism.[68]

Three years earlier Orwell had asked, 'Is [Stalin's regime] Socialism, or is it a peculiarly vicious form of state-capitalism?' (i. 369). But he did not take the anarchist line that the call to defend the USSR 'made by the Communists, and echoed by Churchill and Roosevelt' was a call 'to defend the ruling clique in Russia':

> British and American imperialists have no interests in common with the soviet workers.... The only way to aid the Russian workers is to fight unremittingly the class struggle here in England. Similarly, revolutionary struggle alone provides the only means of destroying German Nazism and Fascism. Only by fighting for the world revolution can the workers everywhere achieve freedom from poverty, tyranny and wars ...[69]

In *1938* Orwell himself had called the slogan 'Guns before butter!' a dodge to deny wage rises: the workers real enemies were 'those who try to trick them into identifying their interests with those of their exploiters, and into forgetting what every manual worker inwardly knows—that modern war is a racket' (i. 368). But when the bombs came he put first things first. By 1940 he was 'attacking pacifism for all [he] was worth' (ii. 34), and in 1941 he noted: 'The most interesting development of the anti-war front has been the interpretation [*sic*—a misprint for 'interpenetration': see *Partisan Review*, 8/1 (March–April 1941), 109] of the pacifist movement by Fascist ideas, especially antisemitism' (ii. 69).

Orwell's moral force was his political independence: his denunciation, in windowpane-clear prose, of *both* private capitalism with its money-based class privilege *and* 'the shallow self-righteousness of the left-wing intelligentsia' (i. 587) holding up the train of the USSR's emperor's robes. Orwell's hatred of propaganda makes it all the more ironic that, within three years of his death, the CIA and the Foreign Office distributed doctored versions of his masterpiece. A cartoon film vetted by the CIA's Psychological Strategy Board suppressed the closing parallel between capitalist and porcine exploitation. In the CIA's happy ending a counter-revolution deposed the pigs.[70] The Foreign Office circulated a comic strip in which Old Major resembled Lenin.[71] That Orwell should have had his purpose tampered with in the name of the 'free world' to shield a system for which he saw 'manifestly no future' (iv. 429) is, of course, disgusting. Yet *Animal Farm* only half fulfilled that purpose, since the pathos of the failure of a specific revolution implies a general statement about the impossibility of *any* revolution. This derives not from latent conservatism or a sour change of political colours,[72] but from the very literary form that makes *Animal Farm* what Edmund Wilson once called 'long-range literature'. Preserving 'the symmetry of the story' meant synopsizing the oppression of the animals parodically and focusing on betrayal of their hopes *after* the Rebellion. Hence the final metamorphosis of the pigs may be read as just a parting shot at them, not necessarily as a backhander at capitalism as well. A serious account of hardships *before* the Rebellion, while still maintaining the link between organizing intelligence and ravenous power-hunger, would merely have divided the interest. But if, as the parable suggests, the alternative to private capitalism is 'Animalism', then better the devil you know. Orwell's conviction that capitalism was deservedly doomed was occulted by the design of *Animal Farm*, which, while raising it to the level of moral satire, simultaneously made it near-perfect material for propagandists of the status quo.

If literary form hindered Orwell's political purpose, it also confirmed the existence of literature stripped of theories. In declaring that he had no fear of a dictatorship of the proletariat but a 'perfect horror of a dictatorship of theorists' Orwell affirmed his faith both in the moral code of ordinary people and in literature. If the dominant theorists of his day have withered, others now proliferate. They suggest that, since words do not perfectly represent reality, they can mean whatever you choose, with the corollary that searching for objective truth (and backing arguments by evidence) is pointless. The only criterion of truth becomes power, with carte blanche to anyone who can wield it. Others theorize that, since reading and writing are conditioned by sex, critical standards should differ for male and female authors. Imagination, once used to transcend sexual barriers, is expected to raise them. In the political and economic sphere, theorists proclaim that civilization has reached its ultimate perfection in unfettered capitalism, as Hegel thought it had in the state, while others 'deconstruct' literature into an expression of Western racism and imperialism. The fairy tale is again a battlefield for political, sociological, and psychological theorists[73] heedless of the grim admission by a famous political exile whom Orwell read with interest: 'Theory is not a note which you can present at any moment to reality for payment.'[74]

Along with the stifling effect of totalitarianism on literature (ii. 163, iv. 88) one of Orwell's bugbears was the 'invasion of literature by politics' (iv. 464). Socialists had no monopoly of mental dishonesty. Rather,

> acceptance of any political discipline seems to be incompatible with literary integrity. This applies equally to movements like Pacifism and Personalism, which claim to be outside the ordinary political struggle. Indeed, the mere sound of words ending in -ism seems to bring the smell of propaganda. Group loyalties are necessary, and yet they are poisonous to literature, so long as literature is the product of individuals. (iv. 468)

Since both left and right have tried to annex *Animal Farm*, it is time literature put in its claim. Totalitarianism may seem less of a threat than in Orwell's day, but with a firm called 'Narration, Ltd' recruiting authors to write propaganda novels 'sponsored' by governments and companies,[75] the literary nature of *Animal Farm* needs affirming. Its political ambiguities are irresolvable, but its universal moral satire emerges more strongly as the USSR fades from memory. In China, where the Communist Party has pragmatically equated private entrepreneurs with workers as a 'productive force' in an effort to broaden its sociological base (as Orwell told socialists to do in *The Road to Wigan Pier*), *Animal Farm* is unlikely to be taken either as a redundant attack on a defunct USSR or as an endorsement of a capitalist status quo, but simply as a warning against power-seekers wielding the jargon of theory to establish tyranny.[76] To Orwell, who defined a real socialist as 'one who wishes ... to see tyranny overthrown',[77] this would have seemed a good symptom. In our theory-bemused West, however, the contradictions of *Animal Farm* may best be circumvented by reading it as literary counter-parody in the perennial struggle for the power to enchant. In his pastiche of a left-wing 'fairy story', Orwell fused artistic and political purpose to chase a twentieth-century Whole Hog out of the flower garden of children's literature.

Notes

1. Letter to G. Orwell, 24 Aug. 1945 (Orwell Archive). Quoted in B. Crick, *George Orwell: A Life* (London, 1982), 491–2. Empson's young son called *Animal Farm* 'very strong Tory propaganda'.

2. Ibid. 489.

3. See G. Woodcock, *The Crystal Spirit* (London, 1967), 158–9; Crick, *George Orwell*, 490.

4. Dwight Macdonald, quoted in V. C. Letemendia, 'Revolution on *Animal Farm*: Orwell's Neglected Commentary', in G. Holderness, B. Loughrey, and N. Yousaf (edd.), *George Orwell* (London, 1998), 24.

5. Volume and page numbers refer to *The Collected Essays, Journalism and Letters of George Orwell*, ed. S. Orwell and I. Angus, 4 vols. (Harmondsworth, 1970).

6. Letter to D. Macdonald, 5 Sep. 1944 (Yale). Quoted in M. Shelden, *Orwell: The Authorised Biography* (London, 1992), 405.

7. All references to *Animal Farm* and to Orwell's prefaces are to George Orwell, *Animal Farm: A Fairy Story*, ed. P. Davison (London, 2000), and the appendices to that edition.

8. Thomas Hobbes, *Leviathan* (Chicago, 1952), I. xiii (p. 85).

9. 'Jonathan Swift: An Imaginary Interview By George Orwell', in *Orwell: The Lost Writings*, ed. W. J. West (New York, 1985), 113.

10. Fyodor Dostoyevsky, *A Raw Youth*, trans. C. Garnett (London, 1916), 219.

11. The parallel gains force from the Bolshevists' obsession with the French Revolution. Trotsky seasons his *History of the Russian Revolution* and *The Revolution Betrayed* with references to Danton, Robespierre, and Bonapartism, calling Stalin's triumph 'The Soviet Thermidor'. In a dramatic debate between Lenin and Kerensky, Lenin demanded: '"Then let us have one of two things: either a bourgeois government with its plans for so-called social reform on paper ... or let us have ... a Government of the proletariat, which had its parallel in 1792 in France."' Kerensky's reply was prophetic: '"We have been referred to 1792 as an example of how we should carry out the revolution of 1917. But how did the French republic of 1792 end? It turned into a base Imperialism, which set back the progress of democracy for many a long year.... You tell us that you fear reaction," he almost screamed; "you say that you want to strengthen our new-won freedom, and yet you propose to lead us the way of France in 1792.... Out of the fiery chaos that you wish to make will arise, like a Phoenix, a dictator"' (H. Pitcher, *Witnesses of the Russian Revolution* (London, 1994), 11214).

12. M. Litvinov, *The Bolshevik Revolution: Its Rise and Meaning* (London, 1918): 'A Collection of Pamphlets, Mainly Political, Formed by George Orwell' (British Library).

13. Ibid. 27.

14. He also gave new meaning to Marx's famous definition of religion: 'Marx did not say, at any rate in that place, that religion is merely a dope handed out from above; he said that it is something the people create for themselves to supply a need that he recognized

to be a real one. "Religion is the sigh of the soul in a soulless world. Religion is the opium of the people." What is he saying except that man does not live by bread alone, that hatred is not enough, that a world worth living in cannot be founded on "realism" and machine-guns?' (ii. 33). Marxism meant that the question of man's place in the universe 'cannot be dealt with while the average human being's preoccupations are necessarily economic. It is all summed up in Marx's saying that after Socialism has arrived, human history can begin' (iii. 83).

15. Leon Trotsky, *My Life* (New York, 1930), 541.

16. T. Cook, 'Upton Sinclair's *The Jungle* and Orwell's *Animal Farm*: A Relationship Explored', *Modern Fiction Studies*, 30/4 (Winter 1984), 696–703.

17. Cook, 'Sinclair's *Jungle*', 697.

18. Arthur Miller, *Timebends: A Life* (London, 1987), 315.

19. Letter to D. Macdonald, 5 Dec. 1946 (Yale). Quoted in Letemendia, 'Revolution on *Animal Farm*', 24 and, in part, in Shelden, *Orwell*, 407.

20. Letter to G. Orwell from T. S. Eliot, 13 July 1944 (copy in Orwell Archive). Quoted in Crick, *George Orwell*, 458.

21. Quoted in Crick, *George Orwell*, 458.

22. Ibid. 123.

23. Litvinov, *The Bolshevik Revolution*, 54.

24. Hobbes, *Leviathan*, 1. xiii (p. 84).

25. Letter to G. Orwell, 24 Aug. 1945 (Orwell Archive). Quoted in Crick, *George Orwell*, 491.

26. J. Reed, *Ten Days That Shook the World* (1919; New York, 1992), 90.

27. Ibid. 26.

28. Ibid. 91–2.

29. Quoted in Pitcher, *Witnesses of the Russian Revolution*, 110–11, 112.

30. R. H. B. Lockhart, *Memoirs of a British Agent* (London, 1932), 238.

31. Trotsky quotes Krupskaya in 1926: 'If Ilych were alive, he would probably already be in prison': *The Revolution Betrayed* (New York, 1995), 93–4.

32. M. Meyer, *Not Prince Hamlet: Literary and Theatrical Memoirs* (London, 1989), 68.

33. For example, even if Orwell had not stressed the pigs' cleverness they would still have had to dominate by intelligence, not education. Letemendia ('Revolution on *Animal Farm*', 17), however, breaches the metaphor in blaming the passivity of the animals on their brief lifespan and 'consequent shortness of their memory', and a class structure fixed by 'their immutable functions on the farm'. In fact, Benjamin, who stresses his longevity, is as passive as the others, and if they are all made victims of zoological limitations the meaning is lost. Their actions, fate, and differences in intelligence must be read as *human*. Lack of previous education is a common *extrinsic* factor, but when the pigs try to teach the animals to read, only Benjamin attains their proficiency—proving the pigs' inborn superiority.

34. Letter to Gollancz, 19 Mar. 1944, quoted in Crick, *George Orwell*, 452.

35. The 'fairy story' or *conte de fées*, a term invented by educated women who in the 1690s gave literary polish to medieval and folk tales, does not have 'political' meaning, although Perrault used it to preach 'morals' endorsing the social order. (Perrault did not call his collection *Contes de fées* but *Histoires ou contes du temps passé: Avec des moralités* (Stories or Tales of Past Times: With Morals).)

36. D. M. Roemer, in M. E. Brown and B. A. Rosenberg (edd.), *Encyclopedia of Folklore and Literature* (Santa Barbara, Calif., 1998), 195, 198.

37. G. K. Chesterton, introduction to *Æsop's Fables*, trans. V. S. Vernon Jones, *illus.* Arthur Rackham (London, 1975), 10.

38. Ibid. 72. Orwell, however, was modern in making his protagonist a *community*. A precedent was Mark Twain's 'The Man That Corrupted Hadleyburg' (1899), in which a self-righteous town revises its motto 'Lead Us Not Into Temptation' to 'Lead Us Into Temptation', after its renowned honesty is shown to be skin-deep.

39. Orwell had already used the horse in an abandoned war novel, 'The Quick and the Dead', where an officer sadistically whips a dying horse named 'old Boxer', 'presumably in the retreat in 1918': Orwell Archive, 'Literary Notebook No. 1', pp. 14–15.

40. It has been claimed that Orwell was directly inspired by his own BBC adaptation of Ignazio Silone's 'The Fox', misleadingly called 'a political allegory set in a pig farm' (*The Lost Writings*, ed. West, 60). Formally it is not 'allegory', but a realistic story in which an anti-fascist Ticino peasant grows to like an injured Italian engineer brought into his house. When the engineer is identified as a local fascist spy the peasant humanely refuses to have him killed by a fellow anti-fascist, only to see him escape with documents leading to mass arrests of Italian workmen. The peasant emotionally identifies the treacherous spy with a prowling fox that has finally been trapped, and hacks it to bits. All the characters, fox included, are flesh and blood, and the story has no relation in form or content to *Animal Farm*. Crick (*George Orwell*, 459) more persuasively cites the 'influence' of Swift's Houyhnhnms, which Orwell regarded as having reached 'the highest stage of totalitarian organization' (iv. 252); but the dynamic of transformation, vital to *Animal Farm*, is absent from the Houyhnhnms' static world.

41. After 1698 *contes de fées* were criticized as extravagant and parodied on the stage: see G. Rouger, introduction to *Coates de Perrault* (Paris, 1967), p. xlviii. They were perennially parodied, e.g. by Voltaire in *The White Bull* (1773–4) and by George MacDonald in the 1860s and Oscar Wilde in the 1890s: see J. Zipes, *Fairy Tales and the Art of Subversion: The Classical Genre for Children and the Process of Civilization* (London, 1983), 104–11, 114–21. Orwell might have read Wilde's parody of the 'happy ending' (e.g. the 'Star Child' becomes a good king, yet 'ruled. he not long ... And he who came after him ruled evilly'). James Thurber, whom Orwell admired (iii. 325), delightfully parodied the fable in *Fables for Our Time* (1940). In 'The Owl Who Was God' Thurber tells how birds and beasts come to worship the owl as God because he can see in the dark (assuming he can see as well in the daytime) and because by luck he answers questions correctly with the few monosyllables he knows. Blindly following him, the animals are hit by a truck in broad daylight, and many, including the owl, are killed. Thurber's moral is: '*You can fool too many of the people too much of the time*': *Vintage Thurber*, 2 vols. (London, 1983), i. 159.

42. Charles Dickens, 'Frauds on the Fairies' (1854), in *Miscellaneous Papers/Edwin Drood* (London, n.d.), 202.

43. Quoted in H. Stone, *Dickens and the Invisible World: Fairy-Tales, Fantasy and Novel-Making* (New York, 1979), 2.

44. 'Frauds on the Fairies', 201.

45. See A. Bony, 'Réalité et imaginaire dans *Hard Times*', *Études anglaises*, 23/2 (Apr.–June 1970), 168–82.

46. Crick, *George Orwell*, 367.

47. See Zipes, *Fairy Tales and the Art of Subversion*, 135–64.

48. G. Trease, *A Whiff of Burnt Boats* (London, 1971), 155, and *Laughter at the Door* (London, 1974), 26, 27. I thank Nicholas Tucker for calling my attention to Trease and to *The Adventures of the Little Pig* (see below).

49. Richards viewed happiness in youth as the best preparation for later misery: 'At least, the poor kid will have had something! He may, at twenty, be hunting for a job and not finding it—why should his fifteenth year be clouded by worrying about that in advance? He may, at thirty get the sack—why tell him so at twelve?' Making children miserable was unjustifiable anyway but 'the adult will be all the more miserable if he was miserable as a child' (i. 537). Richards' honest patriotism, anti-intellectualism, and affection for pre-1914 England would have appealed to the author of *Coming Up for Air*.

50. New York: Workers Library Publishers, 1932.

51. Zipes, *Fairy Tales and the Art of Subversion*, 154–5. Of aristocratic birth, Zur Mühlen (1883–1951) studied Marxism in Switzerland and joined the Communist Party in Frankfurt-am-Main. In 1933 she emigrated to Vienna and in 1938 fled to England. Her tales, aimed at raising the social consciousness of children and offering them models of a fairer world, appeared in communist children's magazines during the 1920s: see J. Zipes (ed.), *The Oxford Companion to Fairy Tales* (Oxford, 2000), 561–2. Her first collection, *Was Peterchens Freunde erzählen* (1921), is in the British Library.

52. Roger Webster.

53. I have tried unsuccessfully to trace Kay or another copyright-holder.

54. A. Mandel-Campbell, 'Water could make your cup runneth over', *Financial Times*, 16–17 Feb. 2002, 'Weekend' section, p. xxli. Private firms have acquired 85% of the world's water distribution (*UBS Investment*, July/Aug. 2001, p. 23). Although NGOs argue that privatization strikes the poorest and that water access should be free or charged at cost price, the World Water Forum does not recognize water as a 'basic human right'. The World Commission on Water, an arm of the World Bank, considers it a profitable resource, especially in poor countries (*Le Monde*, 24 Mar. 2000, p. 40). From the boardroom this looks ideal. If regulators menace profits, firms can invoke job losses. On the other hand, CEOs who boost the share price by sacking workers earn bigger bonuses, and if they have to be sacked in turn they are replaced, as in Orwell's day, by others like themselves, but rewarded for their failure beyond the wildest dreams of Orwell's contemporaries. Privatization, however, sparks conflict. Vivendi Environment was driven out of Tucuman Province, Argentina (*International Herald Tribune*, 27 Aug. 2002, p. 1). Another firm doubled the water price in Bolivia, provoking what has been called the world's first civil war over water (*Le Point*, 30 Aug. 2002, p. 87). Kay's far-fetched metaphor is today's *fait divers*.

55. 'While millions of their countrymen suffered collapsing living standards, declining health and increasing alcoholism, a few [Russians] made enough money to join the ranks of the world's richest men' (*Financial Times*, 6/7 Apr. 2002, p. 1).

56. Max Frisch, 'Über Marionetten', in *Tagebuch 1946–1949* (Zurich, 1964), 154.

57. The Parisian craze for fables and literary *contes de fées* in the late 17th century coincided with one for marionettes (see *Contes de Perrault*, ed. Rouger, 293 n. 2). Perrault himself made the connection; dedicating 'Peau d'âne' he affirmed, 'Qu'en certains moments l'esprit le plus parfait | Peut aimer sans rougir jusqu'aux Marionettes' (ibid. 57). The most sensible Reason, he added, often wearied of its vigil and enjoyed dozing, ingeniously rocked by tales of Ogre and Fairy.

58. See Zipes, *Fairy Tales and the Art of Subversion*, 154–5.

59. See J.-D. Jurgensen, *Orwell, ou la Route de 1984* (Paris, 1983), 154, and J. Cornwell, *Hitler's Pope* (London, 1999), 151 ff.

60. See P. Davison, ed. *The Complete Works of George Orwell* (London, 1998), viii, 116. According to George Woodcock, Orwell justified working for the BBC 'by contending that the right kind of man could at least make propaganda a little cleaner than it would

otherwise have been ... but he soon found there was in fact little he could do, and he left the BBC in disgust' (quoted in Crick; *George Orwell*, 418). (In *Nineteen Eighty-Four* Orwell named the Party's torture chamber, Room 101, after a BBC conference room.) For Orwell, a propagandist aimed not at truth but 'to do as much dirt on his opponent as possible' (iii. 262). Propaganda took 'just as much work as to write something you believe in, with the difference that the finished product is worthless' (iii. 293). Yet he made one exception: 'I have always maintained that every artist is a propagandist. I don't mean a political propagandist. If he has any honesty or talent at all he cannot be that. Most political propaganda is a matter of telling lies, not only about the facts but about your own feelings. But every artist is a propagandist in the sense that he is trying, directly or indirectly, to impose a vision of life that seems to him desirable' (ii. 57). In *Animal Farm* Orwell does this by exposing the *betrayal* of such a vision.

61. Orwell contributed to *Partisan Review* from 1941 to 1946, and praised Dwight Macdonald's review *Politics*. By 1944 he had the New York address of Ruth Fischer (pseud. Elfriede Eisler, 1895–1961), the one-time General Secretary of the German Communist Party and author of *Stalin and German Communism* (iii. 334). Her hatred of Stalin—she never lost her admiration for Lenin—led her to denounce her brother Gerhart as an agent of the Comintern, and her other brother, the composer Hanns Eisler, as a communist 'in a philosophical sense' to the Un-American Activities Committee in 1947; this eventually led, in 1948, to Eisler's expulsion from the United States: E. Bentley (ed.), *Thirty Years of Treason* (London, 1971), 55 ff., 73. Among Orwell's papers in the British Library is a manuscript translation of a German socialist's eyewitness account of the fall of Berlin, other versions of which appeared in Fischer's newsletter 'The Network' (Nov.–Dec. 1945) and in *Politics* (Jan. 1946). Fischer visited Orwell on 17 June 1949 (iv. 565; confirmed to me by Peter Davison).

62. For example, J. R. Carling, *Each for All: A Fairy Play in Three Scenes* (1923); Winifred Young, *Clouds and Sunshine: A Fairy Play* (1922); L. F. Ramsey, *Fairies to the Rescue, a Fairy Play* (1926). H. B. Chipman, *Meri-ka-chak: A Children's Booklet which Carries the Co-operative Message* (n.d.); F. M. Campling, *It's Different Now: A Yarn for Young People* (1939). Some are in the British Library; others are in the Co-operative Union Library, Holyoake House, Hanover, Manchester, or appeared in its sales catalogue.

63. In the first two stories, a 'kindly robber' gives the little pig for Christmas a silver necklace stolen from a fat duchess. He tells the pig to give it to his mother, who complains she owes the farmer back rent:

> 'He's a cruel mean man. He does no work, and makes all the animals pay rent. The horse has to pay rent now for his stables and the fowls for their hen-house, and the cows for the cow-shed.' 'Good heavens,' said the little pig. 'But where do they get the money from?'
>
> His mother began to weep bitterly. 'It's very hard,' she said. 'The fowls have to take their eggs to market to raise the money and the cows have to take their milk and the horse has to carry loads to and fro for the neighbours.' (p. 28)

64. There were probably others. Trotsky's *The Revolution Betrayed* (1937) may have suggested the subject, and even an angle from which to treat it. Describing forced collectivization, Trotsky writes, 'But the most devastating hurricane hit the animal kingdom. The number of horses fell 55 per cent ...' (p. 40).

65. Quoted in Andre Maurois, *Lélia, ou la vie de George Sand* (Verviers, Belgium, 1952), 372, 382 (my translation).

66. London: Freedom Press, 1941.

67. *The Russian Myth*, 26.

68. Ibid. 28–9.

69. Ibid. 30.

70. See F. S. Saunders, Who *Paid the Piper? The CIA and the Cultural Cold War* (London, 1999), 293–5. Saunders remarks, 'Curiously, the critique of America's intelligence bureaucrats echoed the earlier concerns of T. S. Eliot and William Empson, both of whom had written to Orwell in 1944 [*sic*] to point out faults or inconsistencies in the central parable of *Animal Farm*.' Orwell's own 1946 BBC version keeps the last line and praise of more work for less food. Frederic is gone, and 'Farmer 1', who drops his aitches while Napoleon speaks like a gentleman, replaces Pilkington, thus audibly confusing pigs and humans: see P. Davison, *The Complete Works of George Orwell*, viii. 192.

71. See *Guardian*, 17 Mar. 1993, p. 7.

72. Three months after the publication of *Animal Farm* Orwell snubbed an invitation to speak on Yugoslavia for the League of European Freedom because it was 'an essentially Conservative body which claims to defend democracy in Europe but has nothing to say about British imperialism'. He explained: 'I belong to the Left and must work inside it, much as I hate Russian totalitarianism and its poisonous influence in this country' (iv. 49). Simon Leys deplores 'the persistent stupidity of a Left that, instead of at last beginning to read and understand [Orwell] had scandalously permitted the confiscation of its most powerful writer': *Orwell, ou l'horreur de la politique* (Paris, 1984), 46 (my translation).

73. See Zipes, *Fairy Tales and the Art of Subversion*, 60 ff., 179 ff. Zur Mühlen was rediscovered in Germany in the 1960s, starting a wave of 'counter-cultural' children's tales advocating collective control by workers of their labour. England and the United States preferred feminist fairy tales. Zipes, who has edited a volume of them (*Don't Bet on the Prince* (London, 1986)), welcomes the 'upsetting' effect of making Cinderella rebellious, or having Snow White organizing a band of robbers. Mercifully, however, he grants that 'it is extremely difficult to determine exactly what a child will absorb on an unconscious level' (*Fairy Tales and the Art of Subversion*, 191, 57). Orwell himself has drawn feminist fire, the charge being 'not that he treated women badly but that he portrayed them badly. In his novels, the female characters (including the mare in *Animal Farm*) are sketchy or vapid' (D. Honigmann, *Financial Times*, 1–2 June 2000, 'Weekend' section, p. v). If Comrade Orwell wronged Feminist Woman, feminists might recall Eileen Blair's part in *Animal Farm*. Eileen told how, unprecedentedly, her husband would read his day's work to her and welcome her criticisms and suggestions (Crick, *George Orwell*, 451). Her friends attributed the humour in the book to her influence (Shelden, *The Authorised Biography*, 408), and Orwell said that she had helped in planning it (iv. 131). Significantly, he asked her advice, perhaps to help him capture what he called in a broadcast 'the atmosphere of childhood' (*The Lost Writings*, ed. West, 88). She may deserve credit for the tone of the book, including such humorous touches as the mare's frivolous vanity.

74. *The Revolution Betrayed*, 109.

75. *Independent on Sunday*, 1 Sept. 2002, p. 10.

76. The director-adapter Shang Chengjun was necessarily more diplomatic. His play opened near the Great Hall of the People in Beijing, where the Communist Party had just elected its new leaders with all the rigid conformism of *Animal Farm*. Mr Shang knew they might stop his play, but his comment was apt: 'Many people read the book narrow-mindedly ... Sure, [it] satirises the Soviet Union, but I think the phenomenon it describes suits every society and era. I don't want to make a judgment in this play—whether socialism or capitalism is good or not. What I want to express is that no matter which society people

are in, if they want to be their own masters they have responsibilities and duties. If they are indifferent, lazy and don't want to vote, any social system will fail' (*Financial Times*, 16/17 Nov. 2002, p. 3). In Orwell's words, the people must know when to chuck out their leaders—but what if they lose faith in the efficacy of voting?

77. *The Road to Wigan Pier* (Harmondsworth, 1963), 194.

ANNETTE FEDERICO

Making Do:
George Orwell's
Coming Up for Air

In May of 1948, when *Coming Up for Air* (1939) was about to be reissued, George Orwell confessed to Julian Symons that the book "isn't much. Of course you are right about my own character constantly intruding on that of the narrator. I am not a real novelist anyway.... One difficulty I have never solved is that one has masses of experience which one passionately wants to write about, *e.g.*, the part about fishing in that book, and no way of using them up except by disguising them as a novel" (*CEJL* 4: 422). The idea of using fiction to disguise a desire to write about fishing—or the first primroses, or the mating of hares, or comic postcards—shows how much Orwell cared about recording, and so celebrating and dignifying, the pleasures of commonplace activities. His essays on a pint of beer in the perfect pub ("The Moon Under Water"), the ritual of making tea ("A Nice Cup of Tea"), or the spawning of toads, which signals springtime ("Some Thoughts on the Common Toad"), display his delight in the rites and rituals of daily life. Writing about them, "using them up," attests to their coexistence with institutional practices, and reminds us of their irrepressibility. So writing about the pleasures of fishing in *Coming Up for Air* gives fishing cultural space between the ideological battles being waged in Europe in the 1930s. This is important for Orwell because "by retaining one's childhood love of such things as trees, fishes, butterflies, and... toads, one makes a peaceful and decent future a little more probable"

From *Studies in the Novel* 37, no. 1 (Spring 2005): pp. 50–63. © 2005 by the University of North Texas.

(*CEJL* 4: 144). He took great satisfaction in the reflection that certain kinds of private pleasures—reading a novel, fishing, taking a walk—keep going on behind the backs of political and social authorities, those "important persons who would stop me from enjoying this if they could. But luckily they can't" (*CEJL* 4: 144).

Coming Up for Air falls between Orwell's most famously political works: it was published one year after *Homage to Catalonia* (1938), and was the last novel Orwell wrote before *Animal Farm* (1945) and *Nineteen Eighty-Four* (1949). Some literary critics have tended to read the novel as prefiguring the nightmare world of *Nineteen Eight-Four*, as an extended meditation on the common man's passivity and helplessness in a period of impending political crisis; or as a sentimental, even reactionary, compromise of Orwell's leftist politics.[1] In this essay, I want to argue that Orwell's political commitment to democratic socialism—to freedom and self-determination—is very much alive in *Coming Up for Air*. The liberatory potential of the novel is derived less from a position of overt rebellion against the existing order than from a position of faith in the existence of the ordinary as a repository of meaning in a technocratic, politically unstable, and almost entirely secular society. Orwell's political vision of freedom and equality intersects with his journalistic interest in the way ordinary workers and consumers experience the world. *Coming Up for Air* is political precisely as it describes the fissure between authoritative systems of knowledge and official versions of reality—political speeches, newspapers, literature, public lectures—and the concrete, inarticulate dailiness of a lower-middle class person's life.

The narrator of *Coming Up for Air* is George Bowling, a middle-aged suburban insurance agent trying to cope with the changes in English society after the first world war. His voice is funny, friendly, nostalgic, and ironic. Through his thoughts, feelings, and experiences, Orwell reasserts a conviction that political effort incorporates a defense of that which is private, unrecorded, and unofficial. In both *Animal Farm* and *Nineteen-Eighty Four*, utopian system-making and foolproof social methodologies threaten to destroy the instinct for delight in whatever is random, imperfect, or useless, the very things that fall through the cracks of recorded history and that might constitute alternatives to the logic of totalitarianism. In *Nineteen-Eighty Four*, for example, Winston Smith delights in the "litter of odds and ends" in the junk shop (80), he imagines acquiring "scraps of beautiful rubbish" (84), and his dreams of rebellion are inflected with a craving for the everyday, the quotidian: he wishes he were an old married man walking down the streets with his wife, "just as they were doing now, but openly and without fear, talking of trivialities and buying odds and ends for the household" (116). *Coming Up for Air* also asserts the persistence of the trivial. George Bowling's bland world is saturated with beautiful rubbish, the litter of daily life: "portable radios, life-insurance policies, false teeth, aspirins, French letters and concrete garden rollers" (13). George Bowling admits, "Nothing's real in Ellesmere Road except gas-bills, school-fees, boiled cabbage and the office on Monday" (277). In its unembarrassed immersion in the plebeian details of modern lower-middle-class life, these examples suggest a literal inventory of the mundane—and especially in the voice, memories, movements, and locale of an engaging common man; *Coming Up for Air* insists on an unofficial and unaffiliated opposition to totalizing systems of knowledge, of class stratification, and of cultural values.

My reading of this novel has been informed by the cultural and sociological theories of Michel de Certeau, particularly those described in *The Practice of Everyday Life*. Three points, in particular, resonate with Orwell's novel. First, for any person—not just for minority groups or the economically disenfranchised, since "marginality" is pervasive among the "non-producers of culture" (xvii)—reading anything can be construed as "poaching": the subjective, private, possibly subversive unknown travels of a reader through his own texts (170). Second, consumers "make do" with the products, spaces, and points of reference the existing system has to offer (18). And finally, spatial practices—walking in the city, living in houses, cooking, driving—"secretly structure the determining conditions of social life" (96). They are "ploys" that might be developed into an everyday politics of cultural resistance, a "network of antidiscipline" (xv), of stolen pleasures, of manipulating and enjoying. These tactics of the weak against the strong are ethical as well as political; that is, they provide a diversion from the values assumed by totalizing theories of knowledge, and by dominant economic and scientific systems. They are practices that might be derived from an ethics of hope, even if it cannot be formally articulated, rationalized, or made politically feasible. George Bowling's feeling—George Orwell's feeling, perhaps—that "fishing is the opposite of war"(97), that "fishing is somehow typical" of his civilization "before the radio, before aeroplanes, before Hitler" (87), is neither simple escapism nor pointless nostalgia. It is an assertion of hope constructed from memories of commonplace pastimes, activities that may be said to represent "the night-side of societies" (Certeau *Practice* 41): what a society's totalizing institutions do not see or repress.

George Bowling cannot just drop out; he is too old to risk the kind of pointless rebellion of, say, Gordon Comstock in Orwell's *Keep the Aspidistra Flying* (1936). And he's too practical to imagine that people could actually return to nature or innocence or some imagined ideal past. Like George Orwell, George Bowling detests the fake rusticity of "enlightened people" with their "Vegetarianism, simple life, poetry, nature-worship, roll in the dew before breakfast" and the "faked-up Tudor houses" (255) with their "bird-baths and plaster gnomes" (257). George Bowling cannot escape from his environment because the "space of the tactic is the space of the other.... It does not have the means to *keep to itself*, at a distance, in a position of withdrawal" (Certeau *Practice* 37). Stuck in West Bletchley, Orwell's man must make do with intense nostalgia, delinquency, and daydreams.

Orwell describes with frankness and humor the tactical moves of the person nobody notices: fat, forty-five-year old George Bowling, with his vulgar clothes and false teeth, his cheap cigar and his house in the suburbs. George has no illusions about himself. He accepts his particular slot in the social and economic order and he knows how he appears to other people: "a fat middle-aged bloke with a red face" and a "coarse brazen look" (12). His home in West Bletchley is removed from the milieu of intellectuals, corporate privilege, political power, and cultural authority. But he watches the world knowingly and with wariness, from the margins of his class, and the margins of recorded history. He operates in a terrain that is organized by the expanding presence and interests of industry (a jam factory in '28, a bicycle factory in '33), by large building societies, by a branch of the Left Book Club (in '36), and by seeping pretensions to high culture, represented by his wife Hilda's eclectic and short-lived membership in various clubs. George is smart, a bounder and opportunist who is unabashed by the compromises his life has apparently forced upon him. He has given up struggling in his domestic life, accepts that his vapid wife and two horrid kids are just "part of the order of things" (162), and he's smart enough to see the political and moral implications of suburban respectability: "We're all respectable householders—that's to say Tories, yes-men, and bumsuckers" (15). He is Orwell's version of the common man, "wise and mad, lucid and ridiculous" (Certeau *Practice* 2).

George Bowling's ruses and tactics—playing hooky from work, looking in the mirror, shopping, walking, commuting, eating and drinking, attending lectures, reading the headlines, listening to the radio—are disclosed to the reader as to an insider in a largely symbolic project of rebellion. As we read this meandering report from the suburbs, George Bowling's everyday practices become increasingly punctuated by confidential outbursts about the inexpressibility of it all: "You know that feeling" is the novel's principal chord, and it ranges from disgust to amazement to delight. Recovering and trying to articulate feelings and sensory impressions, reconciling self-perception and social reality, and, especially, retrieving memories are sense-making enterprises that need to be organized by language. Like melodrama and many popular utterances, the novel's mode of expression is uncensored, unaccommodating, mushy. He directly addresses the hypocrite reader: "I tell you it was a good world to live in. I belong to it. So do you" (36).

In imaging the reader as friend and interlocutor, and in constantly and directly asking for the reader's participation, Orwell asserts the persistence of a humane desire for companionship and understanding. The first thing repressive regimes do is prevent people from talking to one another. Both John Flory in *Burmese Days* (1934) and Winston Smith in *Nineteen Eighty-Four* desperately crave human conversation, even about trivialities. George Bowling's frank, familiar chitchat is unembarrassed, a confrontation with the facts of his 45-year-old body, his false teeth, his suburban house, his commonplace job, his tedious wife, his "hangover from the past" (23). But these facts cannot become his law. That is what the sentimental journey to Lower Binfield is all about. "I only want to be alive," says George (192), and it is this trivial desire that defines Orwell's politics. To conclude that the novel is defeatist or apocalyptic, that it is only about failure and capitulation to political forces, that is has no moral center, is to deny the ethical importance of both the excessively engaging mode of its narration and the survival tactics it determinedly describes. Reading is a central, daily activity of modern consumer culture, embracing all the literate acts people practice and the textual commodities they consume. Novels, pamphlets, advertising billboards, newspaper headlines, and telegrams tell us what constitutes reality. The production of these narratives of reality is less interesting than the way these different texts are used by consumers in everyday life. To assume that the public (an image never made explicit by the producers of culture) will become what they consume—tabloid newspapers, junk TV, romance novels—takes for granted that assimilating means becoming similar to what is absorbed, rather than, according to Certeau, "'making something similar' to what one is, making it one's own, appropriating or reappropriating it" (*Practice* 166). Reading is based on scriptural models of the reader as the passive recipient of the truth or the law. Professional intellectuals, politicians, broadcasters, journalists, pollsters, critics and reviewers constitute a modern "church of the media." The hierarchy has long been established: "to write is to produce the text; to read is to receive it from someone else without putting one's own mark on it, without remaking it" (Certeau *Practice* 169). The same relationship applies to aural messages. But the reader/listener is not docile; he is also a practitioner. In his hands any text can be remade to give him social leverage. What is captivating and what is boring, what sticks and what is immediately forgotten, what stimulates private memories and gripes, what is filtered out as stupid or irrelevant, constitute "advances and retreats, tactics and games played with the text" (Certeau *Practice* 169). The reader "poaches" on the text, insinuating his own ruses of pleasure and appropriation. "Words become the outlet or product of silent histories" (Certeau *Practice* xxi).

Orwell had a strong sociological bent. He was interested in the attitudes and social identities of contemporary consumers ("Who are these people? Who reads the *Gem* and *Magnet*," he asks in "Boys' Weeklies" [*CEJL* 1: 467]); he was curious about the effects on people of what they read or use as entertainment, and what a commodity's popularity can possibly tell him about his society and his fellow citizens. The fact that many people like vulgar comic postcards is "symptomatically important" to Orwell because such things might constitute a "harmless rebellion against virtue," a "chorus of raspberries" against what he calls his culture's "official literature," discourses that include the prime minister's speeches, solidarity songs, national anthems, Temperance tracts, and papal encyclicals (*CEJL* 2: 164). I think this interest in the consumption of popular culture and the interception of "official literature" by poaching readers informs the creation of George Bowling as an honest nay-sayer, and constitutes the kind of mute disobedience Orwell seems to advocate in "The Art of Donald McGill." Orwell imagines the "silent history" of the common reader as he randomly encounters various texts, from popular entertainment to news and information, from lowbrow fiction to elite masterpieces. George Bowling's frustrated desires for credibility and conviction intersect with his efforts to redefine or reappropriate reality by laying claim to the texts with which he is infused. He evades the competing and pressing messages he gets about what is actually going on.

George Bowling recalls how his father and mother, at the turn of the century, believed everything they read in *The People*, *Hilda's Home Companion*, and *News of the World* (52–53, 60). After the war, though, people changed: "A sort of wave of disbelief was moving across England" (144). The skeptical and ironic reader was about to be hatched: George Bowling has little faith, or even interest, in the production of knowledge represented by the *News Chronicle* and the *Standard*. As he walks along the Strand to Charing Cross, blazing headlines designed to create uncertainty and suspense (to sell papers) demand his visual attention: "LEGS; FRESH DISCOVERIES," and "LEGS; FAMOUS SURGEON'S STATEMENT" (26, 31) announce new facts in a murder case in which a woman's legs were found in a parcel in a railway waiting room. The newsboy's shout, "'Legs! 'Orrible revelations! All the winners! Legs!'" (27), and the poster's eye-smiting headlines announce to the passer-by what is important, what is happening. He must accredit these narratives of violence and power as factual (the famous surgeon's statement must be believed; he is an expert). "Narrated reality constantly tells us what must be believed and what must be done. What can you oppose to the facts? You can only give in, and obey what they 'signify,' like an oracle" (Certeau *Practice* 186).

And yet all the time common people are converting grave and decisive reports into entertainment, into time-fillers, into small talk; media reports are casually manipulated by preoccupied and skeptical consumers. On the train into London, a commercial salesman reading the *Daily Mail* comments idly on the racing news; another chap who is picking his teeth over the *Express* remarks, "'Legs case don't seem to get much forrader'" (23). Glancing at the morning paper, George Bowling does not find much to interest him: "Down in Spain and over in China they were murdering one another as usual" (9). Messages of political crisis are put to private uses, momentarily shelved, half-heartedly believed. As Orwell wrote in one of his *Tribune* essays in 1946, "countless people read the *Daily* ____ while saying frankly that they 'don't believe a word of it'" (*CEJL* 4: 241). George Bowling knows very well, for example, that "the cheer-up stuff they're talking about in the newspapers" really means that war is coming soon (22). He interprets a "positive" report in the *News Chronicle* on British anti-aircraft artillery as bad news for him personally: the big guns might save Woolwich Arsenal, but the bombs are still going to fall on places like Ellesmere Road (22). And he is frightened of the bombs and the machine guns. Yet his anonymity, the fact that he is only watching what goes on from the sidelines, gives him some hope of survival: "ordinary middling chaps like me will be carrying on just as usual" even when the rubber truncheons are brought out (177).

Nevertheless, for George Bowling the news constitutes a possible locus of belief. Both headlines stimulate reflections on morality and religion. "LEGS" leads to a meditation on how moral relativism contributes to the dullness of English murders ("you can't do a good murder unless you believe you're going to roast in hell for it" [27]). "KING ZOG" echoes 30-year-old sermons intoning Og the king of Bashan (33), and begins a train of sensory memories that cluster around the smells, tastes, and sounds of a Sunday in Lower Binfield in 1908: "How it came back to me! That peculiar feeling—it was only a feeling, you couldn't describe it as an activity—that we used to call 'Church'" (34). Today's headlines are tacitly folded into the search for private meaning, a search that worldly George Bowling already knows cannot be fulfilled by either outmoded religious dogma or by utopian politics. But in a secular world, and especially in a society on the brink of war, the remains of belief are passed from one myth—call it "Church"—to other myths, objects, statements, and ideologies, to news bulletins, advertising, political speeches. "It would be vapid to believe that myths disappear with the advent of rationalization," claims Certeau. "If we believed that the streets had been disinfected of myth, we would be deluding ourselves.... They surge up on all sides," and in advertising most of all (*Culture* 19). But there are silent disturbances; desires, dreams, memories get stirred up.

At one point in his story, George has a reverie, a reading memory from the year 1905:

> My favorite place for reading was the loft behind the yard.... I can feel the feeling of it now. A winter day, just warm enough to lie still. I'm lying on my belly with *Chums* open in front of me. A mouse runs up the side of a sack like a clockwork toy, then suddenly stops dead and watches me with his little eyes like tiny jet beads. I'm twelve years old, but I'm Donovan the Dauntless. Two thousand miles up the Amazon I've just pitched my tent, and the roots of the mysterious orchid that blooms once in a hundred years are safe in the tin box under my camp bed. In the forests all around the Hopi-Hopi Indians, who paint their teeth scarlet and skin white men alive, are beating their war-drums. I'm watching the mouse and the mouse is watching me, and I can smell the dust and sainfoin and the cool plastery smell, and I'm up the Amazon, and it's bliss, pure bliss. (104–05)

The description conforms to the novel's antidisciplinary project: apparent passivity conceals radical creativity. Sociopolitical mechanisms of school curricula, book clubs, and the literary canon conceal the common reader's insinuations about the text (Certeau *Practice* 172). Reading is like being in two places at one time (in the loft and up the Amazon), being me and not me (twelve-year-old George and Donovan the Dauntless). The reader is autonomous, already political in his silent transformation of social reality, quietly intent on eluding the "law of information" (Certeau *Practice* 173). George is also intent on eluding the laws of obedience, duty, frugality, and making constructive use of time. Blissful reading is a minor transgression in George's society, where "the idea of doing things because you enjoy them" (160) is heretical.

Besides fishing, what George really wants to do is read. He describes himself as "a considerable reader ... the typical Boots Library subscriber, I always fall for the best-seller of the moment," although he is also a member of the Left Book Club (102). He is the type of consumer who reads whatever other people are reading: *The Good Companions, Bengal Lancer, Hatter's Castle*. He falls for the book of the moment, knowing that he is like a thousand other people. Although he is not particular, George filters his reading through his own embodied experiences. When George reads a romance novel called *Wasted Passion* he says it starts him thinking "about how people—some people—are expected to behave" when confronted with a lover's infidelity. But as a fat man, he could not possibly fling himself down in a paroxysm of weeping like the hero in the book: "It would be downright obscene" (22). He recognizes the novel's prescriptions, but he is always conscious that what he falls for has been marketed to a certain class of readers. Reading as poaching means knowing what you're doing, exercising freedom through the text, re-imagining the text as your own, being impertinent.

Although Orwell was a highly literate man, he was not a snobbish reader. In an essay called "Good Bad Books" he writes, "one can be amused or excited or even moved by a book that one's intellect simply refuses to take seriously" (*CEJL* 4: 21). In other words, one can (many people do) decline the pretensions of "superior" literature, of erudition or artistic experimentation, and read to serve their own purposes. Social institutions, such as formal education, can undermine the reader's relationship with the text. George says it was only later in life that he read "a 'good' book" on his own. "I read the things I wanted to read, and I got more out of them than I ever got out of the stuff they taught me at school" (103). During the war, when George is stuck on the North Cornish Coast at Twelve Mile Dump for a year, he has an opportunity to read anything and everything. "Don't run away with the idea that I suddenly discovered Marcel Proust or Henry James or somebody," he warns. "I wouldn't have read them even if I had" (141). Reading as poaching may be impertinent, or it may politely say no thank you. As he becomes a little more highbrow, he begins to be able to distinguish between "tripe and not tripe," between Elinor Glyn and Arnold Bennett (142, 143). But his solitary, random education, his unsupervised book-learning of a year-and-a-half, without the benefit of experts, becomes important in developing his political awareness: "It did certain things to my mind. It gave me an attitude, a kind of questioning attitude" (143).

But after the war, when he is working as a commercial salesman, George no longer has time to be a highbrow reader (149). When he's on the road he reads nothing but detective stories. Elitist reading practices require, above all, leisure. The highbrow world of art prescribes the way people dispose of time. "A typewriter, some paper, and a little leisure," as Certeau puts it, are necessary for the producers of high culture (*Culture* 142). But for George that world is off limits; he is absorbed in "a frantic struggle to sell things" (149), on "the post-war success dope" to "Get on! Make good!" (154). If back in 1908 or 1916 texts were found at school, after the war one of the realities of modern life is that "the text is society itself [—] urbanistic, industrial, commercial" (Certeau *Practice* 167). Reading has been institutionalized, streamlined, commodified, turned into something represented by a Boots subscription, the Left Book Club, the *News Chronicle*, and political pamphlets. Reading now means receiving information.

So it is important that George poaches not only on Boots's books, but on all forms of official speech. He is as alienated from the gramophone mentality of an anti-Fascist Left Book Club lecturer as he is from the stodgy refrains of his bookish friend Porteous, who is so sealed away in a world of poetry and the Greeks that he never gives a thought to this "German person" who is menacing Europe (185). Orwell's common man has no choice but to navigate his way between the extremes of political action and aesthetic retreat. "I suppose that if the local Left Book Club branch represents Progress, old Porteous stands for Culture" (181). Orwell constructs parallel scenes of persuasion and skepticism. The narrator takes what he can from both authorities and has no allegiance to either. Exposed to the consolations and rationales of poetry and politics, Culture and Progress, he practices "the art of being in between" (Certeau *Practice* 30). But as George Bowling admits, "Neither of them cuts much ice in West Bletchley" (181).

Porteous, a retired public-school master, is the closest representative of Culture in West Bletchley, and George likes him, despite his polite insinuations about George's lack of education (182). When Porteous reads aloud Keats's "Ode to a Nightingale," George enjoys the sounds of the words, although he does not take in their meaning. But the year is 1938 and he has just come from an anti-Fascist lecture. Self-aligned with the millions of "ordinary chaps that I meet everywhere, chaps I run across in pubs, bus drivers and travelling salesmen for hardware firms" (186), he feels the world is coming apart at the seams. "I just felt that this was all bunk. Poetry! What is it? Just a voice, a bit of an eddy in the air" (187). While ordinary chaps "have got a feeling that the world's gone wrong," Porteous, the guardian of high art, does not think Hitler matters. He merely intones. As Porteous breathlessly describes magic casements, George remembers that he has already heard this very same poem, read in the very same way. He thinks, very impertinently, *"He's dead. He's a ghost. All people like that are dead"* (188). George likes Porteous, and it is sometimes a comfort to be in "the classy Oxford" atmosphere of leather armchairs and whisky-and-soda, of pipes, Greek statues, and books from floor to ceiling. "I'm part of the modern world myself," George says, "but I like to hear him talk.... While you listen you aren't in the same world as trams and gas-bills and insurance companies" (183). But only while you listen.

At an anti-fascist lecture, George "turns the tables" on the speaker by getting inside his skull (175), deploying the tactic of a captive audience: to stop listening. By not listening to the substance of the speech, George acquires access to its sense. The speaker is *saying* that Hitler is after us, but he is *seeing* smashing people's faces in with a spanner. He is not talking about going to war, but about having "a good hate" (175, 176), and legitimating that hatred dogmatically through political ideologies and party affiliations, through ownership of the platform, the press, and the podium. George does not align himself with or against the speaker; he merely "starts thinking about [war] again," convinced that "it was going to happen." As with Keats's poem, he takes in the sound but not the discourse of the little lecturer's voice (176). Orwell had common people's lives on his mind very much in 1939 and 1940. He recognized that they were not being helped much by protest literature or leftist poetry, by high art that seemed inaccessible and silly, or by frightening anti-Fascist rhetoric. In "Inside the Whale," his essay on Henry Miller published in 1940, Orwell cites with approval E. M. Forster's description of T. S. Eliot's *Prufrock* (1917) as "'a protest, and a feeble one, and the more congenial for being feeble.... He who could turn aside to complain of ladies and drawing-rooms preserved a tiny drop of our self-respect, he carried on the human heritage'" (*CEJL* 1:524).

Coming Up for Air is also about a middle-aged man's desire for credibility, the desire to be convinced by something: to have a reason to live. Certeau writes, in *Culture in the Plural*, "every action, insofar as it is political, is also 'philosophical'; every action responds to the task of basing a society on reasons for living that belong to *all* and to *each*" (14).[2] When George Bowling pulls over on the road from Westerham to Pudley to look at the primroses that have started to come up, he sees "a little pile of white embers" and a wisp of smoke near a five-barred gate. "Curiously enough," he says, "the thing that suddenly convinced me that life was worth living ... was that bit of fire by the gate" (192). No poet himself, he has a hard time finding the words to explain what he feels. "It's curious that a red ember looks more alive, gives you more of a feeling of life, than any living thing. There's something about it, a kind of intensity, a vibration—I can't think of the exact words. But it lets you know you're alive yourself" (192–93). It creates "a special feeling inside you. Call it peace, if you like. But when I say peace I don't mean absence of war, I mean peace, a feeling in your guts" (195).

Is there a better way to put it? No doubt there is, but George leaves that to the highbrow writers. "A feeling in your guts" is what is resuscitated, and released, and recovered again, in diverse everyday practices and unexpected discoveries that are not elegantly elaborated, not nominated, that just materialize: primroses, the remains of a fire left by a tramp, a pool covered with duckweed. And fishing, with an exclamation point: "Fishing!" (93). A wet, gleaming flounder "with its grey warty back and its white belly and the fresh salty smell of the sea" (100–101). George's feeling about the red ember and the primroses is like his feeling for fish and fishing tackle: "It's not a thing that you can explain or rationalize, it's merely magic" (67). "Daily life," again writes Certeau "is scattered with marvels, a froth on the long rhythms of language and history that is as dazzling as that of writers and artists" (*Culture* 142). To envision the everyday is to be dazzled, sometimes even without the help of skilled spin doctors and professional authors. The politics of everyday practice that Certeau advocates does imply a philosophical position, for this politics has a bearing on our moral involvement with the world—that is, caring about it. George Bowling wonders "why the hell a chap like me should care" about the destiny of Europe when he has to worry about the rent and the kids' school-bills (189). Yet he notices that the primroses have started.

Fishing and reading are spatial practices, organizing activities in George Bowling's project of survival. These activities have some things in common. First, they appear passive (one is just sitting there). Second, they are activities that take place on other people's property: young George literally poaches when he and his brother catch fish in Old Brewer's pool, and then when he tries to hook the enormous carp in the hidden pool at Binfield House; the approach to reading as poaching has been discussed above. Third, fishing and reading must be protected from the intrusion of noisy others. Certeau writes that to read is "to constitute a secret scene, a place one can enter and leave when one wishes; to create dark corners into which no one can see ..." (*Practice* 173). For George Bowling, the scene of fishing is internal, a thing apart from outside influences. Orwell dwells on this: spiteful boys will lie about the size of the fish George caught, but it "didn't matter. I'd been fishing. I'd seen the float dive under the water and felt the fish tugging at the line, and however many lies they told they couldn't take that away from me" (76). The gigantic fish in the dark pool in the woods at Binfield House are his secret. When he is fighting in France in 1915, the sight of perch in a muddy pool takes George right out of the atmosphere of war (96), so powerful are his private memories and pleasurable associations.

Fishing and reading operate not as substitutes for religion or the sacred as such, but as affirmative activities that may be said to constitute an ethics of hope. One critic has suggested that the uncaught carp in *Coming Up for Air* is "a symbol of unfulfilled ambition" (Laskowski 156). Why does it have to mean that? Fishing is literally structured around waiting and *hoping*. George remembers "the kind of passion with which you'd watch the black backs of the fish swarming round, hoping and praying (yes, literally praying) ..." (84). It is a concealed passion, and a blatant transgression, but it is the source of belief, hope, and inspiration. "Everything else has been a bit of a flop" in his life compared with fishing (93). In this everyday leisure activity, this mere hobby, this dark corner invisible to others, there is the possibility of refusing the institutionalized versions of both what is valuable in life and what is real—saying no thank you to the facts and narratives with which he is literally bombarded.

For of course there are competing assertions of reality in George Bowling's world, and in this way the novel does have something in common with *Nineteen Eighty-Four*. "Nothing is real in Ellesmere Road" but mundane routines; nothing is real in the Strand, either—it is all ersatz commodities, "a sort of propaganda floating around" (26), frankfurters made of fish, "everything made out of something else" (27). The most palpable reality for George Bowling is apparently the recollection of smells and tastes and images of daily life in Lower Binfield in 1900, 1908, 1913, yet memory (nostalgia is the pejorative term for it) is also poaching on reality, a sort of anti-museum: it cannot be standardized. When George returns to Lower Binfield, he finds, of course, an industrial town that is as streamlined as London. Worse, it is cluttered with raw red brick buildings, fake Tudor houses, fake wooden walls, fake medieval decor, fake antiqueness—even the beer is adulterated, the "home-made" cakes made of margarine and egg-substitute (222). But when the British air force mistakenly drops a bomb in the village, leaving in its a wake three dead, a demolished grocer's shop, a lot of broken crockery, and (interestingly enough) a leg—"Just a leg, with the trouser still on it and a black boot with a Wood-Milne rubber heel" (265)—George Bowling feels he has been "suddenly shoved up against reality." What had been most real is suddenly revealed as a "dream" he had been dragged out of by the "clang of bursting metal" (262). Depressed but strangely exhilarated—"It was as though the power of prophecy had been given to me," he says (268)—he drives back to the suburbs, past "miles and miles of ugly houses, with people living dull decent lives inside them.... Surely they'll manage somehow, bombs or no bombs, to keep on with the life that they've been used to?" (268–69). Whether that's a hope, a question, or a rationalization, George Bowling comes to the conclusion that for "chaps like me" it will not make the slightest difference if the Fascists gain the upper hand. It will be all the difference for politicians and party members, with their spanners and slogans (177), but for ordinary people, war is a remote event they have no power to influence. They just have to "manage somehow to keep on with the life that they've been used to," to make do with the odds and ends that constitute for Orwell a politics of non-cooperation, of the everyday pleasures that are small gestures toward a faith in humanity, and the love of ordinary things that he thought could make "a peaceful and decent future a little more probable."

Orwell was the most influential political writer of the first half of the twentieth century. Books about him tend to include praise of his prophetic powers, or speculations on his reaction, were he alive, to a few of the big events in the second half of the twentieth century, especially the Vietnam War and the collapse of the Soviet Union. I will be the first to admit that "making do" is no substitute for revolutionary political action, and that is probably why some people have read *Coming Up for Air* as "quietist ... a futile search for a lost past" (Newsinger 59). Irving Howe, in 1950, found it "rather trivial," and Isaac Rosenfeld, writing in the *Partisan Review*, felt that Orwell's "politics suddenly appears to be out of joint" (qtd. in Meyers *George Orwell* 169, 171). Why are there so few sustained critical readings of this novel? Perhaps we have come to expect radical political involvement from George Orwell's books, and this "charming, cheerful minor masterpiece" (the blurb by Harvey Breit on the cover of the 1950 edition) does not quite fit the bill. Yet Orwell once defined politics as "the science of the possible" (*CEJL* 4: 109); Orwell's political, as well as his creative, temperament is consistently stimulated by the mundane, by ordinary activities and common objects. "I am not able," he says in "Why I Write," "and I do not want, completely to abandon the worldview that I acquired in childhood. So long as I remain alive and well I shall continue to feel strongly about prose style, to love the surface of the earth, and to take pleasure in solid objects and scraps of useless information" (*CEJL* 1:6). The kinds of deployments and ruses *Coming Up for Air* makes visible, its wholesale immersion in the interior life of the common man, and its faithful presentation of solid objects should stand as testimony to Orwell's faith in those invisible practices that constitute the possible, the unrecorded tasks and anonymous pursuits of ordinary, decent people. It's not the revolution, but it will have to do.

Notes

1. Raymond Williams links the novel to the discouragement expressed in Orwell's 1940 essay, "Inside the Whale" (Williams 64). George Woodcock, in a perceptive discussion, concludes that *Coming Up for Air* "contains none of the Socialist idealism" of *Homage to Catalonia*; for Woodcock, the "moral" the novel implies is "the defeat of life" (186–87). Jeffrey Meyers ("Orwell's Apocalypse") and Robert Van Dellen also tend to see the novel as largely defeatist. Rita Felski treats it as a "ruthlessly detailed portrayal of the English lower middle class of the 1930s" (35), but she does not perform a sustained analysis and Orwell's is one of several texts she references in her discussion of lower-middle class identity.

2. However, Orwell makes it clear that he believes metaphysical questions cannot be adequately considered as long as people's material well-being is threatened—when they are unemployed, hungry, or afraid of the future. "How right the working classes are in their 'materialism'! How right they are to realise that the belly comes before the soul, not in the scale of values but in point of time!" (*CEJL* 2: 266).

Works Cited

De Certeau, Michel. *Culture in the Plural.* 1974. Trans. Tom Conley. Minneapolis: U of Minnesota P, 1997.

———. *The Practice of Everyday Life*. 1974. Trans. Steven Rendall. Berkeley: U of California P, 1984.

Felski, Rita. "Nothing to Declare: Identity, Shame, and the Lower Middle Class." *PMLA* 115 (2000): 33–45.

Laskowski, William E. "George Orwell and the Tory-Radical Tradition." *The Revised Orwell*. Ed. Jonathan Rose. East Lansing: Michigan State UP, 1992. 149–90.

Meyers, Jeffrey, ed. *George Orwell: The Critical Heritage*. London: Routledge & Kegan Paul, 1975.

———. *Orwell*. New York: W. W. Norton, 2000.

———. "Orwell's Apocalypse: *Coming Up for Air*." *Modern Fiction Studies* 21 (1975): 69–80.

Newsinger, John. *Orwell's Politics*. London: Palgrave, 1999.

Orwell, George. *Coming Up for Air*. New York: Harcourt Brace, 1950.

———. *Nineteen Eighty-Four*. New York: Signet, 1950.

———. *Collected Essays, Journalism, and Letters*. Eds. Sonia Orwell and Ian Angus. 4 vols. Boston: Nonpareil, 1968.

Van Dellen, Robert. "George Orwell's *Coming Up for Air*: The Politics of Powerlessness." *Modern Fiction Studies* 21 (1975): 57–68.

Williams, Raymond. *George Orwell*. New York: Viking, 1971.

Woodcock, George. *The Crystal Spirit: A Study of George Orwell*. 1966. New York: Schocken Books, 1984.

Chronology

1903	Eric Arthur Blair (later to become George Orwell) is born on June 25 in Bengal, India, to a middle-class English family that is connected to the British colonial administration in India and Burma.
1907	Moves to England with his mother and sister.
1911–1916	Schooled at St. Cyprian's.
1917–1921	Attends Eton on scholarship.
1922–1927	Serves with Indian Imperial Police in Burma.
1928–1929	In Paris; works as dishwasher and writer; first articles are published in newspapers.
1930–1934	Lives mainly in London. Publishes articles and translations. *Down and Out in Paris and London* is published in 1933 under the pen name George Orwell. In 1934, *Burmese Days* is published.
1935	*A Clergyman's Daughter* is published.
1936	*Keep the Aspidistra Flying* is published. Marries Eileen O'Shaughnessy. Leaves for Spain in December to join anti-Fascists in Barcelona. Serves four months on the Aragon Front.
1937	*The Road to Wigan Pier* is published. Wounded in the throat, returns to England.
1938	*Homage to Catalonia* is published. Spends several months in a sanatorium to treat his tuberculosis; visits Morocco for winter.

1939	*Coming Up for Air* is published.
1940–43	Publishes *"Inside the Whale" and Other Essays* in 1940. Medically unfit for service in World War II, Orwell joins Home Guard in London. Writes and broadcasts as wartime propagandist for the BBC. In 1941, publishes *The Lion and the Unicorn: Socialism and the English Genius*. In 1943, becomes literary editor of the *Tribune*.
1944	Adopts a child, whom he names Richard Horatio Blair.
1945	Works as correspondent for *The Observer*. Wife dies. *Animal Farm* is published.
1946	Publishes *Critical Essays: Dickens, Dali, and Others*. Rents house in Hebrides, Scottish islands.
1947–1948	Is hospitalized for seven months, starting in December, for tuberculosis.
1949	Publishes *1984*. Marries Sonia Brownell; health continues to decline.
1950	Dies of tuberculosis on January 21. *"Shooting an Elephant" and Other Essays* is published.
1953	*"England, Your England" and Other Essays* is published.
1961	*Collected Essays* is published.

Contributors

HAROLD BLOOM is Sterling Professor of the Humanities at Yale University. He is the author of 30 books, including *Shelley's Mythmaking*, *The Visionary Company*, *Blake's Apocalypse*, *Yeats*, *A Map of Misreading*, *Kabbalah and Criticism*, *Agon: Toward a Theory of Revisionism*, *The American Religion*, *The Western Canon*, and *Omens of Millennium: The Gnosis of Angels, Dreams, and Resurrection*. *The Anxiety of Influence* sets forth Professor Bloom's provocative theory of the literary relationships between the great writers and their predecessors. His most recent books include *Shakespeare: The Invention of the Human*, a 1998 National Book Award finalist, *How to Read and Why*, *Genius: A Mosaic of One Hundred Exemplary Creative Minds*, *Hamlet: Poem Unlimited*, *Where Shall Wisdom Be Found?*, and *Jesus and Yahweh: The Names Divine*. In 1999, Professor Bloom received the prestigious American Academy of Arts and Letters Gold Medal for Criticism. He has also received the International Prize of Catalonia, the Alfonso Reyes Prize of Mexico, and the Hans Christian Andersen Bicentennial Prize of Denmark.

ADRIAAN M. DE LANGE has been a professor of English at Potchefstroom University for Christian Higher Education in South Africa. In addition to publishing *The Influence of Political Bias in Selected Essays of George Orwell*, he co-edited *Conrad in Africa*.

ROGER FOWLER has been Professor of English and Linguistics in the School of Modern Languages and European Studies, University of East Anglia. He published many books, among them *Linguistics and the Novel*, *A Dictionary of Modern Critical Terms*, and *Linguistic Criticism*.

ADRIAN WANNER is a professor of Slavic Languages and Literatures and Comparative Literature at The Pennsylvania State University. Among his book publications are *Baudelaire in Russia* and *Russian Minimalism: From the Prose Poem to the Anti-Story*.

PATRICIA RAE teaches at Queen's University, Kingston, Ontario. She is the author of *The Practical Muse: Pragmatist Poetics in Hulme, Pound, and Stevens*. She also has published essays on twentieth-century British and American literature.

ANTONY SHUTTLEWORTH teaches at Ohio State University. He published *And in Our Time: Vision, Revision, and British Writing of the 1930s* and a piece in *The Isherwood Century*. He also has worked on a study of the writing of Louis MacNeice.

WILLIAM E. CAIN is a professor of English at Wellesley College. He has authored *The Crisis in Criticism* and *F. O. Matthiessen and the Politics of Criticism*. He has edited many titles, including *William Lloyd Garrison and the Fight against Slavery: Selections from* The Liberator.

JAMES M. DECKER teaches at Franciscan University in Clinton, Iowa. He is the author of *Ideology* and *Henry Miller and Narrative Form: Constructing the Self, Rejecting Modernity*. He also has been published in *The Modern Language Review*.

PAUL KIRSCHNER teaches in Geneva. He wrote *Conrad: The Psychologist as Artist* and edited Conrad's *Under Western Eyes* and *Typhoon and Other Stories*.

ANNETTE FEDERICO teaches at James Madison University. She has published *Masculine Identity in Hardy and Gissing* as well as a book on Maria Corelli and late-Victorian literary culture.

Bibliography

Agathocleous, Tanya. *George Orwell: Battling Big Brother.* New York: Oxford University Press, 2000.

Berman, Ronald. *Modernity and Progress: Fitzgerald, Hemingway, Orwell.* Tuscaloosa: University of Alabama Press, 2005.

Bloom, Harold, ed. *Animal Farm.* Philadelphia: Chelsea House Publishers, 1999.

———. *George Orwell's 1984.* Philadelphia: Chelsea House Publishers, 2004.

Bowker, Gordon. *Inside George Orwell.* New York: Palgrave Macmillan, 2003.

Breton, Rob. "Crisis? Whose Crisis? George Orwell and Liberal Guilt." *College Literature* 29, no. 4 (Fall 2002): pp. 47–66.

Burton, Paul. "George Orwell and the Classics." *Classical and Modern Literature: A Quarterly* 25, no. 1 (Spring 2005): pp. 53–75.

Carter, Steven. "The Rites of Memory: Orwell, Pynchon, DeLillo, and the American Millenium." *Prospero: Rivista di culture anglo-germaniche* 6 (1999), pp. 5–21.

Coombes, John E. "Construction of Poverty: Around Orwell's *Down and Out in Paris and London.*" *Cycnos* 11, no. 2 (1994): pp. 75–83.

Fenwick, Gillian. *George Orwell: A Bibliography.* New Castle, Del.: Oak Knoll, 1998.

Gleason, Abbott, Jack Goldsmith, and Martha C. Nussbaum. *On Nineteen Eighty-four: Orwell and Our Future*. Princeton, N.J.: Princeton University Press, 2005.

Gottlieb, Erika. *The Orwell Conundrum: A Cry of Despair or Faith in the Spirit of Man?* Ottawa: Carleton University Press, 1992.

Heptonstall, Geoffrey. "Orwell and Bohemia." *Contemporary Review* 264, no.1539 (April 1994): pp. 211–214.

Hitchens, Christopher. *Orwell's Victory*. London; New York: Allen Lane/Penguin Press, 2002.

———. *Why Orwell Matters*. New York: Basic Books, 2002.

Holderness, Graham, Bryan Loughrey, and Nahem Yousaf. *George Orwell*. New York, N.Y.: St. Martin's, 1998.

Kerr, Douglas. "Colonial Habits: Orwell and Woolf in the Jungle." *English Studies* 78, no. 12 (March 1997): pp. 149–161.

———. "Orwell, Animals, and the East." *Essays in Criticism* 49, no. 3 (July 1999): pp. 234–255.

Kingsbury, Melinda Spencer. "Orwell's Ideology of Style: From 'Politics and the English Language' to *1984*." *Journal of Kentucky Studies* 19 (September 2002): pp. 108–113.

Klawitter, Uwe. *The Theme of Totalitarianism in "English" Fiction: Koestler, Orwell, Vonnegut, Kosinski, Burgess, Atwood, Amis*. Frankfurt am Main; New York: Peter Lang, 1997.

Lyotard, Jean-François. "Bureaucracy: Resistance, Witnessing, Writing." *L'Esprit Createur*, 34, no. 1 (Spring 1994): pp. 101–108.

Meyers, Jeffrey. "George Orwell and the Art of Writing." *Kenyon Review* 27, no. 4 (Fall 2005): pp. 92–114.

———. *George Orwell: The Critical Heritage*. London; New York: Routledge, 1997, 1975.

Meyers, Valerie. *George Orwell*. New York: St. Martin's Press, 1991.

Newsinger, John. "Nineteen Eighty-four since the Collapse of Communism." *Foundation: The Review of Science Fiction* 56 (Autumn 1992): pp. 75–84.

———. *Orwell's Politics*. New York; London: St. Martin's Press; Macmillan Press, 1999.

Pearce, Robert. "Orwell, Tolstoy, and *Animal Farm*." *Reivew of English Studies* 49, no. 193 (February 1998): pp. 64–69.

Rodden, John. *Scenes from an Afterlife: The Legacy of George Orwell*. Wilmington, Del.: ISI Books, 2003.

Rosenfeld, Aaron S. "The 'Scanty Plot': Orwell, Pynchon, and the Poetics of Paranoia." *Twentieth Century Literature: A Scholarly and Critical Journal* 50, no. 4 (Winter 2004): pp. 337–367.

Rossi, John. "Orwell and Patriotism." *Contemporary Review* (August 1992): pp. 95–98.

Schmidt, Mark Ray. "Rebellion, Freedom, and Other Philosophical Issues in Orwell's *1984*." *Publications of the Arkansas Philological Association* 22, no. 1 (Spring 1996): pp. 79–85.

Schweizer, Bernard. *Radicals on the Road: The Politics of English Travel Writing in the 1930s*. Charlottesville: University Press of Virginia, 2001.

Smith, Alan E. "Orwell's Writing Degree Zero: Language and Ideology in *Homage to Catalonia*." *Letras Peninsulares* 11, no. 1 (Spring 1998): pp. 295–307.

Smith, Jimmy Dean. "'A Stench in Genteel Nostrils': The Filth Motif in George Orwell's Cultural Travels." *Kentucky Philological Review* 19 (2005): pp. 43–49.

Stansky, Peter. *From William Morris to Sergeant Pepper: Studies in the Radical Domestic*. Palo Alto, Calif.: Society for the Promotion of Science and Scholarship, 1999.

Stewart, Anthony. *George Orwell, Doubleness, and the Value of Decency*. New York: Routledge, 2003.

Tirohl, Blu. "'We Are the Dead . . . You Are the Dead': An Examination of Sexuality as a Weapon of Revolt in Orwell's *Nineteen Eighty-Four*." *Journal of Gender Studies* 9, no. 1 (March 2000): pp. 55–61.

Trilling, Lionel. *The Moral Obligation To Be Intelligent: Selected Essays*, edited and with an introduction by Leon Wieseltier. New York: Farrar, Straus, Giroux, 2000.

Waterman, David F. *Disordered Bodies and Disrupted Borders: Representations of Resistance in Modern British Literature*. Lanham, Md.: University Press of America, 1999.

West, W. J. *The Larger Evils: Nineteen Eighty-four: The Truth behind the Satire*. Edinburgh: Canongate Press, 1992.

Williams, Raymond. *Orwell*. London: Fontana, 1991.

Wilson, Brendan. "Satire and Subversion: Orwell and the Uses of Anti-Climax." *Connotations: A Journal for Critical Debate* 4, no. 3 (1994–1995): pp. 207–224.

Acknowledgments

"Autobiography: An Analysis of 'Shooting an Elephant'" by Adriaan M. de Lange. From *The Influence of Political Bias in Selected Essays of George Orwell*: pp. 49–60. © 1992 by the Edwin Mellen Press. Reprinted with permission.

"Versions of Realism" by Roger Fowler. From *The Language of George Orwell*: pp. 60–86. © 1995 by Roger Fowler. Reprinted with permission.

"The Underground Man as Big Brother: Dostoevsky's and Orwell's Anti-Utopia" by Adrian Wanner. From *Utopian Studies* Vol. 8, No. 1 (1997), pp. 77–88. © 1997 Society for Utopian Studies. Reprinted with permission.

"Orwell's Heart of Darkness: *The Road to Wigan Pier* as Modernist Anthropology" by Patricia Rae. From *Prose Studies* 22, no. 2 (April 1999): pp. 71–102. © 1999 by Frank Cass & Co. Ltd. Reprinted with permission.

"The Real George Orwell: Dis-simulation in *Homage to Catalonia* and *Coming Up for Air*" by Antony Shuttleworth. From *And in Our Time: Vision, Revision, and British Writing of the 1930s*: pp. 204–220. © 2003 by Rosemont Publishing and Printing Corp. Reprinted with permission.

"Orwell's Perversity: An Approach to the Collected Essays" by William E. Cain. From *George Orwell into the Twenty-first Century*: pp. 215–228. © 2004 by Paradigm Publishers. Reprinted with permission.

"George Orwell's *1984* and Political Ideology" by James M. Decker. From *Ideology*: pp. 146–158. © 2004 by James M. Decker. Reprinted with permission.

"The Dual Purpose of *Animal Farm*" by Paul Kirschner. From *The Review of English Studies* 55, no. 222 (2004): pp. 759–786. © 2004 by Oxford University Press. Reprinted with permission.

"Making Do: George Orwell's *Coming Up for Air*" by Annette Federico. From *Studies in the Novel* 37, no. 1 (Spring 2005): pp. 50–63.© 2005 by the University of North Texas. Reprinted with permission.

Every effort has been made to contact the owners of copyrighted material and secure copyright permission. Articles appearing in this volume generally appear much as they did in their original publication with few or no editorial changes. Those interested in locating the original source will find bibliographic information in the bibliography and acknowledgments sections of this volume.

Index

Characters in literary works are indexed by first name (if any), followed by the name of the work in parentheses